FINANCING YOUR BUSINESS WITH VENTURE CAPITAL

Strategies to Grow Your Enterprise with Outside Investors

FREDERICK D. LIPMAN

PRIMA PUBLISHING

PRIMA PUBLISHING and colophon are registered trademarks of Prima Communications, Inc.

Lipman, Frederick D.
Financing your business with venture capital : strategies to grow your enterprise with outside investors / Frederick Lipman.
    p.   cm.
    Includes index.
    ISBN 0-7615-1460-0
    1. Venture capital.   2. Small business—Finance. I. Title.
    HG4751.L56 1998   98-33965
    658.15'224—dc21   CIP

   99 00 01 02 HH 10 9 8 7 6 5 4 3 2
Printed in the United States of America

This publication is designed to provide accurate and authoritative information (as of June 1998, except as otherwise noted) in regard to the subject matter covered. It is sold with the understanding that the author and publisher are not engaged in rendering legal, accounting, or other professional services. Laws vary from state to state, and if legal advice or other expert assistance is required, the services of a competent professional should be sought.

    The author and publisher specifically disclaim any liability, loss or risk, personal or otherwise, which is incurred as a consequence, directly or indirectly, of the use and application of any of the contents of this book.

How to Order
Single copies may be ordered from Prima Publishing, P.O. Box 1260BK, Rocklin, CA 95677; telephone (916) 632-4400. Quantity discounts are also available. On your letterhead, include information concerning the intended use of the books and the number of books you wish to purchase.

Visit us online at www.primalife.com

To Gail, Keith, Darren, and Kimberly

CONTENTS

ACKNOWLEDGMENTS

I want to acknowledge the helpful comments and editorial efforts of my partners at the Philadelphia office of the law firm of Blank Rome Comisky & McCauley LLP:

Chapters 1, 2, and 3: John W. Fowler, Esq.

Chapters 5 and 16 and Appendix 4: Alan L. Zeiger, Esq.

Chapters 7 and 16: Henry M. Kuller, Esq.

Chapters 9 and 10: Kevin P. Cronin, Esq.

Chapters 11 and 12: Jane K. Storero, Esq.

Chapter 13: Francis E. Dehel, Esq.

Chapters 14 and 15: Barry H. Genkin, Esq.

I absolve the editors from any responsibility for any errors in this book.

I want to specifically acknowledge Stephen M. Sammut who co-lectures with me on venture capital in the MBA program at the Wharton School of Business and at the University of Pennsylvania Law School. Some of the ideas contained in this book were derived from his lectures and from the excellent "bulk pack" which he prepared for the students.

I would also like to thank Ian MacMillan, the George W. Taylor Professor of Entrepreneurial Studies and executive director of the Wharton Entrepreneurial Programs, for his encouragement and support.

Rebecca Stanely, my law firm's librarian, our former librarian, Kit Boyle, Esq., and Benton Gaffney, a paralegal, made important research contributions to this book.

My son, Darren, suggested the title for this book and his contribution is duly acknowledged.

Last but not least, I owe a special debt to my personal secretary, Fran Ratcliffe, who typed the manuscript an unreasonable number of times, and to Valerie Smith who assisted.

INTRODUCTION

This book is intended for entrepreneurs (whether their business is a mature business or only a start-up) who are thinking about the pros and cons of growing with outside capital. The decision as to whether or not to grow a business with outside capital is analyzed, as are the potential strategies for doing so.

This book defines "venture capital" broadly to include not only professionally managed venture capital funds, but also junk-bond financing, private placements to angel investors, and high-risk initial public offerings. This broad definition permits a strategic analysis and comparison of these different growth strategies.

Chapter 1 provides an overall introduction and also gives a strategic example of the quandary faced by the owner of a late-stage business who cannot afford to sell his business because the purchase price will not permit him to maintain his current income. This is a common problem small business owners face.

Chapters 2 and 3 provide additional examples of businesses, some of which should and others that should not seek outside capital.

Chapters 4 and 5 assume that the businessperson wishes to raise outside capital. Chapter 4 provides important advanced planning tips to facilitate capital raising. Chapter 5 gives an overview of the pros and cons of different outside capital alternatives.

Chapter 6 describes the professionally managed venture capital industry. It reminds entrepreneurs that professional managers of these venture capital funds are also entrepreneurs and cautions those seeking capital to thoroughly understand the goals of these professional managers in order to successfully tap this important capital source.

Chapter 7 tells the entrepreneur how to value his or her business in order to understand how much equity dilution he or she will suffer by obtaining venture capital.

Many entrepreneurs are concerned about losing control of their business to venture capitalists. Chapter 8 discusses the elements of control, what constitutes real control, and how one can preserve it.

Chapter 9 describes the important issues in negotiating with a professional venture capitalist.

Chapter 10 summarizes and analyzes the legal provisions of a typical professional venture capital financing.

Chapters 11 and 12 deal with obtaining capital from angel investors as an alternative or possibly a supplement to professional venture capital financing. Chapter 11 describes the different types of angel investors and suggests some methods of locating them. Chapter 12 tells how to conduct an angel investor offering.

Many late-stage companies today are obtaining capital through junk-bond offerings in lieu of going public. Chapter 13 describes using this high-yield debt financing in lieu of a public offering and cites one case in which the equity interest of a venture capitalist was repurchased with the proceeds of junk bonds. Chapter 13 discusses so-called Rule 144A junk-bond offerings for late-stage companies and gives examples of junk-bond offerings conducted by start-up companies that have reasonable cash-flow prospects.

Chapter 14 describes the role of investment bankers in the capital-raising process. Investment banker–sponsored private placements for late-stage companies have become a growing source of venture capital.

Chapter 15 briefly discusses the going-public process and compares the advantages and disadvantages of using third-tier underwriters for a small public offering as an alternative to private venture capital. If you want to know more about the going-public process, readers are referred to my book *Going Public* (Prima, 1997).

Many entrepreneurs are interested in using outside capital to make acquisitions within their industry. Chapter 16 discusses the so-called "roll-up" process, including the recent phenomenon colloquially called "poof" roll-ups.

Chapter 17 is for entrepreneurs who would like to grow their business with outside capital but are afraid of the risk and want to create a "nest-egg" before accepting outside capital. Chapter 17 discusses a method of withdrawing equity from your business known as "leveraged recapitalization," which you might effectuate before seeking outside equity capital.

Finally, Chapter 18 deals with the opportunities and perils facing entrepreneurs who use credit cards to finance their seed stage to start-up businesses.

I have borrowed some material for this book from my prior books entitled *Going Public: Everything You Need to Know to Turn a Private Enterprise into a Publicly Traded Company*, (Prima, 1997) and *How Much Is Your Business Worth: A Step-by-Step Guide to Selling and Ensuring the Maximum Sale Value of Your Business* (Prima, 1996). Those of you who are interested in these subjects are encouraged to read these companion volumes.

CHAPTER 1

BUSINESS GROWTH AND
VENTURE CAPTIAL

T here is no universally accepted definition of "venture
capital." Everyone agrees that a first-round financing of a start-up software firm by a professionally managed
venture capital firm is a "venture capital" transaction.
Not all agree, however, that "bridge" financing to an initial public offering (IPO) of a late-stage company qualifies
as "venture capital" or that a $100 million high-yield note
(junk bond) financing for a well-established family business qualifies.

This book uses a broad definition of "venture capital" to refer to any form of high-risk investing, including
the following:

- A seed capital financing by an angel investor
- Start-up financing by a professionally managed venture capital firm
- A "junk bond" offering of high-yield notes of a late-
  stage company to finance its business plan

1

- A private placement of convertible preferred stock sold by an investment banker, which serves as a bridge to an IPO
- A bank loan that is sufficiently risky to justify the issuance of warrants or options to purchase equity securities of the borrower
- An IPO underwritten by a third-tier underwriter who raises $5 million
- An IPO of a biotech company with immaterial amounts of revenues or profits

TO GROW OR NOT TO GROW: THAT IS THE QUESTION

You should consider venture capital for your business only if you intend to grow the business. Otherwise, you normally will not be able to satisfy the investment return expectations of your investors.

Why would you grow your business? After all, growth involves a lot of hard work and risk. You may expand your business with added capital only to find the business less profitable than it was before the expansion. You could make bad acquisitions and wind up in a bankruptcy proceeding. To add insult to injury, you dilute your equity ownership interest for the future by accepting outside equity capital.

On the other hand, you may have no choice but to grow your business with outside capital. If you are in the seed or start-up stage, outside capital is often necessary. Even if your business is a later stage, fully developed business, you may need outside capital to grow for any of the following reasons:

- Your competitors are growing with outside capital and threaten your market share of the industry.

- You would like to sell your business in a few years, but without significant growth the sales price would be inadequate to satisfy your retirement needs.
- You would like to take your company public but cannot attract a reputable underwriter unless your company is significantly larger.
- You need to grow your company to take advantage of cost efficiencies enjoyed by larger companies in your industry.
- You need to grow your business because technology changes are forcing larger capital expenditures that you cannot finance with internal cash flow and normal bank loans.
- You would like to bring your children into the business, but it is not large enough to pay their salaries as well as yours.

Any of the above reasons would justify growing your business.

Your motivation for growth plays a key role in your ability to attract outside capital; therefore, you must carefully think through your incentive before you approach any outside capital sources. For instance, you would be unlikely to attract outside capital if your proposed growth was solely motivated by your desire to provide jobs for your children.

THE ENTREPRENEUR WHO COULDN'T AFFORD TO SELL HIS BUSINESS

The following example illustrates a typical problem a late-stage company may face.

Example: At age 55, Anthony T. earns approximately $500,000 a year in income from his business. After taxes, he nets $300,000. He would like to sell the business, but cannot get an offer of over $3 million. The roll-up craze (see chapter 16) has not affected his industry, thus he may not receive a higher valuation in the foreseeable future.

Assume that a $3 million sales price translates to $2.2 million after taxes and transaction costs. If Anthony invested the $2.2 million in conservative long-term bonds, he could at most earn $150,000 per year. To maintain his lifestyle, he would have to use a portion of principal each year out of the remaining $2.2 million. This means that his income would decline each year because of the declining principal. At age 55, he may easily outlive his money.

Anthony's own personal savings are small and, in any event, he does not wish to invest his own savings in this growth. Although the prospects for business growth are good, the business will not grow fast enough using internally generated profits and bank debt. He would like to retire no later than by age 65.

Analysis: Anthony T. suffers from a typical problem facing small businesses today. This entrepreneur cannot afford to sell his business. He lacks an easy exit strategy since a sale of the business at age 55 would not provide sufficient funds for him to retire without a severe reduction in lifestyle. He must seriously consider growing the business in order to achieve his exit objective. However, Anthony does not have (nor does he desire to commit) sufficient personal funds for this growth. Since the business does not generate sufficient capital to permit growth unless he reduces his $500,000 per year salary, he should consider seeking outside capital to achieve his exit strategy. Care should be taken in seeking outside capital to find sources who will not object to the $500,000 per year salary. Prior to seeking outside capital, Anthony should consider withdrawing equity from his business in a leveraged recapitalization, if the business is not highly leveraged (see chapter 17).

An alternative to seeking outside capital would be for him to never exit the business and to instead "milk" the business until he dies, or possibly sell the business to a key employee with a long-term note. These are reasonable solutions *only* if the business is not likely to deteriorate over time. If the risk of business deterioration over time is real, these alternatives may not be viable.

THE BENEFITS OF GROWTH

Growing your business can have a disproportionate effect on the valuation of the business. Many businesses sell for a multiple of earnings before interest, taxes, and depreciation/amortization (so-called "EBITDA"). Others are valued using a discounted cash-flow method of valuation. The disproportionate effect of growth results from the higher multipliers of EBITDA (for EBITDA valuations) and lower discount rates (for discounted cash-flow valuation) that are applied to valuing a larger business compared to a smaller business in the same industry. In addition, well-structured growth results in cost-saving efficiencies.

With regard to value, you cannot compare a business worth less than $5 million with a business in the same industry worth more than $50 million. The business worth over $50 million generally sells for a higher multiplier of EBITDA. Likewise, you cannot analogize a business worth $50 million with one worth $500 million in the same industry. While a business worth less than $5 million may sell for only four times EBITDA, a business in the same industry worth over $500 million can today sell for eight or more times EBITDA.

This arises in part because buyers prefer larger-sized businesses, which are more dominant in their field, and financial buyers are typically not interested in businesses worth less than $20 million.

This suggests that a good strategy to build your value prior to your exit date is to engage in strategic mergers or roll-ups (discussed in chapter 16). By "building up" your business during the presale years through mergers and other acquisitions, you will have a much more attractive target when it comes time for you to sell, since a larger business sells at a higher multiple of the EBITDA.

For example, assume your business has $10 million in revenues, and $1 million of earnings before interest, taxes, depreciation, and amortization. Assume that your business would normally sell at a multiplier of five times EBITDA for a total purchase price of $5 million (less debt). By increasing your business to $50 million in revenues, and assuming your EBITDA percentage remained a constant 10 percent of revenues (resulting in an EBITDA of $5 million on $50 million in revenues), your business could now be worth six times (rather than five times) your EBITDA, thus resulting in a new purchase price of $30 million (less debt). If, as a result of cost savings from your growth, your EBITDA percentage to revenues rose from 10 percent to 12 percent, thus resulting in a $6 million EBITDA, your business could then be worth $36 million (less debt). Thus, even though you increased your EBITDA six-fold (from $1 million to $6 million), the value of your business increased more than seven times (from $5 million to $36 million).

STRATEGIC CHOICES

An entrepreneur has a bewildering array of strategic choices to make in growing his or her business. These choices depend upon the stage of the business (start-up or mature), the type of business, and the personal objectives of the entrepreneur.

At some point, the entrepreneur may have to select among one or more of the following strategies:

- Grow the business through internally generated earnings and bank financing only.
- Grow the business through joint ventures or other corporate partnering.
- Grow the business through franchising.
- Grow the business with outside capital supplied by professionally managed venture capital firms or by angels.
- Grow the business with junk-bond financing.
- Grow the business through a public offering.

Not all of these strategic alternatives are available for every business. For example, many businesses do not lend themselves to franchising (because there is nothing to franchise) or junk-bond financing (because the business does not generate the cash flow to pay the interest on the junk-bond notes).

Some of the strategies substitute for others. For example, instead of seeking outside equity capital, the entrepreneur may enter into a joint venture or other corporate partnership arrangement, which would eliminate the need for outside equity capital.

Franchising, if a reasonable option for your business, can also substitute for outside equity capital. The franchising process provides cash from initial franchise fees and a percentage of the franchisee revenues. The trade-off is that you must perform services for these fees and relinquish an exclusive market share to your franchisee.

Not all the strategic alternatives are mutually exclusive. For example, your company may not be large enough to attract an underwriter for an IPO, even though that is your primary objective; but your business may be large enough to attract venture capital to permit the company's growth until it becomes an attractive IPO candidate.

Many entrepreneurs prefer to grow through internally generated earnings and normal bank debt. They cherish their freedom and independence and prefer not to have to answer to any equity partners. This is particularly true of family businesses in which owners have no intention of exiting the business through a sale (other than to a relative) or IPO.

Sometimes the strategic alternatives available to a businessperson are quite clear. If your company is on the verge of bankruptcy or in a seed stage, you have little choice but to seek outside capital.

However, most entrepreneurs have numerous strategic choices available to them and selecting from these alternatives is among the most difficult business decisions they face.

LEVERAGED RECAPITALIZATION

Some entrepreneurs do not wish to take the risk of growth with outside capital. Although they prefer their business to grow, these entrepreneurs do not wish to risk their existing equity on the significant growth required to permit an IPO.

If you are an entrepreneur who does not want to risk your existing equity in the business, you should consider a leveraged recapitalization. This strategy permits the entrepreneur to withdraw equity out of his or her business by obtaining loans that are not personally guaranteed and using the proceeds to pay the entrepreneur a large dividend equal to their equity withdrawal. The use of leveraged recapitalizations to create a "nest egg" is discussed more fully in chapter 17, entitled "Withdrawing Equity from Your Business."

Example: At age 45, Joyce M.'s three retail stores are doing well and she would like to grow the business until she qualifies for an IPO. She has been advised that her retail chain must grow to at least $125 million in sales to qualify for an IPO and she must show increasing profits. To create $125 million in sales, she will need to open an additional 12 retail stores. She will require outside equity capital as well as bank financing to grow to 15 stores. Her business, which is owned by a Subchapter S corporation, currently has no outside bank debt and has a $5 million net worth. Since retail businesses often go bankrupt after they grow, Joyce would like to have a personal "nest egg" before she solicits outside capital so that no matter what happens, she and her family are protected. She could create such a fund by having the Subchapter S corporation borrow from a bank as much as can be obtained without a personal guarantee and then declaring a dividend to herself of a portion of the proceeds of the bank loan.

Comment: Since venture capitalists are unlikely to ever agree to an equity withdrawal by the entrepreneur prior to an IPO, the entrepreneur is wise to effectuate the equity withdrawal *prior* to seeking outside capital from a venture capitalist.

STAGES OF BUSINESS

The strategic alternatives available to an entrepreneur vary greatly with the growth stage of his or her business. In general, the more advanced the growth stage, the more financing alternatives are available. In contrast, businesses in the seed stage have very few financing alternatives.

For example, a later stage business might consider a growth strategy using debt leverage, such as a Rule 144A junk-bond financing discussed in chapter 13. Such an alternative would not normally be available to a start-up company.

In contrast, start-up companies are limited to the following forms of financing:

- Friends and family
- Credit cards
- Angel investors
- Professionally managed venture capital

Stages

The following is a brief description of the stages of a business as taught at the Harvard Business School.* However, there is no agreement as to what constitutes a business "stage."

> *Seed Financing* is the earliest stage of funding. A small investment (typically $25,000 to $300,000) is made to support an entrepreneur's exploration of an idea. Often there is no business plan, an incomplete management team, and little assurance that the basic technology or business concept is feasible. Sometimes, when the product technology is well established, seed money is raised simply to finance

---

*From Daniel R. Scherlis and William A. Sahlman, "A Method for Valuing High-Risk, Long-Term Investments: The 'Venture Capital Method,'" note 288-006. Boston: Harvard Business School, 1987. Excerpted and reprinted by permission.

the recruitment of key management and the writing of a business plan, both of which are generally necessary for start-up funding. Seed investors expect to provide basic business advice, and perhaps even office facilities, for their entrepreneurs. Seed investors often apply discount rates of over 80 percent to the projects in which they invest.

Start-Up Financing entails the commitment of more significant funds to an organization that is prepared to commence operations. A start-up should be able to demonstrate a competitive advantage. Most high-technology firms should have a product in prototype form embodying a proprietary technology. A research-oriented venture, such as a biotechnology firm, might instead exhibit an impressive research staff. Low-technology ventures, such as specialty retailing or entertainment, should have a powerful concept with preemption advantages and a superior management. Investors in start-up ventures frequently provide assistance to management in recruiting key personnel, establishing sound management practices, and providing access to suppliers, banks, and potential customers. Start-up investors apply discount rates of 50 percent to 70 percent.

First-Stage Financing is provided to on-going businesses. A first-stage company is generally not profitable, but it normally has an established organization, a working product, and, preferably, some revenues. First-stage funds are usually used to establish a company's first major marketing efforts, and to hire sales and support personnel in anticipation of higher sales volume. Often, funds are also applied to product enhancements or product line expansion. First-stage investors attempt to monitor closely a venture's head count, ensuring that staffing levels correspond to attainable sales levels. They often become more actively involved as problems develop in production or sales, and are prepared to replace key managers as necessary, sometimes filling in key positions themselves while searching for new managers. Discount rates applied to a first-stage venture are generally 40 percent to 60 percent.

Second-Stage Financing is typically provided for working capital and fixed asset needs to support the growth of a company with active production, sustainable sales, and, preferably, some profits. Whereas earlier-stage funds were largely dedicated toward proving a venture's viability, second- and later-stage capital is oriented toward the expansion of a tested contender. Since the capital invested in the later stages is more likely to pay for assets rather than operating expenses, it is more readily recoverable in the event of liquidation, thus lowering the overall risk to the investors. Second-stage investors do not generally expect to become actively involved in problem-solving as often as first-stage investors do. They do monitor performance closely, generally by comparison to a business plan. Discount rates for second-stage investments range from 30 percent to 50 percent.

Bridge Financing is intended to carry a company until its IPO. Although an IPO is not yet appropriate due to market timing or the size and performance of the company, it is generally expected within a year after the bridge. Bridge investors might provide funds to satisfy ongoing capital needs, with the expectation of selling out again in the IPO as part of a secondary offering (an offering of shareholders', as distinct from company, stock). Alternately, bridge investors might apply some or all of their funds to buy out early-stage investors who are anxious to liquidate their holdings. Such an investor often expects to hold the stock past the IPO date, as a long-term investment. Bridge investors are generally passive investors. They apply discount rates of 20 percent to 35 percent.

Restart Financing, also known as emergency or sustaining financing, is raised for a troubled firm, at a price significantly below that of the previous round. Although the venture is performing well below expectations, the round will be priced low enough to offer a high expected rate of return, one result of which is likely to be substantial dilution of any previous investors that do not participate in the restart financing.

Internal Rate of Return

Table 1.1 provides a "rule of thumb" for the internal rate of return required by professionally managed venture funds.

Table 1.1   Stages of Venture Capital
Rule of Thumb Required Return

Description	Internal Rate of Return*
Seed/start-up	60–100%
Development + mgmt. team	50–60%
Revenues/expansion	40–50%
Profitable/cash-poor	30–40%
Rapid growth	25–35%
Bridge to cash out	20% +

*Before applying subjective factors

Chapter 2

Strategic Considerations

The decision to grow your business with outside capital is a difficult one for most entrepreneurs and involves weighing personal and business objectives.

Venture capital can take any of the following forms:

- Sale of high-yield notes (so-called "junk bonds")
- Sale of convertible notes or notes with warrants
- Sale of convertible preferred stock
- Sale of common stock

The prejudice against outside capital is natural for established businesses. Few entrepreneurs want to take on a partner. This is especially true if you have started and grown the business with your own capital or the capital of family and friends. In addition, suppliers of outside capital generally impose restrictions on your business. Some require veto over certain major decisions, board of directors' participation, and limitations on your compensation. Despite these disadvantages, accepting outside capital can still make good sense. Although wanting to own 100 percent of your business is natural, owning a smaller proportion of a much larger business may be wiser. This is particularly true if you wish ultimately to go public or to sell the business at an attractive price.

If your business has a good cash flow, junk bonds may offer you a method of obtaining outside capital without diluting your equity ownership.

PUBLICLY TRADED COMPANIES VS. PRIVATE COMPANIES

An "illiquidity discount" is generally applied to the value of the stock of a privately held company. This illiquidity discount reduces the stock value of a private company by 33 percent or more compared to the stock of an identical publicly traded company, since a private company cannot offer investors the liquidity of the public market place.

As a general rule, if you are raising capital, the faster you can be in a position to offer stock that can be publicly traded to outside investors, the smaller your personal equity dilution will be.

FACTORS TO CONSIDER

The following factors will bear on your decision to accept outside capital:

- Your personal exit strategy
- Your ability and willingness to make your business attractive to sources of outside capital

- Your ability and willingness to accommodate the "hassle" of due diligence, capital raising, and the subsequent growth of your business
- The competitive situation in your industry
- Your age and health

Exit Strategy

Any outside investor in your business will typically want an exit strategy. Three main exit strategies are:

- Selling your business
- Going public
- Having your company buy back the investment

The time frame for these exit strategies varies with the nature of the investors and their personal goals. Venture capitalists typically have exit strategies that vary in time from three to ten years. Most prefer an exit set no later than at five years.

If your personal exit strategy does not coincide with the exit strategy of your outside investors, you should think twice before taking outside capital. For example, if you have no desire to sell your company or go public in five years, but your investor wants an exit in five years, you have no choice but to buy back the equity. Yet, your company may not have the funds to afford the buy-back in five years and you may be forced to sell your business prematurely.

If you possess a family-owned business and want to give the business to your children, who will pay for your retirement with company funds, you are not a good candidate for outside capital. One possible exception would be if your children have an exit strategy that would accommodate an outside investor.

Some professionally managed venture capitalist firms require a so-called "drag-along" clause in their legal documents, particularly in early-stage investments. This clause requires that you sell your company if they want to sell. Obviously, if you have no desire to sell the company, you should avoid these venture capitalists.

It is not necessary to sell your company to accommodate the exit objectives of outside investors. Going public is a perfectly acceptable exit strategy. Going public permits you to raise public funds at attractive prices, creates liquidity for outside investors, and may permit you to continue to control the company after the public offering.

Example: At age 50, George N. is the owner of a family business started by his grandfather. He would like to leave the business to his children, one of whom already works in the business. However, his business, which is a niche publishing business, is not doing well. Competition from larger publishers, who have greater capital resources and better distribution channels, is seriously hurting sales and profitability.

George needs outside capital to grow the publishing business, but there is a limit on what the banks will finance. He does not want to sell the business in five years and has no desire to go public unless he is absolutely forced to do so. Therefore, his strategy in attracting outside equity capital is to agree to buy back the investment after five years with internally generated profits combined (if necessary) with other outside capital that might be obtained at that time. If he is unable to buy back the investment in five years, his fallback is to go public. However, he should recognize that the IPO fallback is questionable since (1) there might not be an attractive IPO market in five years and (2) his business might not be sufficiently appealing to attract an underwriter.

Analysis: George N. has decided on the best from among many bad choices. Doing nothing means further erosion of the business. Yet seeking outside equity capital creates the risk that the business cannot buy back the investment in five years and that an IPO won't work, thereby resulting in the sale of the business at an unattractive price. Even if the IPO does work, he risks losing family control of the business.

Personal Goals

If you are tired of working so hard and want to cut back, think twice before accepting outside capital. Investors are looking for someone to score a "home run" with their money. A tired executive is unlikely to accomplish that objective.

If you want to spend more time with your family, think twice before accepting outside capital. Of course, if your second-in-command can handle your job almost as well as you, you might kick yourself up to Chairman of the Board of your company and let your second-in-command run the show. This permits you to slow down while at the same time permitting your business to raise outside capital.

Some businesspeople find it difficult to delegate. If that describes you, it is unlikely that the "kick yourself up-stairs" strategy will really work.

Competition

If your business must have outside capital to stay competitive, you may have no choice but to seek outside capital. Many industries today are going through so-called roll-ups. These roll-ups are resulting in large public companies that are well capitalized and willing to purchase a dominant market share. You may be unable to effectively compete with these companies without outside capital to grow your business.

Age and Health

Your age or health may adversely affect your ability to raise outside capital. Passive investors want management in place who will facilitate their exit strategy. If you are 75 years old or in poor health (regardless of age), your ability to attract outside investors will be seriously impaired unless your second-in-command is an impressive individual capable of leading your company.

Likewise, if you are 22 years old (regardless of your health), you may find it difficult to attract investors because of your relative youth. You should consider surrounding yourself with more seasoned executives before approaching outside investors.

POSTPONE OUTSIDE CAPITAL AS LONG AS POSSIBLE

The discount rates on seed-stage venture capital run 80 percent or more per annum compounded. One seed-stage professionally managed venture capital firm has announced a discount rate of 100 percent per annum. That means that the investment must project to produce a return of 100 percent per year, compounded, on each $1 million investment in the company until the exit date—that is, a sale or an IPO. Thus, if the exit date is five years after the investment and the investment is $1 million, the investor expects to receive $32 million upon a sale or an IPO (that is, $1 million compounded at 100 percent per year).

On the other hand, the discount rate on second-stage companies can be as low as 20 percent to 35 percent per annum.

Moral: The longer you wait to seek outside capital, the less equity dilution you suffer.

DON'T WAIT TOO LONG

Some entrepreneurs wait too long before seeking outside capital. They are so concerned with retaining 100 percent of the equity in and control of their business that they miss nonrecurring market opportunities to grow their business. For example, if a significant strategic merger becomes available in your industry, it may be advisable to seize that opportunity even if you have to dilute your equity ownership earlier than you wish.

Moral: Weigh equity dilution against the market opportunity available to grow your business.

The next chapter gives you concrete examples of companies that are either good or bad candidates to grow with outside capital. See which is most analogous to your own company.

CHAPTER 3

STRATEGIC EXAMPLES

The following are examples of entrepreneurs who might wish to seek outside capital. In each example, the age of the entrepreneur is a factor. You will also note that in each example, to achieve the entrepreneur's personal exit strategies, the businessperson may have little choice but to seek outside capital.

Example 1: At age 45, Sarah R.'s niche business is part of an industry composed of a large number of small family-owned businesses. A large public company has been acquiring these businesses in a so-called roll-up. The large public company will be a substantial competitor for her business because of its greater capital and market clout and has shown itself willing to cut prices to increase its market share.

Sarah has a young family and is not ready to sell her business and retire. She would like to grow the business to make it more of a market force, with the

view of ultimately taking it public or selling it in ten
years. However, her internally generated earnings do
not provide her with sufficient expansion capital. She is
fearful of taking on too much bank debt because of the
cyclical nature of her business.

Thus, both her growth strategy and personal exit objectives are stymied without outside capital.

Example 2: At age 35, Felix P.'s business is just beginning to turn cash-positive. It has taken five years to
get the business to this point and he has exhausted his
personal capital sources. The business has great
growth potential, but insufficient capital to finance
any further growth.

Example 3: At age 25, Carol S. has just graduated from
a prestigious Ivy League business school and has developed an Internet business with great potential. Her
family and friends provided the initial $500,000 in seed
capital. However, she needs at least an additional $1
million to expand her marketing program and thereby
enable her business to rest on a more solid footing.

Example 4: At age 65 Malcolm L. and his brother
Martin (age 63) would like to sell their business to
Malcolm's son and Martin's son-in-law, both of whom
are active in the business. Malcolm's son (age 35) and
Martin's son-in-law (age 30) do not have any significant
capital and need a partner to help pay the $30 million
purchase price their father and father-in-law are asking
for the business.

The following are examples of entrepreneurs who
should not solicit or accept outside capital:

Example 1: At age 55, Dorothy M. likes running the
family-owned business she inherited from her father.

Her children, ages 20 and 22, are in college and are not certain they want to join her business upon graduation. She has no desire to go public or to sell the business either now or in the future and prefers to keep the business in the family. Thus, her personal objectives do not coincide with the exit strategies of outside investors.

Example 2: At age 40, Manuel E. would like to grow the business he founded. He has difficulty answering to outside investors. He could finance his growth strategy with a joint venture or other corporate partnership arrangement that does not require him to give up any equity in his business. Alternatively, he could sell franchises to finance his growth. Either alternative is more attractive to him than having an equity partner.

Example 3: At age 35, Inge F.'s niche business has been growing nicely using internally generated funds and bank debt. No competitors appear on the horizon to threaten her growth. She is not keen on selling the business in five years, which might be the exit objective of an outside investor. She doubts that her business would be an attractive IPO candidate in five years, and is not particularly enamored with making her compensation public information, as would be required in a public offering.

Example 4: At age 25, Kevin C.'s start-up business desperately needs at least $1 million in outside equity capital. However, the venture capitalists who have approached him have placed a very low pre-money valuation on the business, namely $500,000. If he accepts the $1 million from the venture capitalist, they will own 66% of the equity in his business, computed as follows:

$$\frac{\$1 \text{ million}}{\$1.5 \text{ million}} = 66\%$$

Kevin will effectively become an employee with some equity incentives. That was not his objective when he started the business. Therefore, he has decided to reduce his business costs to the bone and move to his parents' home to reduce personal expenses, thereby permitting him to take less salary. His strategy is to try to grow the business without outside equity until it is large enough to justify a higher pre-money valuation from venture capitalists so that he does not lose control of the business.

Example 5: At age 24, Betsy B. would like to obtain outside capital for her business, but has not developed sufficient concrete uses for the additional capital, nor does she have a business plan that would be impressive to an investor.

She should not solicit outside capital until she knows exactly how she will use the outside capital and creates a sophisticated business plan.

If you decide that your business is a good candidate for outside capital, the next chapter gives you seven important advance planning steps.

CHAPTER 4

ADVANCED PLANNING TO RAISE CAPITAL

The following are the seven most important steps to take prior to seeking outside capital:

- Hire an outstanding professional team.
- Create a business plan.
- Understand the thinking of your proposed capital sources.
- Strengthen your management and board.
- Create protection against competition.
- Unless your business is a start-up, obtain audited or auditable financial statements.
- Eliminate deal killers.

HIRE AN OUTSTANDING PROFESSIONAL TEAM

Your professional team should consist of an experienced securities lawyer, an accountant, and a financial advisor.

Securities Lawyer

If you plan to seek funds from the venture fund community, your lawyer should ideally have the following three attributes:

- Contacts in the capital sources you expect to tap
- Prior experience in negotiating and structuring deals with those capital sources
- Securities law expertise

Your lawyer should have direct experience in the capital raising process that you propose. For example, if you will be seeking funds from the professionally managed venture fund community, your lawyer should have contacts in that community, prior experience in negotiating and structuring deals with professionally managed ventures capital funds and securities law expertise.

Likewise, if you propose to tap the angel community, your lawyer should be able to introduce you to possible angels as well as have prior experience in an angel offering and securities law expertise.

If your proposed lawyer has securities law expertise, but no contacts, keep looking. A lawyer who can introduce you to your proposed capital sources can be very valuable. If you choose an attorney who has no contacts with capital sources, you are shortchanging yourself.

You should be able to find a securities lawyer in the major corporate law firms in your community who has all the attributes described.

Accountant

Your accounting firm is an important part of your professional team if you are a later-stage business. The audited financial statement of a later-stage business will be important to your capital source. The greater the prestige of your accounting firm, the greater the comfort your capital sources will feel.

If you plan an IPO, most underwriters will require an accounting firm with a national or international reputation.

If you are in the seed or start-up stages, your historical financial statements are less important to your capital source. Therefore, your accountant is a less important player than during later stages. Nonetheless, using a prestigious accounting firm may help lend credibility to your company and increase the potential sources of capital available for referral to your company. Choosing a strong regional accounting firm may also lead to introduction to angels and other capital sources.

The use of a prestigious law firm and accounting firm can be helpful in increasing your credibility with potential capital sources. It helps demonstrate your commitment to use professionals who can stay with the company through an IPO or a sale.

Financial Advisor

If neither you nor your chief financial officer (assuming you have one) have prior experience in raising capital, hiring a financial advisor is wise. The financial advisor serves in three roles:

- Assists in preparing a business plan
- Opens doors to potential capital sources
- Negotiates the terms and conditions with capital sources

Great care must be taken in selecting a financial advisor. You need a person who has hands-on prior experience in negotiating with your likely capital sources. Check the references of your financial advisor carefully, both directly and through your securities lawyer and accountant. Talk to entrepreneurs who are alleged to be "satisfied" prior customers of your potential financial advisor.

Some financial advisors will operate on a complete or partial contingent fee—that is, their fee will depend upon the monies actually raised. The contingent fee arrangement is usually not considered a problem if the capital source is a single venture fund. However, if the capital source involves a private placement to numerous "accredited investors," a partial or complete contingent fee raises a question as to whether the financial advisor is required to be registered as a "broker-dealer" or "agent" under federal and state securities law. Since most financial advisors are not properly registered, a contingent fee raises a question as to the legality of your offering. Although this area of the law is murky (and kept so by the SEC), it is best to avoid a contingent fee arrangement in a retail angel offering.

DEVELOP A BUSINESS PLAN

Prior to selecting your capital source, you should have prepared a business plan. The business plan is essential to raising capital for all but very late-stage companies.

Most entrepreneurs need outside professional help to put together an appealing business plan. If you have never sought outside capital previously, you are well advised not to attempt this task alone. Even if you have a good chief financial officer or controller, if they lack prior experience in raising outside capital from your intended sources, you will probably not be able to prepare a winning business plan.

Many outside consultants and professionals purport to be experts in preparing business plans. However, you must carefully check their qualifications. If they have never successfully raised capital from similar capital sources, look elsewhere.

Even if you use an experienced outside consultant, your ideas and input are critical to a winning business plan. Professional venture capitalists easily spot "canned" business plans.

Particular care should be used in preparing the short "Executive Summary" of your business plan. Many venture capitalists stop reading business plans if the first page or two of the Executive Summary does not appeal to them.

Your outside consultant or professional should also be used to advise you how to deal with a professionally managed venture capital fund or other capital source. An initial mistake in your first meeting may result in no second meeting.

Business plans many times contain statements and projections that may create issues under the antifraud provisions of federal and state securities laws. Therefore, you would be wise to require investors to sign subscription agreements in which they warrant and represent that they are relying solely on the offering or disclosure document in making their investment decision and not on the business plan.

A well-drafted subscription agreement will require the investor to indemnify, or compensate, the company and its control persons if such warranty or representation is false. Such indemnification agreements have been upheld by the courts and serve as shields against investor lawsuits based upon alleged material misstatements or material omissions contained in the business plan.

Understand the Thinking of Your Capital Sources

No businessperson would consider trying to negotiate a major sale of their goods or services without fully understanding customers' needs. Yet, many entrepreneurs have no hesitancy in talking to capital sources without fully understanding their goals and objectives. Treat capital sources as if they were important customers of your business and study them as if you were making a major sale to them.

If your likely capital source is a professionally managed venture capital fund, read chapter 6 of this book and study the types of investments in which the fund has engaged before completing your business plan. Obtain at least the following information concerning the professionally managed venture capital fund:

- What are the fund's preferred industries?
- Would an investment in your company exhaust the remaining uninvested funds? (The last investment of a fund may have an advantage since the fund manager may not want to start their next fund until their prior fund is fully invested.)
- What is the typical "hurdle rate" of the fund? ("Hurdle rate" is the average rate of return the fund expects on its investments and on companies at your stage of development.)
- What stage of business development does the fund prefer for investment? (In other words, why waste your time on a fund with later-stage preferences, if you need seed capital?)

You also need to know what IPOs have occurred in your industry recently and what multiple of projected income the underwriter used in computing the public offering price. These details are important to know so you can convince the venture capital fund of the proper valuation of your business, after applying discounts to reflect the earlier stage of your business. Demonstrating knowledge of recent IPOs in your industry will enable you to impress potential investors with your sophistication.

STRENGTHEN YOUR MANAGEMENT
AND BOARD OF DIRECTORS

The quality of management is the single most important factor to capital sources, particular professionally managed venture funds. Arthur Rock, the dean of the venture capitalists, stated in the *Harvard Business Review* (Nov.–Dec. 1987):

> As a venture capitalist, I am often asked for my views on why some entrepreneurs succeed and others fail. Obviously, there are no cut-and-dried answers to that question. Still, a few general observations about how I evaluate new businesses should shed some light on what I think it takes to make an entrepreneurial venture thrive and grow.
>
> Over the past 30 years, I estimate that I looked at an average of one business plan per day, or about 300 a year, in addition to the large numbers of phone calls and business plans that simply are not appropriate. Of the 300 likely plans, I may invest in only one or two a year; and even among those carefully chosen few, I'd say that a good half fail to perform up to expectations. The problem with those companies (and with the ventures I choose *not* to take part in) is rarely one of strategy. Good ideas and good products are a dime a dozen. Good execution and good management—in a word, good *people*—are rare.
>
> To put it another way, strategy is easy, but tactics—the day-to-day and month-to-month decisions

required to manage a business—are hard. That is why I generally pay more attention to the people who prepare a business plan than to the proposal itself.

CREATE PROTECTIONS AGAINST COMPETITION

One of the key characteristics that appeals to capital sources is the protection the company has against competitors. Protections based solely on the cheapest price for your goods or services are normally considered less important than patents, trade secrets, and similar kinds of intellectual property protections. Therefore, you must be prepared to answer the question as to how your business will fare against its competitors, actual or potential, and what barriers exist against competitors.

You would be wise to review your business operation with a patent lawyer to determine whether anything you do is patentable. If some patent protection is arguably available, try to file your patent applications before seeking outside capital.

OBTAIN AUDITED OR AUDITABLE FINANCIAL STATEMENTS

Unless your company is in the seed or start-up stage, most investors want the comfort of having audited financial statements for at least the most recently completed fiscal year. If you are seeking bridge financing into an IPO, you will want to demonstrate to your investors that you can qualify for an IPO by satisfying the SEC's requirements for audited financial statements. An IPO will generally require three years of audited financial statements (two years in the case of certain small businesses). If your IPO is planned for more than one year after the bridge financing, you can include as your third year the period after the bridge financing and, under such circumstances, you will only need two years of audited financial statements.

An audited financial statement provides the investor with a greater assurance of your financial results. In addition, professional venture capitalists are happier if you use a prestigious international auditing firm to perform your audits, since they usually retain such a firm to perform their own audits.

If you normally use a good regional accounting firm, it is probably unnecessary to change auditors on the eve of your financing.

Even if you do not obtain an audited financial statement, at least obtain an auditable financial statement for the three years prior to the proposed financing. An auditable financial statement permits you to complete the audit retroactively at the time of the financing.

ELIMINATE DEAL KILLERS

Eliminate all "deal killers" before you seek outside capital. Once you have made a decision to seek financing, immediately examine your business, with the help of your corporate attorney, to determine whether you have deal killers or other impediments to a financing.

Following are typical examples of deal killers if the resulting contingent liability is large in relation to the value of your business:

- Illegal or improper payments to customers or suppliers or their employees
- Environmental liabilities
- Litigation liabilities

- Tax liabilities resulting from misclassification of employees as independent contractors
- Unfunded pension obligations and multi-employer pension plan liabilities
- Product warranty obligations of unreasonable scope or length

Once you have completed your advance planning steps, decide which capital sources and forms of investment you intend to select. The next chapter offers you an overview of your capital choices.

CHAPTER 5

OVERVIEW OF CAPITAL CHOICES

O nce you decide you want outside venture capital, you have four major sources available:

1. Professionally Managed Venture Capital Funds
2. An Angel Investor Offering
3. An Investment Banker–Sponsored Private Placement (primarily for later-stage companies)
4. An IPO

Each of these choices is examined in succeeding chapters.

If you rank the choices in terms of the least dilution to your equity interest, they are as follows:

Least: An IPO

Middle: Angel Offering and Investment Banker– Sponsored Private Placement

Most: Professionally Managed Venture Capital Funds

However, if you rank the capital choices in terms of transaction costs, the order is quite different:

Least: Professionally Managed Venture Capital Funds

Middle: Angel Offering and Investment Banker–Sponsored Private Placement

Most: An IPO

Following in Table 5.1 are the major sources of investment capital according to the *Venture Capital Journal*:

TABLE 5.1   MAJOR SOURCES OF INVESTMENT CAPITAL*

	1978	1995	1996
Banks/Insurance	16 %	5 %	18 %
Foundations/Endowments	9	20	22
Pension Funds	15	40	38
Corporations	10	18	2
Families/Individuals	32	8	17
Other	18	6	3

*Reprinted with permission of Securities Data Publishing: New York.

Omitted from the chart are federal, state, and local governmental programs. Although these programs are not within the scope of the book, governmental financing has provided seed and start-up capital for many businesses, particularly high-tech businesses.

Table 5.2 reflects sources of all outside capital, including bank loans, at various stages of corporate development:

TABLE 5.2 SOURCES OF BUSINESS DEVELOPMENT FINANCING

Stage of Development	Risk Profile and Principal Risk Elements	Financial Characteristics	Typical Financing Sources
Seed and Start-Up	*Highest:* Management, Product, Market, Financial	Losses Minimal assets Negative cash flow	Equity of founders and family Government programs Angels and professionally managed venture capital
Growth	*Moderate:* Management, Financial	Break-even to profitable Rapidly growing assets Negative or modestly positive cash flow	Bank loans and mezzanine financing* Leases Private equity (early growth) Public equity (later growth) Strategic alliances
Maturity	*Lowest:* Competition	Profitable Stable asset levels Positive cash flow	Bank loans and mezzanine financing Public and private equity placements Strategic alliances

*Mezzanine financing refers to later-stage financing that combines debt and equity.

ADVANTAGES AND DISADVANTAGES OF PROFESSIONALLY MANAGED VENTURE CAPITAL

The major advantages of seeking venture capital from professionally managed venture capital funds are:

- You have a sophisticated partner who can help guide your company through the pitfalls of growth.

- Your association with the professionally managed fund creates credibility and lends prestige to your company, thereby facilitating further financing, including an IPO.
- A good venture capitalist will introduce you to opportunities that would otherwise not become available to you.

The major disadvantages of seeking venture capital from professionally managed funds are:

- Your company will experience a significantly lower valuation, thereby diluting your personal equity position.
- Covenants and veto powers will be imposed by the legal documentation of the venture capitalist.
- If you fail to achieve your projections and need further venture capital financing, you can expect to be significantly penalized in your equity percentage and can potentially lose control of your company.

Management still has certain bargaining leverage even if they miss their projections, provided the venture capitalist still needs management to operate the business. Venture capitalists recognize the need for management incentives, even if management requires more capital than originally anticipated in the business plan.

If a second venture capital group is required to finance the business, they will typically expect the first venture capital group to leave enough equity to provide adequate incentive to management. Thus, it is not unusual for the second venture capital group to refuse to fund if the first venture capital group fully exercises the anti-dilution rights and this results in management having an inadequate equity percentage.

You should not count on this protection; instead, assume that if the company requires more rounds of capital than anticipated by the business plan, you will be significantly penalized and probably lose control of your business.

FORMS OF FINANCING

The following are the major forms of financing:

- Notes or other debt instruments (leases, for example)
- Preferred stock
- Common stock
- Warrants or other options to purchase equity

From the entrepreneur's viewpoint, selling debt securities (such as notes) is the optimum vehicle for raising capital since the entrepreneur prefers no equity dilution.

However, debt securities require that your business have actual or prospective cash flow to service the interest and principal payments on the debt. If that cash flow is questionable, the investor will undoubtedly want an "equity kicker" to compensate for this additional risk. The "equity kicker" will typically take the form of a warrant or other option to purchase common stock, usually at a nominal exercise price (for example, $.01 per share). The use of high-risk debt securities to finance your business is discussed in chapter 13.

Even if you are required to give an "equity kicker" to your investor, the equity dilution to you may be significantly less than if all the investment were made in common or preferred stock.

However, if the "equity kicker" is too high a percentage of your company, then consider the feasibility of a common or preferred stock financing. In determining what is "too high" a percentage of your company, consider the fact that the investor would receive back his or her entire investment, and still retain the "equity kicker." If your company were unable to repay the debt, your company could wind up in bankruptcy and your equity might be lost.

Theoretically, from the investor's viewpoint, debt securities with an equity kicker are an ideal investment form. The debt securities permit the investor to receive back their entire investment and still retain their equity kicker. However, the downside of debt securities from the investor's viewpoint is that they should, because of the decreased risk, receive a smaller percentage of the equity than they would have received if all their funds had been invested in equity.

Early-stage professionally managed venture capital firms rarely lend money to a company because they want to maximize the percentage of equity they acquire. Equity, in contrast to debt, provides the venture capitalist with unlimited upside potential if the business does well. Most early-stage companies do not have the cash flow to service debt securities.

Professional venture capitalists typically invest in preferred stock of the company convertible into common stock of the company. The use of preferred stock by professional venture capitalists is motivated partly by tradition and custom and partly because venture capitalists want to maximize the equity percentage they acquire.

Preferred stock typically permits the venture capital a liquidation preference over the common stock, the imposition of certain covenants on the company, veto rights over significant corporate actions, and a dividend preference. A "liquidation preference" means that if the company is sold or otherwise liquidated, the preferred stockholders can receive their investment (plus accrued but unpaid dividends) before any distribution is made to the entrepreneur who holds common stock. The liquidation preference usually equals the original investment made by the venture capitalist plus the amount of accrued but unpaid dividends (typically the equivalent of interest).

Selling preferred stock, rather than debt securities, permits the company to reflect the investment as additional shareholder equity rather than additional debt. This may permit the company to obtain trade credit because the company will reflect substantial shareholder equity in their balance sheet.

The preferred stock typically issued to the venture capitalist is actually not permanent equity, but is quasi-debt. The preferred stock is typically redeemable at the investor's option, in three to seven years (or earlier if certain default events occur). Most state laws prohibit a redemption of the preferred stock if the company would be rendered insolvent (that is, unable to pay its debts in the ordinary course of business).

Because of these redemption provisions, the SEC prohibits publicly traded companies from reflecting this redeemable preferred stock under the "Stockholders Equity" section of the balance sheet of a publicly traded company. However, private companies are still permitted under generally accepted accounting principles to reflect the preferred stock under "Stockholders Equity."

From the entrepreneur's viewpoint, if the company's cash flow cannot service debt securities or the entrepreneur does not wish to take that risk, the next preference should be to issue common stock, not preferred stock. Common stock typically has no redemption rights, liquidation preference, covenants, or veto rights, and places the investor in the same risk position as the entrepreneur.

Therefore, many angel offerings are structured with common stock and not preferred stock. In some cases, the common stock sold to angels is either of a non-voting or limited-voting class, with the entrepreneur retaining the voting class of common stock to assure control.

Example: Your company has received the following offers from different venture capitalists:

Offer No. 1 A $5 million loan, with a five-year bullet maturity (i.e., the principal is due and payable in a single payment at the date of maturity of the note—in this case, at the end of five years), interest at 8 percent per annum payable monthly, and warrants to purchase 30 percent of your company's common stock exercisable at a nominal price. As entrepreneur, you do not have to personally guarantee repayment of the loan.

Offer No. 2 $5 million to purchase your company's preferred stock, which has a dividend rate of 15 percent per annum (payable only on liquidation or redemption), redeemable at the holder's option after five years (or earlier upon certain default events), and convertible into 40 percent of your company's common stock. The covenants and veto rights in Offer No. 2 are identical to those in Offer No. 1.

Analysis: Offer No. 1 permits your company 10 percent less equity dilution than Offer No. 2. However, the trade-off is that your company must, under Offer No. 1, repay all the original capital plus interest and the venture capitalist still retains warrants to purchase 30 percent of your company's common stock. In the event of a default on the loan made pursuant to Offer No. 1, your company could be placed in bankruptcy and your equity might be eliminated.

Offer No. 2 dilutes the entrepreneur more than Offer No. 1, but that dilution may be justified by the fact that if the venture capitalist redeems the preferred stock after five years, the venture capitalist loses its equity completely and the entrepreneur resumes ownership of 100 percent of the equity. Under most state laws, the preferred stockholder cannot force redemption if the company would be rendered insolvent. Offsetting these advantages is the fact that Offer No. 2 would require the payment of a 15 percent per annum dividend rate in the event of liquidation or redemption of the preferred stock, in contrast to the 8 percent per annum interest rate in Offer No. 1.

If the business does well and can repay the $5-million loan plus interest, Offer No. 1 is the better choice for the entrepreneur. However, some entrepreneurs may sleep better at night with Offer No. 2. Of course, the best deal, if available, is usually a common-stock offering, but that is not an option in this example.

TAX-ADVANTAGED INVESTMENTS

If your company is a C corporation and sells to an investor stock (whether common or preferred) that was "qualified small-business stock" originally issued after August 10, 1993, and held for five years, the federal income tax rate on the gain will only be 14% (Section 1202 of the Internal Revenue Code). The limit on the tax exclusion is the greater of $10 million or ten times the aggregate-adjusted basis for all "qualified small-business stock" issued by the corporation and disposed of by your investors during a tax year. A special rollover provision permits an investor to satisfy the five-year holding period by selling qualified small-business stock held for more than six months and replacing it with qualified small-business stock of a different company during the five-year period.

"Qualified small-business stock" refers generally to a corporation engaged in manufacture, wholesale, or retail whose aggregate gross assets do not exceed $50 million (subject to qualification and exceptions). The corporation must meet active business requirements during substantially all of the period the investor held the stock.

Both venture capitalists and angel investors may well prefer to invest in stock that qualifies for the 50 percent exclusion.

If you decide to try to access professionally managed venture capital funds, understanding the organization and goals of these funds and how to select one is essential. These subjects are covered in the next chapter.

CHAPTER 6

PROFESSIONALLY MANAGED VENTURE CAPITAL

As most of us know, major companies such as Microsoft, Genentech, Intel, Digital Equipment Corporation, Federal Express, Compaq, and Sun Microsystems were financed with professionally managed venture capital.

Venture capital, in the sense of private risk capital, has existed in every society in one form or another. For example, in ancient Rome, Marcus Licinius Crossus, reportedly the richest man in Julius Caesar's Rome, financed many private enterprises.

Few businesses qualify for financing under the rigorous standards of the professional venture capitalist. Most businesses obtain their start-up capital from the personal resources of their founders and the founders' family and friends. After that start-up capital is exhausted, and assuming the businesses do not qualify for bank financing, they must seek capital from wealthy individuals and other nonprofessionally managed sources.

Although professional venture capitalists manage billions of dollars of funds, wealthy individuals probably provide an even larger pool of venture capital. However, because of their lack of organization, reaching these investors is difficult. Investment bankers, brokers, and other intermediaries play an important role in locating such capital.

The term "venture capital" is used loosely in the investment community to refer to a wide variety of investment strategies. These strategies range from very high-risk investments in seed or start-up companies to investors who provide only bridge financing to mature companies about to go public. Therefore, an analysis is required in determining whether a self-characterized "venture capitalist" is in fact a classic venture capital investor.

INDUSTRY OVERVIEW

According to the *1997 Annual Report of the National Venture Capital Association,* a total of 867 private equity funds existed as of December 31, 1997, of which 621 funds were classified as "venture funds," broken down as follows in Table 6.1:

TABLE 6.1   PRIVATE EQUITY FUNDS*

Fund Type	No.
Early/Seed Focused	220
Balance Focused	343
Later Stage Focused	58
All Venture	621
Buyout Funds	211
Mezzanine Debt	35
All Private Equity	867

*Reprinted with permission of VentureOne Corp., San Francisco.

Today's professional venture capital investor is looking for investments that have potential returns significantly exceeding normal investments. An overall return of 25 percent to 35 percent more per year is expected. This investor will typically reject hundreds of proposals before narrowing his or her sights on investments meeting its rigid criteria.

Of every ten investments he or she makes, a venture capitalist expects to lose money on at least five, to have no return or mediocre returns on four investments, and to do spectacularly well on one investment. That one investment must make up for all of the other losses. Thus, although venture capitalists hope for overall returns 25 percent to 35 percent or more per year, they can only achieve that objective if their one profitable investment has a return that is a multiple of 35 percent per year.

Table 6.2 demonstrates the actual performance of all private equity funds over a 20-year period:

TABLE 6.2   PERFORMANCE OF PRIVATE EQUITY FUNDS
AS OF 12/31/97*

Net IRR (%) to Investors for Investment Horizon Ending 12/31/97 for Private Equity Funds					
Fund Type	No.	1 Year	3 Years	5 Years	10 Years	20 Years
Early/Seed Focused	220	33.8	48.9	31.1	18.3	17.8
Balance Focused	343	22.6	37.3	25.3	14.9	13.8
Later Stage Focused	58	41.4	42.7	37.0	23.9	20.2
All Venture	621	29.5	41.2	28.1	16.7	15.4
Buyout Funds	211	22.1	21.3	21.7	19.9	21.2
Mezzanine Debt	35	10.3	13.9	15.1	10.7	11.1
All Private Equity	867	24.0	27.1	23.7	18.0	17.7

*Reprinted with permission of VentureOne Corp., San Francisco.

The investment goals of the venture capitalist can only be achieved by selecting investees that have huge potential growth and the management skills to achieve such growth. Certain kinds of businesses, such as high-technology–based companies, can achieve that goal. Other businesses, such as stable service businesses and local retail businesses, typically do not have the growth potential the venture capitalist is seeking.

Some large investment funds (such as state pension plans) invest a very small percentage of their portfolio in venture capital. Major corporations will also occasionally make small investments in tangentially related businesses.

Many investment advisory firms exist to professionally manage and invest venture capital funds. The venture capital funds are typically provided by institutional investors (for example: state pension funds, endowments, foundations, corporations) and wealthy individuals who do not possess the expertise to practice this specialized high-risk, high-reward investment strategy. These investment advisors tend to specialize in certain industries in which they believe they have the greatest expertise. Thus, some funds invest only in biotechnology companies, or only in computer software companies, and so on.

SOURCES OF FUNDS

Venture capitalists typically create investment funds or pools of money ranging in size from $25 to $100 million, with each investor (typically a limited partner) putting up $1 to $10 million. The venture fund is designed to exist for ten or twelve years, after which the remaining money and stock in companies is returned to the investors. A $100-million fund would have investments in 25 to 50 companies in its portfolio. The period for a first investment in new companies usually lasts three to five years, after which the remaining funds are used for subsequent financing for those companies that survive.

Table 6.3 illustrates the sources of venture capital funds:

**TABLE 6.3   CAPITAL COMMITMENTS ($BILLIONS)
BY LIMITED PARTNER TYPE (1979–1997)***

Limited Partner Type	1979	1997
Corporations	0.10	2.50
Endowments & Foundations	0.06	1.66
Foreign Investors	0.09	0.42
Individuals & Families	0.14	1.25
Insurance Companies	0.02	0.62
Pension Funds	0.19	3.95
Total	0.60	10.40

*Reprinted with permission of VentureOne Corp., San Francisco.

DESCRIPTION OF A VENTURE CAPITAL FUND

The following is a brief description of a typical venture capital fund according to a recent study by the Federal Reserve Bank of Philadelphia.

- **Organization of the Fund.** The typical venture capital fund is organized as a limited partnership, in which the venture capitalist—the *general partner*—invests 1 percent of the funds and the other investors—the *limited partners*—invest the remainder. Investors make an initial investment and also a commitment to provide funds up to some maximum dollar amount during the life of the fund. Limited partnerships have a fixed maturity, usually ten years for venture capital funds, with an option to extend the life of the fund up to three years. At the end of the fund's life, all cash and securities on hand are distributed to the fund's investors.

- **Management of the Fund.** As general partner, the venture capitalist plays an active role in managing the portfolio, but the fund's limited partners are not permitted to plan an active management role. However, the fund's investors do have limited voting rights concerning some decisions, for example, whether the fund's life should be extended at maturity. Investors also exercise some control through covenants, contractually agreed rules that place restrictions on the investment decisions of the venture capitalist. For example, one common covenant limits personal investments by fund managers in portfolio firms.

- **Compensation Scheme.** The venture capitalist's compensation has both a fixed and a variable component. The fixed component is a management fee, usually 2 to 3 percent of the funds already invested. The variable component is approximately 20 percent of the fund's profits—often called the *carried interest*—which is commonly paid to the venture capitalist only after investors have recovered their investment. (However, this strict priority scheme is not universal.) The remaining 80 percent of the fund's profits go to the investors.

SEED-STAGE FUNDS

Very few funds devote themselves exclusively to seed-stage companies. The reasons for that phenomenon are:

- As professionally managed funds have grown larger, there is more pressure on fund managers to increase the minimum size of their investments. Since the investment needs of seed and start-up is small, the investment size does not meet the minimum.
- It takes as much due diligence effort to make a small investment in a seed or start-up as a later-stage company.
- Seed and start-up companies are viewed as riskier than later-stage companies, and that risk is not necessarily completely compensated for by higher hurdle rates.

The size of professionally managed funds has increased as so-called "gatekeepers" of the large state pension funds have increased the minimum size of the investment in a venture capital fund. Gatekeepers for some large state pension funds use the "10 and 10 rule." That is, the minimum investment is $10 million into a venture fund, and investment cannot constitute more than 10 percent of the total invested.

As a result, venture capital funds that are funded by state retirement plans tend to be large. If a venture capital fund has over $100 million, fund managers find it difficult to justify an investment of only $500,000 in seed-stage or start-up.

The increasing size of professionally managed funds from 1980 to 1997 is illustrated in Table 6.4.

The lack of early-stage professionally managed venture capital funds has encouraged state and local governments to establish small venture funds to encourage economic development. For example, the Ben Franklin Technology Center of Southeastern Pennsylvania provides seed funding to entrepreneurs of up to $50,000 and has programs that provide further funding thereafter up to $250,000. In addition, various pockets of the federal government may

Table 6.4   Capital Under Management*
Summary Statistics

	1980	1987	1997
No. of Firms in Existence	71	317	371
No. of Funds in Existence	92	593	603
No. of Professionals	551	1,637	1,969
No. of First-Time Funds	14	15	47
No. of Funds Raised	29	87	143
Capital Raised This Year ($Billions)	0.4	3.4	10.4
Capital Under Management ($Billions)	2.2	20.0	45.6
Avg. Firm Size to Date ($Millions)	31.0	63.2	123.0
Avg. Fund Size to Date ($Millions)	23.9	33.8	75.7
Avg. Fund Raised ($Millions)	26.7	27.5	93.0
Largest Fund Raised to Date ($Millions)	167.0	1,175.0	2,022.0
Largest 10% Firms Manage ($Millions)	1.0	8.7	35.5
Largest 10% Firms Manage (%)	47%	44%	78%

*Reprinted with permission of VentureOne Corp., San Francisco.

provide early-stage financing in certain niche areas, including the so-called SBIR program.

Canadian Venture Capital

Canada, with a population approximately one-tenth as large as that of the United States, has an active venture capital community, which is described in Appendix 5. The Canadian venture capital industry is virtually identical to that of the United States, with the possible exception of labor-sponsored venture capital. Certain entities associated with Canadian labor unions are entitled to solicit venture capital funds from the public, as described in Appendix 5.

SELECTING A VENTURE CAPITALIST

The five basic criteria for selecting the most appropriate venture capitalist for your business are:

* Location
* Stage of development
* Industry specialization
* Capital required
* Leadership

Information concerning the profile of particular venture capitalists can be found in the brochures of the venture capital firms and standard publications, such as Lister and Harnish, *Directory of Venture Capital* (John Wiley & Sons, Inc., 1996) and Pratts' *Guide to Venture Capital* (Securities Data Publishing Company, 1997). The Lister book provides information on minimum investment requirements, which is not currently contained in Pratts'.

Location

Venture capitalists prefer to finance local companies. It is easier to perform due diligence and to monitor the company after the investment.

Some venture capitalists have a "two-hour rule." If it takes more than two hours to reach your office or plant from their office, you are less likely to be financed.

If location were the only factor, you would substantially increase your chances for financing if you were located in California (Silicon Valley preferably), as demonstrated in Table 6.5.

TABLE 6.5   DISBURSEMENTS BY STATE (1997)*

State	Companies	% of Total	Investment ($Billion)	% of Total
California	858	35.0	4.9	37.1
Massachusetts	274	11.2	1.4	10.4
Texas	121	4.9	0.8	6.2
New York	108	4.4	0.6	4.5
New Jersey	76	3.1	0.4	3.2
Illinois	60	2.4	0.4	3.0
Pennsylvania	84	3.4	0.4	2.8
Florida	52	2.1	0.4	2.8
Colorado	72	2.9	0.3	2.6
Washington	63	2.6	0.3	2.5
All Others	661	26.6	3.1	23.8
Total	2,429		13.1	

*Reprinted with permission of VentureOne Corp., San Francisco.

In fact, some companies located in an area with few venture capitalists have had to relocate to Silicon Valley to obtain financing.

Table 6.6, which reflects venture capital disbursements by regions, indicates the dominant position of Silicon Valley.

If your area is well-stocked with venture capitalists, a local venture capitalist is important if you expect to be financed by a national group of venture capitalists. Any venture capital syndicate would expect participation by a local venture capitalist who can monitor the investment.

TABLE 6.6   VENTURE CAPITAL DISBURSEMENTS ($MILLIONS)
BY REGION (1980-1997)*

Region	1980	1990	1997
Northern California	186.4	976.3	3,688.8
Northeast	171.7	998.6	2,694.0
Midwest	49.0	402.5	1,307.3
Southeast	55.2	286.9	1,245.4
Southern California	67.0	405.2	1,209.4
Southwest	91.4	310.4	978.7
Mid-Atlantic	55.9	306.6	898.1
Rocky Mountain	42.4	123.3	443.9
Northwest	12.8	92.6	415.7
Unknown	0.0	13.0	198.3
Total	731.8	3,915.5	13,079.5

*Reprinted with permission of VentureOne Corp., San Francisco.

Stage of Development

Each venture capitalist has a profile of the ideal stage of the company's development they would prefer for investment. Most larger venture capitalists prefer late-stage companies.

If your company is in the seed stage, you are probably wasting your time seeking capital from a later-stage venture capitalist. Focus your efforts in venture capitalists who are interested in early-stage investments.

One possible exception to this rule is if you are within the industry specialization of a normally late-stage venture capitalist and have an exciting management team and business concept. Even normally late-stage venture capitalists will occasionally take a flier on an earlier-stage company in these circumstances.

Some venture capital companies advertise that they will do start-up financing. However, because of the inconsistent usage of the word "start-up," they really mean first-stage investing.

Table 6.7 indicates venture capital disbursement by stage:

TABLE 6.7   VENTURE CAPITAL DISBURSEMENTS ($MILLIONS)
BY STAGE (1980–1997)*

Stage	1980	1990	1997
Expansion	208.4	1,731.9	5,329.2
Early	369.7	1,192.1	3,436.3
Later	68.6	618.9	2,997.0
Buyout	85.0	374.3	1,301.3
Total	731.8	3,917.2	13,063.9

*Reprinted with permission of VentureOne Corp., San Francisco.

Industry Specialization

All venture capitalists prefer certain industries and, in certain cases, specialize in their preferred industries. Tailor your search for a venture capitalist to the industry specialization the venture capitalist advertises.

Table 6.8 reflects 1997 venture capital disbursements by industry groups.

Amount of Capital Required

Early-stage companies generally find that larger venture capitalists prefer late-stage companies. Venture capitalists

TABLE 6.8   VENTURE CAPITAL DISBURSEMENTS BY INDUSTRY (1997)*

	All Investments		Initial Investments	
Industry Group	No. of Companies	Investment Amount ($Billions)	No. of Companies	Investment Amount ($Billions)
Information Technology	1,326	7.4	699	2.8
Med/Health/Life Science	497	2.9	231	1.0
Non-Technology	606	2.8	366	1.6
Total	2,429	13.1	1,296	5.4

*Reprinted with permission of VentureOne Corp., San Francisco.

with large funds to invest generally have a larger minimum investment. These minimum investment requirements may well exceed the needs of an early-stage company.

The economics of the venture capital industry dictate this phenomenon. As noted, it takes as much effort to invest $1 million as it does to invest $5 million. If the venture capital fund exceeds $100 million, it makes sense to create a $5-million minimum with up to 20 potential investments. A $1 million minimum would require up to 100 potential investments to exhaust the fund.

This phenomenon can be seen in Table 6.7, which reflects the trend toward expansion and later-stage funds from 1980 to 1997.

Leadership

Many venture capital firms prefer a passive role in investments. It is preferable to select a firm that is willing to assume a leadership role in the investment. The leader will then syndicate the investment to the passive venture capital funds.

APPROACHING A VENTURE CAPITALIST

You would do best to approach a venture capitalist through an intermediary known to and respected by the venture capitalist. Your attorney or financial advisor can help you in this regard.

CHECK OUT YOUR VENTURE CAPITALIST

Venture capital firms can vary significantly in their philosophy, culture, and approach to investee companies. Try to obtain the names and phone numbers of the founders and chief executive officers of the companies in which the venture firm has invested and check out the firm to the extent feasible. The so-called "vulture capitalist" can be avoided with some intelligent due diligence.

After you have selected a venture capital fund, the most important issue to you is how much equity you will have to give up to obtain an investment. This is determined by the valuation of your business, discussed in the next chapter.

CHAPTER 7

VALUING YOUR BUSINESS

T he value of your business before you receive an injection of equity is called its "pre-money" value and the value after the injection is the "post-money" value. Your pre- and post-money values determine how much equity you have to give up to outside investors. For example, if the pre-money value of your business is $4 million and outside investors are injecting $1 million of equity capital into your business, your outside investors should receive rights to 20 percent of your equity. This is computed as follows:

$$\frac{\$1 \text{ million}}{\$4 \text{ million} + \$1 \text{ million}} = \frac{1}{5} = 20\%$$

The numerator of the fraction is the outside equity capital injection and the denominator is the sum of (a) your pre-money value and (b) the amount of the outside equity capital injection.

Most professional venture capitalists compute the post-money value of the business at the projected exit date, and discount that figure to the present, before deciding the equity capital percentage they will require of your business. Thus, in the example, the venture capitalist may compute a post-money value of $5 million for your business by discounting a projected exit-date value of $50 million back to $5 million; therefore, its $1-million investment justifies a 20 percent equity interest.

Using the post-money valuation permits the venture capitalist to factor into the valuation the effect of the $1-million capital injection on the future projections of your business.

Most venture capitalists compute the post-money valuation of your business by using a discounted cash-flow method of valuation (described in the next section). The valuation is designed to permit the venture capitalist to achieve its so-called "hurdle rate," the minimum yearly investment return the venture capitalist expects before considering an investment.

For example, if the hurdle rate of the venture capitalist is 35 percent per annum, the post-money valuation will reflect the likely valuation of the business when the exit occurs (for example, in five years), discounted by a minimum of 35 percent per annum. The discounting rate will probably significantly exceed the 35 percent hurdle rate to allow for the possible risk that the exit valuation will not be achieved. As noted, a seed-stage business may have a 100 percent per year discount rate.

The exit valuation may be based upon a sale or an IPO valuation, or some combination. Thus, the venture capitalist's valuation analysis begins with a comparison of your company to other companies in your industry that have been sold or gone public. Once appropriate analyses are obtained, the discount rates are applied to reflect the expected hurdle rate and the risk that your business never reaches the exit objectives.

> **Tip:** The greater the time until the exit date, the greater the total discount for determining the present value of your business. If you can reasonably accelerate the exit date in your projections, you can generally achieve a higher present valuation for the business and, therefore, less equity dilution. The only exception is if by postponing the exit date you can increase the valuation by a significant amount greater than the yearly discount rate.

The pre-money value of your business is typically set forth in the term sheet provided to you by the venture capitalist. However, as explained in chapter 9, the pre-money value of your business contained in the term sheet may be rendered virtually meaningless by certain other clauses (such as participating-preferred stock, high redemption prices, and so on) also in the term sheet.

DISCOUNTED CASH-FLOW METHOD

The discounted cash-flow method of valuation is typically used for both early-stage business with no earnings as well as late-stage businesses as a method of double-checking the valuation obtained through other valuation methods discussed in this chapter.

Under this method of valuation, you look at future cash flows projected from the operations and discount them in accordance with time and risk factors. The higher the risk, the higher the discount factor.

The discounted cash-flow method begins with a projection of revenues and operating profit. These projected financial results are then adjusted for nonrecurring and nonoperating items of income and expense, and are reduced by taxes. The projected operating profit estimates (after taxes) are then further adjusted by adding back depreciation/amortization and deducting net investments in working capital and capital expenditures.

At the end of a given period, typically five or ten years, a "terminal" or "residual" value is calculated for the business. This "terminal" or "residual" value is then combined with the discount and flows to produce an overall valuation for the business. The "terminal" or "residual" value used by venture capitalists is the exit valuation. As noted, the exit valuation will be based on analogous companies that have been sold or are publicly traded.

The net equity value of the business, including the residual value, is then determined by deducting the market value of interest-bearing debt and adding the market value of nonoperating assets that remain in the business. An example of this calculation is contained in Table 7.1.

Obviously, a cash flow ten years from today is not worth the same amount to the investor as a current cash flow. Thus, the formula tends to give little current value to cash flows that are too far in the future.

Tip: The earlier the exit date set forth in your business plan, the higher the valuation of your business. Thus, if you have a choice of exiting in year 3 or year 5 at the same valuation, choose year 3. The business will only be more valuable with a year 5 exit date if the valuation growth between year 3 and year 5 exceeds the discount rate.

TABLE 7.1 DISCOUNTED CASH-FLOW VALUATION (000 OMITTED IN $ AMOUNTS)

	Year 1	Year 2	Year 3	Year 4	Year 5	Terminal Value
Revenues	$30,000	$45,000	$50,000	$55,000	$62,000	
EBIT	3,264	3,825	4,322	4,884	5,519	
Income taxes (cash basis)	1,110	1,301	1,469	1,661	1,876	
Net operating income	2,154	2,524	2,853	3,223	3,643	30,358
Cash flow adjustments						
Plus: Depreciation	1,392	1,800	2,034	2,298	2,597	
Less: Net change in working capital	(405)	(731)	(168)	(204)	(244)	
Capital expenditures	(1,966)	(3,675)	(4,161)	(4,398)	(4,697)	
Free cash flows	1,175	(82)	558	919	1,299	
Net present value at 12%	1,049	(65)	397	584	737	17,226

Total corporate value $19,928

Less: Market value of debt   12,528

Shareholder value $ 7,400

Discount Factor

The discount factor applied to the cash flows is arrived at by using various formulas, one of which is the Capital Asset Pricing Model. The Capital Asset Pricing Model sets the discount rate at the weighted average cost of equity and debt capital.

The Capital Asset Pricing Model estimates the future cost of a corporation's equity through a multi-factor equation and then determines the after-tax expected future costs of the corporation's debt. The final step is to compute the weighted average cost of capital, which is the weighted average cost of both equity and debt.

The weighted average cost of equity is computed by using the following equation: $re = rf + B (rm - rf)$, which can be defined as follows:

re = expected future cost of equity

rf = risk-free rate of return

B   = the Beta factor, which is a measurement of market risk with the figure 1 equaling a normative risk. One court has defined the Beta factor as "the nondiversified risk associated with the economy as a whole as it affects this firm."

rm = the market risk premium for this particular business

The "rm" factor together with the Beta factor in the equation has the effect of discounting the future cash flows by the risk of their nonoccurrence. The greater the risk of the projected cash flow not occurring, the higher the expected future cost of equity.

Your historical financial results are only relevant to this discounted cash-flow method to the extent that they give credence to the projections of future cash flow.

Other Valuation Methods

The discounted cash-flow valuation method is not the only method used by venture capitalists. Following are some of the other valuation methods.

Comparable Company Method of Valuation

The comparable company method of valuation typically involves comparing your company to the market capitalization and multiples of certain financial criteria (such as net income; projected net income; earnings before interest and taxes; earnings before depreciation, amortization, interest, and taxes; revenues and book value) of comparable public companies. Market capitalization refers to the public-trading price of the stock multiplied by the number of outstanding shares. Thus, if a comparable public company had a public-trading price of $20.00 per share and 2 million shares were outstanding, the overall market capitalization of that comparable public company would be $40 million.

The market capitalization method of valuation contains a number of defects. The trading price of shares of a public company does not normally reflect any control premium unless the company is expected to be sold shortly. Consequently, the public-trading price may significantly understate the overall value of the comparable public company in a sale situation where a control premium is paid for the shares.

In addition, comparing a publicly held company with a privately held company is difficult. Shares of public companies typically trade at a price that reflects the liquidity available to shareholders, which is not available to shareholders of a privately held company. As a result, privately held companies tend to sell at a discount compared to comparable publicly held companies. The problems with using market capitalization comparisons do not necessarily mean that this method of valuation is defective, since multiples of other financial criteria are also compared to the public company, such as the EBITDA multiple, in using the comparable company method of valuation.

Comparable Transaction Method of Valuation

Where information is available on the sale of comparable companies (whether public or private), this information is very valuable in assessing the value of your company. However, great care must be taken in using this information, since every company is unique and significant differences may exist between your company and the so-called "comparable company."

One major problem with this method is the lack of sufficient information that would enable you to judge how "comparable" another company is to yours. For example, your company may have one customer which accounts for 15 percent of your sales—a negative factor. You may not be able to determine whether the so-called comparable company had this same negative factor. Therefore, information on the sale price of the comparable company may be difficult to assess and should be taken with a grain of salt.

EBITDA Method

A number of fully developed businesses are valued by venture capitalists based on a multiple of accounting earnings or income before interest, taxes, depreciation, and amortization (the so-called "EBITDA") less debt. The EBITDA method is typically used for later-stage businesses, particularly where a sale exit is most probable.

Before applying the multiple, EBITDA is adjusted to remove expenses and revenue that will not be carried forward. These adjustments can be quite substantial for a closely held business that pays excessive compensation and perquisite to the owner and his or her family. Many investors will also subtract from the EBITDA any required yearly capital expenditures.

The adjusted EBITDA is then multiplied to obtain an "enterprise value." The multipliers typically range from four to seven times adjusted EBITDA. The pre-money investment value of the business is obtained by subtracting the company's debt from its enterprise value.

Asset-Accumulation Method

This method involves accumulating the going concern value of each of the specific assets of your business. This includes off-balance sheet assets, such as customer lists, product market identification, and value of your trained workforce, in addition to your balance-sheet assets. In computing going-concern value, three standard appraisal methods are utilized:

- Cost approach
- Income approach
- Market approach

The replacement cost of certain off-balance sheet intangible assets may be utilized to value them on the theory that a buyer could have to pay replacement cost to duplicate these assets. For example, if a buyer were to start your business from scratch, the buyer would have to incur costs until a trained management team and workforce could be assembled. These costs could be considered to be the value of your management team and workforce. A similar value could be applied to appraise your other intangible assets.

The value of your balance sheet and off-balance sheet assets is then combined to calculate the total value of your entire business.

Other Valuation Formulas

A myriad of other valuation formulas are used today.

If your business is asset-intensive, some economists suggest that your business value is equal to your "hard-assets" plus "goodwill." Hard-assets refer to the total fair-market value (which can be replacement cost) of your fixed assets and equipment, leasehold improvements, accounts receivable, and inventory. Your goodwill is your discretionary cash for one year—that is, the amount of cash you received as salary and dividends.

Another formula used for smaller businesses focuses on the seller's discretionary cash per year and multiplies this figure by 2.2727 to arrive at a sale price.

None of these or the many other formulas currently in use are universally applied. What is important is that you understand the particular valuation formula most likely to be applied to your business.

MINIMUM VALUE FORMULAS

The minimum value of your business is the higher of (a) its value to service acquisition debt or (b) its liquidation value.

Acquisition-Debt Value (Leverage Buyout Analysis)

If your business produces positive cash flow before interest, taxes, and depreciation/amortization (EBITDA), that cash flow can service (that is, pay interest and principal) a certain amount of acquisition debt for the buyer. The amount of acquisition debt that can be so serviced is the minimum value for your business, particularly to a financial buyer.

For example, assume that the excess cash flow of your business (EBITDA) is $500,000 per year, and that, based upon current interest rates, this $500,000 is sufficient to pay the interest and principal due on $3 million of bank debt that matures over a five-year loan term (exclusive of the balloon principal payment in the fifth year, which can be refinanced). The minimum value of your business would be $3 million, particularly to a financial buyer.

The amount of debt senior lenders will provide for a given business without an equity component has a limit. Therefore, once that debt limit is reached, your cash flow must be sufficiently high to be able to attract equity investors.

In this sense, you can determine the minimum value of your business using a leveraged buyout analysis.

Liquidation Value

Some businesses are only worth the liquidation value of their assets. Liquidation value refers to the price the owners would receive in an orderly liquidation—not in a fire sale. These businesses are typically not producing positive cash flow and do not have prospects of doing so.

SPECIFIC FACTORS THAT AFFECT VALUATION

Your business may have specific favorable and unfavorable factors that increase or decrease its valuation. The following list contains several examples.

Factors Increasing Valuation	Factors Decreasing Valuation
• Strong customer relationships at all levels	• Weak customer relationships and frequent turnover
• Proprietary products or services	• Lack of proprietary products or services
• No single customer accounts for more than 5 percent of revenues or profits	• A single customer accounts for over 15 percent of revenues or profits
• Strong management team (important mainly to financial buyers)	• A weak management team (so-called "one-man show" syndrome)
• Excellent employee turnover and relations	• Poor employee turnover and relations
• Consistent revenue and earnings trends	• Inconsistent revenue and earnings trends
• Plant and equipment in good repair	• Plant or equipment have been neglected and require significant repairs

You must analyze the strengths and weaknesses of your business and be prepared to point out the strengths and acknowledge the weaknesses, which the investor will probably discover in its due diligence process.

The two most important issues to an entrepreneur are (1) to obtain the highest valuation for his business and (2) to keep control of the business after the investment. The next chapter explains control issues.

Chapter 8

Keeping Control of Your Business

In general, whoever controls the majority of the members of your company's board of directors, controls your company under state corporate laws.

The board of directors, not the shareholders, controls all of the following major decisions:

Decision: Hire or fire officers or other employees
Who Decides: Solely board of directors, not shareholders

Decision: Incur debt
Who Decides: Solely board of directors, not shareholders

Decision: Enter into new line of business within "purpose" clause of charter
Who Decides: Solely board of directors, not shareholders

Decision: Purchase assets
Who Decides: Solely board of directors, not shareholders

Decision: Issue more common or preferred stock
without exceeding authorized number
of such shares in charter
Who Decides: Solely board of directors, not shareholders

Decision: Sale of some assets but not substantially all assets
Who Decides: Solely board of directors, not shareholders

Decision: Register shares under securities laws
Who Decides: Solely board of directors, not shareholders

Decisions on which shareholders must vote under state corporate laws generally include only the following:

- Charter amendment
- Merger, consolidation, or sale of substantially all assets
- Dissolution or division
- Election and removal of directors (unless staggered terms)

Following are the decisions that generally can be initiated only by the board of directors and must have prior board approval regardless of the wishes of the shareholders:

- Mergers, consolidations, or sale of substantially all assets
- In some cases (particularly public companies), charter amendments, dissolutions, and divisions

Thus, until the directors are replaced by the share-holders, the board of directors is in control. Even the replacement of directors by shareholders can be significantly delayed if the terms of the directors are staggered.

CONTROL PREMIUMS

Under most state laws, a controlling shareholder of a corporation is entitled to a premium from the sale of a controlling block of stock and need not share that premium with other shareholders. However, selling corporate office or management control by itself (that is, accompanied by no stock or insufficient stock to carry voting control) is illegal, as is selling to a looter or appropriating a corporate asset to the personal benefit of a control person.

According to § 5.16 of the American Law Institute's *Principles of Corporate Governance: Analysis and Recommendations (1994):*

> a controlling shareholder . . . has the same right to dispose of voting equity securities as . . . any other shareholder, including the right to dispose of those securities for a price that is not made proportionally available to other shareholders, but the controlling shareholder does not satisfy the duty of fair dealing to the other shareholders if:
>
> (a) The controlling shareholder does not make disclosure concerning the transaction . . . to other shareholders with whom the controlling shareholder deals in connection with the transaction; or
>
> (b) It is apparent from the circumstances that the purchaser is likely to violate the duty of fair dealing . . . in such a way as to obtain a significant financial benefit for the purchaser or an associate. . . .

As a *Comment* to § 5.16 states:

> Judicial decisions generally have allowed control-
> ling shareholders to sell their shares at a premium
> above the market price existing prior to the disclo-
> sure of the transaction without having required
> either that the premium be shared with other share-
> holders or that the transaction be restructured so
> that all shareholders could participate on the same
> terms. Sed, e.g., *Zetlin v. Hanson Holdings, Inc.* 48
> N.Y.2d 684, 421 N.Y.S.2d 877, 397 N.E.2d 387
> (1979); *Clagget v. Hutchinson,* 583 F.2d 1259 (4th
> Cir.1978); *Yerke v. Batman,* 376 N.E.2d 1211
> (Ind.App.1978); *Ritchie v. McGrath,* 1 Kan.App.2d
> 481, 571 P.2d 17 (1977). Section 5.16 follows these
> decisions and rejects the competing equal opportu-
> nity rule, which would require a premium to be
> initially offered to or later shared by all sharehold-
> ers on a pro-rata basis.

EXAMPLE OF CONTROL PROVISIONS

The typical venture capital agreement contained in Appendix 3 reflects the following provision concerning control
of the board of directors of the investee company:

> The Board of Directors shall consist of six members.
> The Holders of the Series A Preferred Stock shall
> have the right to elect two directors. The Holders of
> the Common Stock shall have the right to elect two
> directors. The Holders of Preferred Stock and the
> Holders of the Common Stock voting as a single class
> shall have the right to elect two officers of the cor-
> poration to serve as directors.

The professional venture capitalist typically purchases preferred stock, rather than common stock, of your company. In this case the venture capitalist purchased what is called Series A Preferred Stock, which is convertible into common stock.

The Series A Preferred Stock is entitled to elect two directors out of six. Clearly this is not a majority of the board. The common stock elects two directors out of the six directors. Two of the six directors are elected jointly by the holders of preferred stock and the holders of common stock voting as a "single class"; they must be officers of the company.

The two officers of the company are clearly the swing directors. If they vote with the two directors elected by the Series A Preferred Stock, control passes to the holders of the preferred stock.

So long as there are more shares of common stock than shares of Series A Preferred Stock, the common stock will prevail because both common and preferred stock vote as a "single class." However, that is not the end of the analysis because of the following provisions in the agreement:

- Clause (iii) of Section 7.6 of the venture capitalist's Stock Purchase Agreement (page 263, line 28 of Appendix 3) provides that the two swing directors are elected by the holders of the majority of the outstanding common stock *and* the holders of a majority of the outstanding Series A Preferred Stock, voting as separate classes. The effect of this provision is to afford the Series A Preferred Stock a veto right over who becomes a swing director.

- The two swing directors must be officers and the chief executive officer is appointed and removable by the Series A Preferred Stock (see Section 4(a) of the Amended and Restated Articles of Incorporation, commencing on page 284, line 6). Since the two officer swing directors report to the chief executive officer, who is in turn appointed and removed by the Series A Preferred Stock, it is likely that the economic interests of the two officer swing directors will be aligned with the interests of the chief executive officer. Since the chief executive officer is both hired and fired by the Series A Preferred Stock, it seems likely that he would align himself with the interests of the Series A Preferred Stock.

- The compensation committee of the board of directors is controlled by the preferred stock designees (see Section 7.7(k) of Stock Purchase Agreement on page 266 of Appendix 3). Since the compensation of the two officer swing directors is controlled by the compensation committee and the compensation committee is controlled by the Series A Preferred Stock, it is likely that the two officer swing directors will vote with the preferred stock.

- Section 7 of the Amended and Restated Articles of Incorporation (commencing on page 286 of Appendix 3) provides redemption rights, at the option of the Series A Preferred Stock, as early as six months after the date of the venture capital investment if the company fails to achieve a positive net income (see page 287). If the company fails to be profitable within the six-month period, the redemption rights of the preferred stock give the holders of the Series A Preferred Stock the right to receive back their investment out of funds legally available for that purpose. This leverage could permit the holders of the Series A Preferred Stock to control the company even if none of the prior provisions were effective.

TAG-ALONG CLAUSE

Most professional venture capitalists use the so-called
"tag-along" clause to make certain that they share in any
control premium. The clause permits the venture capital
to "tag along" on any sale of stock by the entrepreneur
and requires the venture capitalist to receive the same
price per share, thus insuring a proportionate sharing of
any control premium. An example of such a clause is contained in Appendix 3, page 319, paragraph 3.

Once a professionally managed venture capital fund
has decided to make an investment, it will provide you
with a term sheet such as the one contained in Appendix
1. You are now ready to negotiate.

CHAPTER 9

NEGOTIATING WITH A PROFESSIONAL VENTURE CAPITALIST

Despite popular belief to the contrary, you can negotiate with a venture capitalist. How much you can negotiate will depend upon your bargaining strength.

Bargaining strength is directly related in part on what other strategic alternatives you have and in part on the venture capitalist. If you wait until your situation is desperate to obtain venture capital, you will have almost no bargaining power. To enhance your bargaining power with the venture capitalist, you should attempt to attract as many venture capitalists as possible to your company. However, that strategy may not be effective if the venture capitalists decide to cooperate rather than compete.

A better strategy is to have angel investors waiting in the wings or to obtain a letter of intent from the underwriter for a small IPO.

You need to package your business in the most attractive manner you can and obtain professional help—an attorney and a business advisor who are experienced in

venture capital investments—to assist you in your negotiations. If you have personal venture capital experience,
you may be able to dispense with the business advisor.

Ten Major Issues in Negotiating Venture Capital Investment

The following outlines ten major issues in negotiating with
a professionally managed venture capital fund:

Valuation

- How much is your business worth? (The greater its
  value, the less equity dilution you suffer for the same
  amount of investment.)

Funding of Investment

- Is the entire investment paid at closing, or is the
  investment paid over time?

Control of Board of Directors

- Who elects the majority of board members? (See
  chapter 8.)

    If officers are board members, who controls their
  compensation (that is, composition of board compensation committee)?

Form of Investment

- Preferred stock, common stock, and/or notes (convertible or not) and/or warrants?

If Investment Is in Preferred Stock

- What dividend rate and when does it commence?
- What liquidation rights?
- What conversion rights? (Do accrued but unpaid dividends also convert?)
- Is preferred stock participating or not?
- What voting rights for directors and on other shareholder issues?
- What special protections (such as veto rights) are given to preferred stock over corporate actions?
- What redemption rights are given to holders of preferred stock and to company?
- What anti-dilution protections—full-ratchet or weighted-average (how determined?)—and other protective clauses?

Management Incentives and Disincentives

- *Incentives:* Stock options and other incentive plans?
- *Disincentive:* Forfeiture of stock if employment is terminated?

Employment Contracts

- For whom?
- Term?
- Compensation?

Protection of Proprietary Information

- What protection is afforded to proprietary information?

Stockholders' Agreement

- Tag-along rights?
- Drag-along rights and other provisions?

Registration Rights

- How early can investor require registration?
- How many demand registration rights and piggy-back rights?
- Other covenants?

Valuation Issues

The negotiations begin with the venture capitalist providing you with a term sheet, which is a brief summary of the major deal terms. A term sheet for a recent early-stage investment is set forth in Appendix 1.

The valuation of your business determines the amount of equity you must give to the venture capitalist in exchange for his investment in your business. As discussed in chapter 7, the percentage of the equity to which the venture capitalist is entitled is determined by the following formula:

$$\frac{\text{amount of investment in company}}{\text{pre-money value of company + amount of investment in company}}$$

The term "pre-money" value of your company refers to its value prior to the investment. For example, if your company has a pre-money value of $1 million and the venture capitalist is investing $500,000 in your company, the venture capitalist is entitled to 33 percent of your equity, computed as follows:

$$\frac{\$500,000}{\$1 \text{ million} + \$500,000} = 33 \tfrac{1}{3}\%$$

The term "post-money" valuation refers to the value of the business after the investment. In the above example, the post-money evaluation is $1.5 million.

In most negotiations, venture capitalists will advise you as to what they consider to be the pre-money value of your business. However, a better strategy for entrepreneurs is to develop their own valuation model and to convince the venture capitalist of the correctness of this valuation.

Your business advisor is your best source of information on pre-money valuation. A competent business advisor will be able to provide you with analogies to other businesses, particularly publicly traded companies, and extrapolate a pre-money valuation from these analogies. Since the valuation of the business involves more educated guesses than science, your business advisor's educated guesses are just as good as the venture capitalist's educated guesses and should be given to the venture capitalist early in the negotiation.

SUBTLE METHODS OF DECREASING VALUATION

Venture capitalists use at least six methods to increase the percentage of equity in your company to which they are entitled through the legal drafting of the venture capital agreement. These methods are:

- Requiring you to issue participating-preferred instead of nonparticipating-preferred stock
- Requiring accrued dividends on preferred stock to be converted into additional equity
- Requiring full-ratchet anti-dilution clauses, rather than average-price anti-dilution clauses
- If the investment is made in stages, accruing preferred-stock dividends on each of the staged investments before all has been received
- Counting stock options as outstanding stock
- High redemption prices and miscellaneous methods

Participating vs. Nonparticipating Preferred Stock

The characteristics of the preferred stock that must be issued to the venture capitalist can significantly affect the valuation of your business.

The term sheet in Appendix 1 reflects a pre-money valuation of $4.75 million and the injection in stages of $3.5 million into the company. In return, the venture capitalist receives shares of "participating-preferred stock" of the company. One would presume that the post-money valuation of the business would therefore be $8.25 million ($4.75 million + $3.5 million).

Shares of "participating-preferred stock" permit the holder to receive, in the event of the sale or other liquidation of the business, their original investment back (plus accrued but unpaid dividends).

For example, suppose all assets of the business were sold for $8.25 million in cash plus the assumption by the buyer of all of its liabilities. Under these circumstances, $8.25 million would be available for distribution among all holders of preferred stock and common stock.

With a "participating" preferred stock, the holder of the preferred stock receives the first slice of the $8.25 million by taking back their original investment of $3.5 million.

Although the term sheet in Appendix 1 is ambiguous, the $3.5 million may also be increased by accrued but unpaid dividends at the rate of 4 percent per annum (which is the rate set forth in the term sheet for dividend accruals). For purposes of this computation, we assume that the accrued but unpaid dividends are not added to the $3.5 million.

The payment of $3.5 million to the preferred stock reduces the amount available to further distribution to $4.75 million ($8.25 million less $3.5 million). The remaining $4.75 million is then divided between the participating-preferred stock and the common stock in accordance with the ratio of preferred stock investment ($3.5 million) over the pre-money value of $4.75 million plus the $3.5 million, or 42 percent.

Thus, the percentage of the remaining $4.75 million paid to the participating preferred stock is computed as follows:

42 percent of $4.75 million =
$1.995 million to preferred stock

58 percent of $4.75 million =
$2.755 million to common stock

The effect of this sale of the business at $8.25 million is that the preferred stock receives a total of $5.495 million ($1.995 million + $3.5 million) and common stock receives a total of $2.755 million.

If the common stock receives only $2.755 million out of sale proceeds totaling $8.25 million, what is the meaning of the $4.75 million "pre-money" value set forth in the term sheet? The answer is that it has no meaning because participating-preferred stock is to be received by the venture capitalist.

The correct pre-money value of this business is really only $2.755 million. The entrepreneur who believes the term sheet "pre-money" valuation of $4.75 million is incorrect. The only purpose of the $4.75 million "pre-money" value in the term sheet was to provide a mechanism to divide the sale or liquidation proceeds after the original investment of the preferred stock had been returned.

If the preferred stock had not been "participating," but instead was "non-participating," the $4.75-million pre-money valuation would have been correct. Under those circumstances the preferred stock would not have been entitled to receive its original investment (possibly plus 4 percent dividend) before the split with the common stock. Thus, if the assets of the company had been sold for $8.25 million and the buyer had assumed all liabilities, the $8.25 million would have been divided as follows, using the 42 percent to 58 percent division between the preferred stock and common stock:

42 percent of $8.25 million =
$3.5 million (with rounding) to the preferred stock
58 percent of $8.25 million =
$4.75 million to the common stock

Moral: Understanding the true valuation of your business requires a detailed legal and business analysis of the terms of the preferred stock.

Converting Accrued Dividends into Additional Equity

The preferred stock typically purchased by the venture capitalist contains a dividend rate. In Appendix 1, the dividend rate is 4 percent per annum. The 4 percent per annum dividend is applied to the original investment of $3.5 million and increases the liquidation preference of the preferred stock each year by 4 percent. Some venture capitalists, in computing the number of shares of common stock into which the preferred stock is convertible, also require that the accrued dividends, as well as the original investment, be convertible. The venture capitalists do not require such conversion in the agreement set forth in Appendix 3.

The previous discussion assumes that the accrued but unpaid dividend on the preferred stock does not increase the conversion percentage of the preferred stock. If such unpaid dividends did increase the conversion percentage of the preferred stock, the split would become more unfavorable for the common stock.

For example, if nonparticipating-preferred stock had an accrued dividend rate of 4 percent per annum, convertible into additional shares of common stock, and was outstanding for five years before the sale at $8.25 million, the split could be computed as follows: preferred stock receives at least 47 percent of proceeds (versus 42 percent if dividend was not convertible into additional common stock) and common stock receives at most 53 percent of proceeds (versus 58 percent if dividend was not convertible into additional common stock).

Anti-Dilution Clauses

Two general types of anti-dilution clauses are used by professional venture capitalists in their legal documents:

- Full-ratchet anti-dilution clause
- Weighted-average anti-dilution clause

In the full-ratchet anti-dilution clause, if the company issues more stock after the closing of the venture capital financing at a lower valuation than that used by the venture capitalist at the closing, the venture capitalist obtains the benefit of the lower valuation. For example, in the venture capital agreement set forth in Appendix 3, the company issued 50,000 shares of Series A Convertible Preferred Stock at $20 per share to the investors. Each of the 50,000 shares of Series A Preferred Stock is convertible into 50,000 shares of Common Stock, which represents approximately 32 percent of the common stock.

If after the closing, the company were to issue shares at $10 per share, the conversion rate on the Series A Convertible Preferred Stock would increase so that the 50,000 shares of preferred stock would convert into 100,000 shares of common stock, or approximately 46 percent of the company. This reduces the entrepreneur's percentage of the company by an additional 14 percent and increases the venture capitalist's percentage by the same amount.

The problem with the full-ratchet anti-dilution clause is that the increase in the venture capitalist's percentage occurs even if only one share is issued at $10 per share. The full-ratchet clause does not proportionalize the dilution by the number of shares actually issued below the initial valuation of the venture capitalist.

The weighted-average anti-dilution clause takes into account how many shares were issued at $10 per share. Thus, if only one share were issued at $10 per share, there would be virtually no change in the percentage of the common stock to which the venture capitalist was entitled upon conversion of its preferred stock.

Even the weighted-average clauses can be unfair to the entrepreneur if these clauses have either of the following characteristics:

- The clause does not average sales above the venture capitalist's valuation (for example, $20 per share) with sales below that price.

- The clause measures dilution by looking only to the number of preferred shares outstanding before and after the dilutive event, rather than considering the total number of shares of common stock computed on a fully diluted basis (that is, treating convertible securities as if they were converted and stock options as if they were exercised).

Although professional venture capitalists will require either a full-ratchet or weighted-average anti-dilution clause, angels do not necessarily require such clauses. This is a matter of negotiation with the angel. In many cases, it is possible to sell common stock of your company to angels, so that these anti-dilution provisions never become an issue.

Dilution Through Certain Types of Staged Financing

Staged financing refers to a financing structure in which the venture capitalist's funds are not paid in full at the closing. Your business may not be able to absorb all of the investment immediately; therefore, it makes sense to provide the money in installments.

In early-stage companies, the venture capitalist may require the achievement of certain milestones as a condition to further investment. This reduces the venture capitalist's risk and requires you to demonstrate the ability of your business to achieve these milestones before you receive further funding.

Staged financing does not reduce the pre-money valuation of your business unless one of the following two provisions is contained in the venture capital agreement:

- The venture capitalist receives preferred stock representing all of his or her investment at closing even though not all the venture capitalist's money is invested at closing and preferred stock dividends on all of the investments start to accrue at closing.

- In the case of investment based on milestones, your company is worth significantly more upon achievement of the milestones than the valuation initially given by the venture capitalist.

An example of the first form of dilution can be found in the venture capital agreement set forth in Appendix 3. In that agreement, the venture capitalist invests $1 million in exchange for 50,000 shares of Series A Convertible Preferred Stock of a software company known as ABC, Inc. The cost per share is $20. The venture capitalist pays $500,000 at the closing and is required to pay $500,000 six months after the closing; this obligation is evidenced by a promissory note bearing no interest executed by the venture capitalist.

Even though only $500,000 is paid at the closing, all 50,000 shares of Series A Convertible Preferred Stock are issued at the closing. As a result of issuing all 50,000 shares at closing, not just the 25,000 preferred shares that were paid for by the $500,000, the common stockholders are diluted by the accrual of dividends on the 25,000 preferred shares not yet paid for. Since these dividends accrue at the rate of $3 per year, the dividend preference on the preferred stock has been increased by $37,500 (25,000 × $1.50 per share for six months), even though no interest is paid on the $500,000 note.

Counting Stock Options As Outstanding Stock

If the venture capitalist's valuation shows that he or she is entitled to 33⅓ percent of your equity for his or her investment in your company, and your company has 6,000 shares of common stock outstanding, the venture capitalist should clearly receive preferred stock convertible into 3,000 shares of your common stock. The 3,000 shares produces a fraction of 33⅓ percent of the total of 9,000 shares of common stock outstanding after the conversion of the preferred stock (6,000 existing shares of common stock plus an additional 3,000 resulting from the conversion of preferred stock).

If your company also has employee stock options outstanding for 600 shares of common stock in the foregoing example, some venture capitalists would want their preferred stock convertible into 3,200 shares of common stock, rather than 3,000 shares of common stock. Their theory is that they should not be diluted by employee stock options, if and when they are exercised.

This argument has some merit if the employee stock options have exercise prices for common stock below the price paid per share for common stock by the venture capitalists (assuming the preferred stock was converted to common stock). However, some venture capitalists require the inclusion of employee stock options in the calculation even if the option exercise price equals or exceeds the price paid per share by the venture capitalist.

The effect is that the entrepreneur's equity percentage is diluted by the outstanding employee stock options, thereby indirectly reducing the valuation of the entrepreneur's share of the company. Employee stock options are many times issued in lieu of salary, which would otherwise have been borne by the business as a whole. Therefore, one may argue that saddling the entrepreneur with the entire cost of the employee stock options is unfair.

High Redemption Prices and Miscellaneous Methods

The typical venture capitalist will require your company to buy his or her preferred stock shares through a redemption right exercisable three to seven years after the date of the investment. The redemption right is intended to afford the venture capitalist an exit if your company is not sold and does not effectuate an IPO that provides for a satisfactory return to the venture capitalist.

Usually, the redemption price is equal to the original investment plus the amount of the accrued but unpaid dividends. However, some venture capitalists require a redemption price that is three or more times the original investment, often accompanied by a similar liquidation preference.

For example, suppose a venture capitalist declares that your company has a pre-money valuation of $10 million and the venture capitalist invests $5 million (thereby creating a $15 million post-money valuation for your company). The venture capitalist would typically acquire preferred stock convertible into one-third of your outstanding common stock (after conversion). If the venture capitalist requires a redemption right after five years that entitles him to receive three times the original investment (i.e., $3 \times \$5$ million, or $15 million), this redemption right completely undermines the original $10 million pre-money valuation. Thus, if the business were sold after five years for $15 million, all of the proceeds would belong to the venture capitalist because of the redemption right or similar liquidation preference. You and the other common stockholders of your company would not benefit from the sale until the valuation exceeded $15 million and then only to the extent of the excess.

If the business were sold for $17 million, only $2 million would be distributed to the common stockholders, thereby rendering meaningless the $10 million pre-money valuation.

There are various other methods used by venture capitalists that undermine the pre-money valuation contained in the venture capitalist's term sheet. For example, some venture capitalists increase the conversion right of their preferred stock if certain goals are not satisfied. Other venture capitalists obtain warrants that entitle them to purchase additional common stock of your company for a nominal consideration if certain adverse events occur.

There is no limit to the number of methods that can be used by a venture capitalist to effectively change the valuation of your business. A careful review of the term sheet by a knowledgeable securities lawyer who has experience in this area should detect these subtle methods of undermining the pre-money valuation given to you by the venture capitalist.

Control of the Company

Most professional venture capitalists do not require you to give them control of your business; however, some do. You should initially inquire as to this issue before selecting a venture capitalist.

The board of directors of a corporation makes all significant decisions of importance to the corporation, as noted in chapter 8. The shareholders have certain veto rights on major transactions and elect the board. Therefore, the venture capital agreement must be carefully examined to determine who controls your board of directors.

Control of the shareholder vote, as illustrated in chapter 8, is much less important to the entrepreneur than is control of the board vote. Control of the board vote means that the entrepreneur needs a majority of all board members, assuming that each has one vote.

The typical venture capitalist will require representation on your board of directors. Many venture capitalists require a board of directors consisting of five persons, two selected by the common stock (which you control), two selected by the preferred stock (which the venture capitalist controls), and one director who is either independent or selected from among the officers. The tie-breaking director may be elected by the preferred stock and common stock voting together. If there are more shares of common stock than shares of preferred stock, the common stock will likely control that selection.

However, some venture capital agreements permit the preferred stock a veto right over the selection of the tie-breaking directors (see chapter 8). If the tie-breaking director is to be selected from among the officers, the entrepreneur should ask who controls the compensation of those officers. If the majority of the board of directors' compensation committee board of directors must consist of the venture capitalist's representatives, the tie-breaking director may not be completely neutral.

Even though professional venture capitalists do not require you to give up control, they typically will (1) give themselves veto rights over any major corporate action and (2) provide both overt and subtle methods of exercising control. These veto rights typically include the following subjects at a minimum:

- Issuing more stock
- Buying back stock
- Dividends
- Sales, mergers, consolidations, or dissolution
- Changes in your company's charter or bylaws

Professionally managed venture capitalists may also require veto rights over the following decisions:

- Selection or termination of the CEO
- Incurrence of debt
- Changes in board structure or in your business

Redemption Rights

Another control mechanism utilized by professionally managed venture capitalists is to permit their preferred stock to be redeemable on certain events. Typically, the redemption rights will become effective around the fifth year. However, some venture capitalists add provisions permitting redemption even earlier if certain milestones or projections in the business plan are not met.

This redemption right gives venture capitalists an important control mechanism. If they can force the company to repurchase the preferred stock (plus accumulated but unpaid dividends), they can exercise substantial influence over the company, particularly if the company cannot afford to redeem the preferred stock.

Most state corporate statutes do not permit a forced redemption of stock if the redemption would cause the company to be unable to satisfy its other debts in the ordinary course of business. State law may also contain other limitations on the legal ability of the venture capitalist to force redemption.

Drag-Along Rights

A "drag-along" clause permits the venture capitalist to force the sale of the company, including the stock of the entrepreneur. It is used by some, but not all, professional venture capitalists, particularly in early-stage business. An example of a "drag-along" clause is contained in Appendix 3, page 321, paragraph 8.

If the venture capitalist insists upon a "drag-along" clause, the entrepreneur should attempt to eliminate it or place significant limitations on the use of this powerful clause. The existence of a "drag-along" clause also provides significant leverage and control to the venture capitalist.

If the "drag-along" clause cannot be eliminated, you might negotiate with a venture capitalist for possible limitations on the "drag-along" clause, such as the following:

- Limiting the ability to exercise the "drag-along" clause for the first several years on the theory that a

sale should not be forced until management has had a reasonable opportunity to operate the business
- Limiting the ability to exercise the "drag-along" clause to situations in which the goals of the business plan have not been satisfied by a wide margin over a significant period of time
- Conditioning the venture capitalist's right to exercise the "drag-along" clause on a right of first refusal given to the entrepreneur, or at least the right to make the first offer to purchase the business

FORM OF INVESTMENTS

Professional venture capitalists will typically require your company to issue preferred stock, convertible into common stock, in exchange for their investment. The preferred stock will typically contain provisions permitting the holder to force the company to redeem it at the end of five years, and earlier if certain conditions occur. In effect, the preferred stock investment of the venture capitalist is really just a disguised long-term debt, convertible into your stock if things go well.

There are three major reasons for requiring your company to issue preferred stock:

- If your company is liquidated, the venture capitalists will receive their money as preferred stockholders (plus accrued but unpaid dividends) prior to any distribution on the common stock. For this purpose, "liquidation" may include a sale or merger.
- For purposes of balance-sheet presentation, preferred stock might be classified under the stockholder equity section of your balance sheet. If the venture capitalist received notes, they would be viewed as an

additional liability of the company, thereby making your company less attractive to potential suppliers and bankers.

- The use of preferred stock also permits the preferred stockholders, voting as a separate class, to have veto rights over certain corporation transactions.

If the venture capitalist uses preferred stock, the following issues would typically be covered in the term sheet:

- What is the dividend rate and when does it commence?

  Note: The dividend rate, typically ranging from 4 percent to 15 percent per annum on the original investment by the venture capitalist, is actually a form of disguised interest, which adds to the liquidation preference of the preferred stock. If the company is sold or otherwise liquidated, in some term sheets the accrued dividends are convertible into additional shares of common stock.

- What liquidation rights?

  Note: The liquidation rights are typically equal to the original investment by the venture capitalist plus accrued but unpaid dividends.

- What conversion rights (do accrued but unpaid dividends also convert)?

  Note: The right of the preferred stock to be converted into common stock is determined by the pre-money valuation of your business. See chapter 7.

- Is preferred stock participating or not?

  Note: Participating-preferred stock typically permits the venture capitalist, in the event of a sale or other liquidation, to receive back the original investment and the right to convert to a certain percentage of your common stock for purposes of dividing the remaining proceeds. Nonparticipating-preferred stock does not permit the venture capitalist to receive back the original investment in addition to the right to convert into common stock.

- What voting rights for directors and on other shareholder issues?

- What special protections (such as veto rights) are given preferred stock over corporate actions?

- What redemption rights are given to holder of preferred stock and to company?

  Note: A "redemption right" is the right of the preferred stock to demand the repayment from the company, usually of the original investment plus accrued but unpaid dividends. Typically, the preferred stock redemption rights commence five years after the date of the original investment or earlier if certain default events occur.

- Anti-dilution protections—full-ratchet, weighted-average (how determined?) and other protective clauses?

The terms of the preferred stock should be negotiated, to the extent the entrepreneur has bargaining power, to avoid provisions that overtly or subtly reduce the valuation of the company as previously set forth. For example, efforts should be made to avoid conversion rights with respect to accrued but unpaid dividends. So-called "participating" preferred stock should be avoided because of its equity dilution, and weighted-average dilution clauses should be negotiated in lieu of so-called full-ratchet clauses.

MANAGEMENT INCENTIVES AND DISINCENTIVES

Your negotiation with a venture capitalist should include the reservation of a certain percentage of shares of common stock for your key employees. Typically, venture capitalists will permit a reservation of 5 percent to 10 percent of the outstanding common stock for that purpose.

However, certain venture capitalists will consider the reserved stock as if it were part of the outstanding shares of common stock for purposes of computing the pre-money valuation of your company and the percentage of your company's stock to which they are entitled for their investment. Thus, if the venture capitalist is entitled to one-third of your outstanding stock in exchange for his or her investment, the one-third will also apply to your reserved management stock. Under these circumstances, the reserved stock will be diluting your own equity interest.

Venture capitalists differ on this issue; you may, therefore, be able to negotiate a provision whereby the reserved stock does not increase the percentage of shares to which the venture capitalist is entitled.

Venture capitalists typically will not object to a stock-option plan in which the option price is based upon the valuation given to the company by the venture capitalist. This gives the key employees an incentive to grow the company above the venture capitalist's valuation. If no growth occurs, the option becomes valueless.

Venture capitalists also provide disincentives to the key employees, including the entrepreneur, if they terminate their employment with the company. These disincentives are usually provided for in a stock-restriction agreement that requires the forfeiture of a percentage of the key employee's stockholdings if he or she leaves employment or is terminated with cause.

An example of such an agreement, which provides for the forfeiture of up to 60 percent of the key employee's stock, is contained in the Stock Restriction Agreement of Appendix 3 commencing on page 301. The Stock Restriction Agreement contained in Appendix 3, provides for the forfeiture of the full 60 percent of the stock if the termination occurs within one year after the closing. The forfeiture percentage decreases each year thereafter until the fourth anniversary of the investment, when the forfeiture provision lapses.

EMPLOYMENT CONTRACTS AND AGREEMENTS

The professional venture capitalist will typically require the entrepreneur and his or her key employees to enter into employment contracts and agreements to preserve proprietary information and to prevent competition. An example of such an employment agreement is contained in Appendix 3, beginning on page 325; and an example of an agreement protecting proprietary information and to prevent competition is also contained in Appendix 3, starting on page 289.

Typically, the employment contract is reserved for the top two executives, whereas all key employees (and possibly all employees) are required to sign the employee agreement protecting proprietary information.

The entrepreneur should not take great comfort in his or her employment contracts. The primary purpose of the employment contract is to legally bind the entrepreneur to a minimum period of employment and a fixed compensation.

If the entrepreneur does not control the board of directors, nothing can prevent the board of directors from terminating the entrepreneur's employment even before the end of the term of the employment contract. This is true whether or not the entrepreneur has created any "cause" for the termination. If your employment is terminated in breach of the employment agreement, you must mitigate damages by seeking another position and offsetting any income earned from this other position against the damages caused by the premature termination of your employment contract.

If you wish to assure yourself that you cannot be fired by the board of directors, and assuming that you are a member of the board, you must negotiate a clause in the corporate charter that requires unanimous consent of the board for any employment contract termination. Merely placing a clause in the employment agreement that you cannot be terminated during the term of the contract is legally ineffective since the board of directors normally has a legal right to breach any executive employment contract.

It may also be worthwhile to place a clause in the employment contract eliminating any duty you might have to mitigate damages for breach of the employment contract by the company. The effect of such a clause would be that, if you were terminated without cause, the company would owe you compensation for the remaining term of the contract, and that compensation could not be reduced by any income you earn elsewhere.

STOCKHOLDERS' AGREEMENT

The Stockholders' Agreement typically prevents you from selling your stock without giving a right of first refusal to the preferred stockholders. It may also contain the "tag-along" and "drag-along" clauses previously discussed. An example of a Stockholders' Agreement is contained in Exhibit D of Appendix 3, commencing on page 316.

REGISTRATION RIGHTS

Professional venture capitalists typically require the company, upon request, to register their stock under the Securities Act of 1933. The costs of preparing and filing such a registration statement can be considerable, generally exceeding $200,000 for a first-time registrant.

The professional venture capitalist requires registration rights in order to facilitate a public-offering exit strategy. Since only the company can register stock under the Securities Act of 1933, the professional venture capitalist registration rights clause contractually requires the company to register upon request a minimum percentage of the preferred stock. An example of such a clause is contained in Section 6 of Appendix 3, which commences on page 245.

It would be foolish for the professional venture capitalist to request registration unless an underwriter or other purchaser of the stock was ready to acquire the stock once the registration became effective. However, the existence of the registration rights clause creates leverage, which the entrepreneur should attempt to reasonably limit.

For example, most venture capitalists will negotiate extending the date when the registration rights commence from one year to two or more years after the initial investment. Since only the company can file a registration statement with the Securities and Exchange Commission under the Securities Act of 1933, the entrepreneur may also need a registration rights covenant if the entrepreneur could lose control of the board of directors. In such a situation, the entrepreneur could find himself with a significant amount of stock that could not be publicly sold after the IPO (with the possible exception of sales under Rule 144, which permits at least 1 percent of the outstanding stock to be sold every three months if certain conditions are satisfied).

OTHER COVENANTS

The typical venture capital agreement contains a variety of covenants, such as:

- A requirement that monthly, quarterly, and annual financial reports be sent to preferred stockholders
- A requirement to permit preferred stock investors certain observation rights, including the right to attend Board of Director meetings
- A requirement not to issue employee stock options without approval of the compensation committee of the board of directors (which is usually controlled by the venture capitalist)
- A requirement to give preemptive rights for any new stock issuance to holders of preferred stock
- A requirement to maintain life insurance on the life of the entrepreneur(s), payable solely to the company, usually in an amount at least equal to the venture capital investment
- A requirement as to the number of preferred stockholder designees who must sit on the board of directors and its compensation committee
- A requirement to pay tax and maintain adequate insurance, preserve corporate existence, comply with laws, maintain adequate books and records, maintain properties and assets, comply with ERISA, and so on
- A requirement to obtain approval by the majority of the preferred stock for capital and operating expense budgets, cash-flow projections, profit-and-loss projections, and the company's business plan
- A requirement to obtain approval from the compensation committee of the board of directors (typically controlled by venture capital designees) of all compensation and fringe benefits for officers
- Limitations on transactions with affiliates and major corporation transactions
- Prohibition on repurchase of shares or charter or bylaw amendments or changes in the nature of the business

Many (but not all) of these covenants disappear when the company has a qualified IPO.

A "qualified public offering" typically requires an IPO at a valuation of at least five to six times the price per share paid by the venture capitalist, which raises a minimum amount of IPO proceeds (typically $20 million or more). If there is an IPO, but it is not a "qualified public offering," the covenants will continue in effect.

However, most underwriters typically insist upon changes in the covenants as a condition to the underwriting. If the IPO valuation gives some benefit to the venture capitalist (even though not the five to six multiple), most professional venture capitalists will negotiate covenant changes.

An example of these covenants is contained in Section 7 of Appendix 3, commencing on page 259.

These covenants are fairly standard; therefore, it is difficult to negotiate major changes. However, you can usually make minor changes to certain clauses in appropriate circumstances.

For example, many venture capitalists may waive the requirement for monthly financial statements and budgets and will agree to quarterly or semiannual financial statements and budgets. Likewise, the amount of life insurance on the entrepreneur's life may be negotiable if the cost is too high.

CHAPTER 10

SUMMARY AND ANALYSIS OF A VENTURE CAPITAL AGREEMENT

T he following is a brief summary of a professionally managed venture capital agreement, which appears in Appendix 3 of this book. The company was a developer of software that was to be sold at retail for the purpose of assisting investors with their portfolios. The agreements represent first drafts as furnished by counsel for the professionally managed venture capital firm.

The total investment was $1 million and the professionally managed venture capital firm, called XYZ, Ltd., purchased 50,000 shares of Series A Preferred Stock of the company, ABC, Inc., at $20 per share. Following are details of the scenario.

1. A proposed Stock Purchase Agreement relating to the sale of ABC, Inc. to the investors listed on Schedule I (collectively called the "Investors" or "XYZ, Ltd.") of 50,000 shares of a newly created class of Series A Convertible Preferred Stock. The purchase price for each share is $20. Thus ABC, Inc. will

receive a total of $1 million. The proposed closing date was three months later. On the closing date, 50 percent of the purchase price ($10 per share) is payable in cash or by check or wire, and the balance is evidenced by a promissory note due December 31st of the year in which the closing occurred.

2. The Stock Purchase Agreement also contains the following major terms: (a) Section 2 contains extensive warranties and representations by ABC, Inc., and Section 3 contains warranties and representations by the Investors designed primarily to ensure that the transaction satisfies the private placement exemption in Section 4(2) of the 1933 Act (see chapter 12); (b) Section 4 contains extensive conditions precedent to the obligations of the Investors to close, including a due-diligence "out," and Section 5 contains limited conditions precedent to the obligation of ABC, Inc. to close; (c) Section 6 contains a requirement for ABC, Inc. to register the Series A Convertible Preferred Stock under the 1933 Act (which could be required by the Investor as early as one year after the date of the Agreement); (d) Section 7 contains covenants relating to the operation of ABC, Inc., reports to Investors, the composition of board committees, and so forth.

3. The proposed Amended and Restated Articles of Incorporation of ABC, Inc. which reflect the rights and privileges of the newly created preferred stock and common stock of ABC, Inc. These Amended and Restated Articles of Incorporation are to be filed on the closing date of the Stock Purchase Agreement. The Series A Preferred Stock has, among others, the following major characteristics:

(a) a cumulative annual dividend of at least $3 per share (effectively, a 15 percent yield based on the $20 purchase price);

(b) a liquidation preference of $20 plus all accrued but unpaid dividends;

(c) the right to convert each share of Series A Preferred Stock, at the holder's option, into one share of common stock of ABC, Inc. (subject to anti-dilution adjustments);

(d) a right to elect two of the six directors of ABC, Inc. (the common stock has the right to elect two directors, and the holders of the preferred stock and the common stock voting as a single class elect the remaining two directors from among the officers of ABC, Inc.);

(e) the right to vote on non-director election issues presented to the shareholders, based on one vote for each share of common stock into which the preferred stock could then be converted;

(f) a protective provision that requires the consent of the majority of outstanding Series A Preferred Stockholders to consent to certain major transactions; and

(g) the right to redeem the preferred stock, at the holder's option, upon the earlier of (i) five years after closing, (ii) the death of either of the founders, or (iii) the failure of ABC, Inc. to satisfy certain financial ratios and tests.

(The Amended and Restated Articles of Incorporation are attached to the Stock Purchase Agreement as Exhibit A.)

4. A proposed Employee Agreement to be executed by ABC, Inc. and all officers and employees of ABC, Inc., which provides (among other things): (a) that ABC, Inc. is the owner of all information of a commercial value in ABC's business, (b) that the employee must maintain all such proprietary

information in confidence, and (c) that all inventions produced by the employee must be disclosed to ABC, Inc., which would become the sole owner of such inventions. This document is attached to the Stock Purchase Agreement as Exhibit B.

5. A proposed Stock Restriction Agreement to be executed by ABC, Inc. and each employee of ABC, Inc., who is a holder of its common stock, in which the employee grants ABC, Inc. an option to purchase that common stock from the employee at a nominal price if the employee status is terminated, voluntarily or involuntarily. An escrow agent is established to hold the employee's common stock. This document is attached to the Stock Purchase Agreement as Exhibit C.

6. A proposed Stockholder's Agreement to be executed by ABC, Inc., the Investors, and each existing holder of the common stock of ABC, Inc. (whether or not an employee) in which each holder of common stock agrees as follows:

   (a) not to transfer such shares of common stock except as permitted by the Stockholder's Agreement;

   (b) to grant a right of first refusal to ABC, Inc. for any proposed disposition of common stock;

   (c) to require such common stockholder to permit Investors to participate in sales of such common stock;

   (d) to require the common stockholder to agree that (if requested by ABC, Inc. or any representative of the underwriters) such common shareholders will not sell such common stock for a 90-day period following the effective date of the Registration Statement filed by ABC, Inc. under the 1933 Act;

    (e) to require the common stockholder to agree to join in any agreement to which the holders of a majority of outstanding preferred shares are parties that provides for the sale of all of the capital stock of ABC, Inc. to any third party. This document is attached as Exhibit D to the Stock Purchase Agreement.

7. A proposed Employment Agreement to be executed by ABC, Inc. and its two principal executives, which provides for their employment for two years after the date of the Stock Purchase Agreement. This document is attached as Exhibit E to the Stock Purchase Agreement.

8. A proposed Term Note to be executed by each Investor for an amount equal to 50 percent of the stock purchase price, which is due and payable without interest on December 31 of the year of closing the financing. This note is to be delivered at the proposed closing in June of the year of closing. This document is attached as Exhibit F to the Stock Purchase Agreement.

EXPLANATION OF SPECIFIC CLAUSES

Minimum Capital Raised: No investor shall be obligated to purchase any shares of Series A Preferred Stock at the Closing unless an aggregate of at least 90 percent of the total number of shares of Series A Preferred Stock to be sold hereunder pursuant to Section 1.1(b) are purchased concurrently therewith.

Explanation: This clause permits the investor to refuse to close the transaction and invest his money in the company if less than 90 percent of the total funds to be invested by all investors are paid at the closing. The purpose of this clause is to protect each investor so that he or she is not obligated to close unless there is a sufficient amount of money to fund the business plan.

ABC, Inc. needs similar protection. Otherwise, if the investors so wished, ABC, Inc. could be forced to close even though (for example) only $100,000 was paid by all investors at the closing. Without similar protection as that offered to the Investors, ABC, Inc. could be forced to give two directorships to the Series A Convertible Preferred Stock and other protection and veto rights that may not be justified by the amount of capital provided by the investors. In addition, ABC, Inc. may need a minimum "critical mass" of funds to accomplish its business objectives.

Liquidation Preference: In the event of any liquidation, dissolution, or winding up of the corporation, either voluntary or involuntary, the holders of Series A Preferred Stock shall be entitled to receive, prior and in preference to any distribution of any of the assets of this corporation to the holders of Common Stock by reason of their ownership thereof, an amount per share equal to the sum of (i) $20.00 for each outstanding share of Series A Preferred Stock and (ii) all accumulations of unpaid dividends in each share of Series A Preferred Stock.

Explanation: The purpose of this clause is to make it clear that in the event of a sale or other liquidation of the company, the holders of the preferred stock would receive their money first, plus accrued but unpaid dividends, before any distribution is made to the holders of common stock. Thus, if the dividend rate is 15 percent per annum, and the company were sold after five years, preferred stock could receive $20 per share plus $3 per year of accrued dividends (15 percent of $20), or a total of $35, prior to any payment to holders of common stock. Alternatively, the preferred stock could convert into common stock on a share-for-share basis and would do so if the common shareholders would be receiving a higher distribution than $35 per share.

Conversion Rights: Each share of Series A Preferred Stock shall be convertible, at the option of the holder thereof, at any time after the date of issuance of such share, at the office of this corporation or any transfer agent for the Series A Preferred Stock, into such number of fully paid and nonassessable shares of Common Stock as is determined by dividing $20.00 (the "Original Conversion Price") by the Conversion Price at the time in effect for such share. The initial Conversion Price per share or shares of Series A Preferred Stock shall be the Original Conversion Price.

Explanation: This is a somewhat complicated way of saying that each share of preferred stock is convertible into one share of common stock. In effect, by dividing $20 by $20, the result would be 1; therefore, one share of common stock would be issued upon conversion for each year of preferred stock.

The purpose of this formula is to be able to change the denominator of the fraction in the event shares are issued below $20 per share so that the preferred stock gets the benefit of additional shares of common stock. For example if shares were issued at $10 per share after the initial venture capital investment, the numerator of the fraction would continue to be $20 and the denominator of the fraction would be changed to $10. The result is that two shares of common stock would be issued for each share of preferred stock.

Conversion Price Adjustments of Preferred Stock:
The Conversion Price shall be subject to adjustment from time to time as follows: (i) (A) If the corporation shall issue any Additional Stock (as defined below) for a consideration per share less than the Conversion Price in effect immediately prior to the issuance of such Additional Stock, the Conversion Price in effect immediately prior to each such issuance shall forthwith be decreased to a price equal to the least consideration per share received by the corporation for such Additional Stock.

Explanation: This is what is called a "full-rachet" antidilution clause. If, as in the example above, shares are issued for $10 per share after the venture capitalist has paid $20 per share, the clause instructs the reader to reduce the denominator of the fraction in the previous example from $20 to $10. This results in the issuance of two shares of common stock for one share of preferred stock, as noted above.

Protective Provisions: So long as shares of Series A Preferred Stock are outstanding, this corporation shall not without first obtaining the approval (by vote or written consent) of the holders of at least a majority of the then outstanding shares of Series A Preferred Stock:

(a) sell, lease, convey, or otherwise dispose of any substantial part of its technology, property, or business, or merge with or into or consolidate with any other corporation (other than a wholly owned subsidiary corporation), or effect any transaction or series of related transactions in which more than 50 percent of the voting power of the corporation is disposed of;

(b) alter or change the rights, preferences, or privileges of the shares of Series A Preferred Stock so as to affect adversely the shares;

(c) amend its Articles, except for the filing of Statements of Reduction of Authorized Shares, or bylaws;

(d) create any new series of stock or any other securities convertible into equity securities of the corporation having a preference over, or being on a parity with, the Series A Preferred Stock with respect to voting, dividends, liquidation rights, or otherwise;

(e) do any act or thing which would result in taxation of the holders of shares of the Series A Preferred Stock under Section 305 of the Internal Revenue Code of 1986, as amended (or any comparable provision of the Internal Revenue Code as hereafter from time to time amended);

(f) issue any Additional Stock except for the issuance of up to 15,813 shares of Common Stock to employees of the Company pursuant to an employee benefit plan approved by the directors of the corporation;

(g) adopt or amend any employee benefit plan or arrangement providing for compensation or benefits to any of the ten most highly compensated employees of, or consultants to, the Company; or

(h) declare any dividend on any class or series of stock other than the Series A Preferred Stock, or repurchase shares of any class or series.

Explanation: The purpose of these provisions is to give a veto power to the holders of the majority of preferred stock over a number of corporate actions that could affect their interests. Examples include a sale of any substantial part of its technology, issuing additional stock, declaring a dividend, and so on. This provision gives substantial control over major business decisions to the venture capitalist.

Redemption Rights: The Redemption Date shall be the earliest of the following dates or events: (i) five (5) years after closing; (ii) the death of either entrepreneur 1 or entrepreneur 2; (iii) the failure to appoint on or before December 31 [of year of closing] a Chief Executive Officer acceptable to the holders of a majority of the Series A Preferred Stock; (iv) the rejection by the Board of Directors of three candidates for Chief Executive Officer proposed by the holders of a majority of the Series A Preferred Stock; or (v) the failure of the Company to meet any of the following financial ratios or results, computed in accordance with generally accepted accounting principles consistently applied, at any time: (1) maintain a ratio of operating expenses to sales of not more than 75 percent, 70 percent, and 67 percent during the years ended December 31 [year of closing and first and second year after closing], respectively; (2) maintain a ratio of current assets to current liabilities of at least 110 percent at all times; (3) maintain a ratio of total debt to equity of not more than 50 percent at all times; (4) achieve positive net income for the three-month period ending December 31 [of the year of closing]; and (5) achieve net revenues of at least $2,500,000, $4,900,000, and $6,800,000 in the years ended December 31 [first, second, and third year after closing], respectively.

Explanation: The purpose of this clause is to permit the venture capitalist to receive back his or her original investment plus accrued but unpaid dividends if certain unfavorable events occur or, in any event, five years from the date of the investment. Although the venture capitalist will typically buy preferred stock, the preferred stock has debt characteristics. The primary debt characteristic is the optional maturity date in five years.

The unfavorable events listed in this clause are typically taken from the business plan. Thus, the business plan probably projected revenues of $6,800,000 in the third year after the closing. The attorney for the venture capitalist took this figure and provided in the charter that if the company were unable to satisfy this revenue projection, the venture capitalist could get its original investment returned plus accrued but unpaid dividends, at the option of the venture capitalist.

This type of redemption clause is typical in a venture capital agreement and is usually the subject of extensive negotiations with the entrepreneur.

State laws may prohibit the venture capitalist from actually redeeming preferred stock if it would cause the company to become insolvent (that is, unable to pay its debts in the ordinary course of business) or result in its liabilities (plus any preferred liquidation preference) exceeding its assets.

Exit Clauses

Venture capital investors typically negotiate registration rights covenants to permit the public sale of the investment and other provisions designed to ultimately force either the purchase of the investment by the company or the sale of the entire company. Examples of these clauses can be found in the following provisions of the venture capital agreement contained in Appendix 3 of this book: Section 6 of the Venture Capital Agreement (Registration Rights commencing on page 245); Section 7 of Exhibit A of the Venture Capital Agreement (Redemption Rights commencing on page 286); Sections 3 and 8 of Exhibit D of the Venture Capital Agreement (the so-called "tag-along" and "drag-along" provisions, respectively, pages 319 and 321).

The "tag-along" clause (also called the "co-sale" clause) permits the venture capital investors the right to participate in sales of the company stock by founders and other major shareholders. Since outside parties may pay a premium for a controlling interest in the business, a "co-sale" clause allows the venture capital investors to share in this premium. In addition, the "co-sale" clause permits the venture capitalist to sell its interest in the corporation to the new controlling purchaser who may have different objectives from the founders.

The "drag-along" clause (also called the "forced-sale" clause) permits the venture capital investors to force the founders to sell their interest in the corporation if the venture capitalist has received an acceptable offer. This is a harsh clause since the founders can be forced to divest themselves of their equity interest in the business. The justification for this clause is that the venture capitalists may not be able to sell their interest in the business unless the founder's interest is sold along with their own, since the purchaser may wish 100 percent of the equity of the business.

EMPLOYMENT AGREEMENTS

Venture capitalists typically require an employment agreement from the entrepreneur to lock in his or her services. (See Exhibit E of Appendix 3 on page 325).

How valuable are the Employment Agreements to the two principal executives of ABC, Inc., if control of the board of directors changes? The board of directors could fire these executives in breach of their Employment Agreement and pay damages to the executive (subject to the executive's duty to mitigate damages). Note also that the termination of employment appears to trigger repurchase rights for the Company under Section 1 of the Stock Restriction Agreement (page 301) with respect to the executive's common-stock holdings in ABC, Inc.

If you decide that a professionally managed venture fund is not your ideal source for capital, you should consider angel investors and conducting an angel-investor offering, which are discussed in the next two chapters; a junk-bond offering (chapter 12) that can be made to either angel or institutional investors (chapter 13); an investment banker–sponsored private placement (chapter 14); or an IPO (chapter 15).

CHAPTER 11

ANGEL INVESTORS

A ngel investors are high-net-worth individuals who are willing to invest in developing companies. Apple Computer got its first round of outside capital from an angel. In 1977, an early Intel executive and shareholder invested $91,000 into Apple and guaranteed another $250,000 in credit lines. At the time of the Apple IPO in 1980, the angel was allegedly worth $154 million.

Most estimates put the amount of angel capital invested in 1997 in the United States at approximately $50 billion. Of that amount, $40 billion supposedly came from friends and family and was invested primarily in privately held small businesses. This type of angel money is called "3F money," for friends, family, and fools.

A recent phenomenon is the appearance of professional angels consisting of successful entrepreneurs who have already exited (that is, enjoyed the fruits of an IPO or sale) and are looking to do it again with another promising entrepreneur.

Angels vary widely in personality, methodology, and goals. On one end of the spectrum is the unsophisticated investor who likes a particular entrepreneur or business and views his or her investment no differently than gambling in a casino. These investors, sometimes called "recreational investors," like the idea of being identified with a particular company. They enjoy bragging about the investment to their friends at their club or on a golf course. They typically purchase either common stock or high-yield notes (either convertible or with warrants) and do not impose restrictions on the entrepreneur. These recreational investors are sufficiently wealthy so that the loss of the entire investment would not remotely affect them any more than a gambling loss would.

The other end of the angel investor spectrum is the sophisticated angel who views the investment as a business. While not as sophisticated as a professional venture capitalist, these investors exhibit a significant amount of due diligence and invest only in businesses they fully understand.

These sophisticated angels tend to purchase preferred stock or convertible notes, and never common stock, so they will always be senior to the entrepreneur who holds common stock. Entrepreneurs should expect significant operating restrictions in any agreement with the sophisticated angel, who thinks and talks like a professional venture capitalist. It is not unusual for these investors to refuse to invest in a company because no member of their group has investment experience in that company's type of business.

THE ARCHANGEL

Many angel investors operate in groups, the leader of which is called the archangel. The archangel for the recreational investor is typically the first to invest his money, with the remaining group members following on his heels. The archangel for sophisticated investors typically arranges for the due diligence for the group and negotiates all business terms.

STRUCTURING DEALS FOR ANGELS

The structuring of the angel transaction will depend upon the nature of probable angels, sophisticated or unsophisticated.

If your target market is sophisticated angels, you would best approach them with an outstanding business plan and an impressive management team. You would probably waste your money by creating an offering or disclosure document prior to obtaining their input since these sophisticated angels will be giving you a term sheet similar to that prepared by a professional venture capitalist. Only after you have received their term sheet and finalized your negotiations is it worth your while to create an offering document.

Some companies never create an offering or disclosure document when dealing with very sophisticated angels, particularly when the group consists of fewer than five investors. Instead, they create a "risk factor" document, which discloses all investment risks they can think of. This is a much shorter and less costly document to prepare than a full-offering or disclosure document.

If your target market is recreational investors, then a full-offering or disclosure document is advisable. These recreational investors will typically not negotiate terms. Therefore, you are better off structuring the offering for them on a take-it-or-leave-it basis. The offering or disclosure document should not be prepared until you have had informal conversations with these investors to discuss the nature of the transaction and received some encouragement.

INVESTOR TERMS

Both sophisticated and recreational angel investors want to know that they are being treated fairly, that everyone gets the same deal.

However, investors who take more risks are entitled to something extra. Therefore, the earliest round of investors should have some price or other advantage (such as warrants) over later investors.

You may need early investors to provide enough funds to pay legal, accounting, and printing costs for the offering or disclosure document used in late rounds. Therefore, it is permissible to allow these investors an edge either through a lower valuation, a warrant, or otherwise.

FINDING ANGELS

There is no one scientific way to locate angels, except through networking. Many brokers, investment advisors, lawyers, and accountants are aware of angel networks. You have to locate these intermediaries and try to interact with them.

When one angel investor turns you down, ask him or her about other angels who might have an interest.

Since sophisticated angels like to invest in businesses they know, try to find other businesspeople who have been in a similar business. If businesses have recently been sold in your industry, the sellers might be logical angels.

A Web site for angels is now being developed. However, this new site is unlikely to be an important source for angels for many years to come.

One reason is that angels, like professionally managed venture capitalists, prefer to invest locally. Therefore, a Web site listing the angels located within your region would be more helpful than a national site.

A second reason is that angels do not want to identify themselves, for fear of being bothered by a multitude of entrepreneurs. The new Web site accommodates to that concern by keeping the name and address of the angel secret until the angel approves its disclosure. However, many angels do not trust the secrecy of the Web.

Finally, many recreational angels, who do not view investing as a business, would not like to see themselves listed on a Web site.

WEB-SITE ANGELS

Angel sites listed on the Internet are:

ACE-Net (The Angel Capital Electronic Network sponsored by the U.S. Small Business Administration)	www.sba.gov/advo
America's Business Funding Directory	www.businessfinance.com
American Entrepreneurs for Economic Growth	www.aeeg.org
American Venture Magazine	www.businessexchange.com
The Angel Network Membership Guestbook	www.eillc.com/angel.htm
BizPlanIt	www.bizplanit.com
British Venture Capital Association	www.brainstorm.co.uk/ BVCA/
Business Angels P/L	www.businessangels.com.au

Capital Matchmaker	www.matchmaker.org
The Capital Network	www.thecapitalnetwork.com
CONNECTNet	www.darwin1.ucsd.edu:8000/connect/index.html
DataMerge Inc.	www.datamerge.com
Entrepreneur Investments, LLC	www/eillc.com/what.htm; www.eillc.com/index3.htm; www.eillc.com/
European Venture Capital Association	www.evca.com
Finance Hub	www.financehub.com
Garage.com	www.garage.com
Idea Cafe	www.ideacafe.com
Industry Canada Strategis	http://strategis.ic.gc.ca
INNOVEST	www.innovest.org
International Capital Resources Guide	www.icrnet.com
The Investment Exchange	www.tinvex.com
MoneyHunter	www.moneyhunter.com
National Venture Capital Association	www.nvca.org
Sacramento Area Venture Capital Network	www.foothill.net/svcn/
SCOR-NET	www.scor-net.com
The Venture Capital Marketplace	www.v-capital.com.au
Venture Capital Online	www.vcapital.com
Venture Capital Resource Library	www.vfinance.com

The Venture Site   www.venturesite.co.uk

Venturenet   www.venturenet.org

Most of the sites offer services for the entrepreneur to locate potential angels. Care should be exercised in using these sites to avoid potential scams. Entrepreneurs are cautioned not to pay up-front fees to the sponsors of these sites and to have a securities lawyer review any legal documentation.

CORPORATE ANGELS

A growing number of corporations have developed venture capital divisions designed to nurture companies that fit into the corporate strategy. For example, Intel Corporation supposedly made 100 venture capital investments in 1997, twice as many as the year before.

It is not unusual for large corporations to make large expenditures for research and development for their own operations. However, many of these research development investments turn out to be less than productive, primarily because of the lack of internal incentives within the organization.

Corporate investors generally can afford higher valuations because of their focus on "strategic" rather than financial returns. While some corporate investors seek early-stage opportunities—some even want portfolio company board seats—others want a more passive role with a company that has worked out the bugs. Intel is one of the most active corporate venture players, reportedly spending some $300 million on about 100 transactions last year. The chip maker generally invests between $1 million and $5 million in each deal. Intel typically does not want board seats or to manage the day-to-day company operations.

ANGEL NETWORKS

The following is a list of angel networks:

Atlanta Development Authority (ADA)
230 Peachtree Street, N.W., Suite 2100
Atlanta, GA 30303
404-658-7000

Atlanta Venture Forum, Inc. (AVF)
2800 One Atlantic Center
1201 W. Peachtree Street
Atlanta, GA 30339-3450
404-873-8522

Capital Network, Inc. (TCN)
3925 West Braker Lane, Suite 406
Austin, TX 78759-5321
512-305-0826

Council for Entrepreneurial Development (CED)
P.O. Box 13353
104 Alexander Drive
Research Triangle Park, NC 27709
919-549-7500

Datamerge, Inc.
4521 E. Virginia Avenue, Suite 201
Denver, CO 80222
303-320-8361

Environmental Investor's Newsletter
6230 Wilshire Blvd., Suite 1158
Los Angeles, CA 90048
213-466-3297/800-995-1903

Indianapolis Small Business Development Corp. (ISBD)
One N. Capitol Avenue, Suite 1275
Indianapolis, IN 46204
317-264-2820

International Capital Resources (ICR)
388 Market Street, Suite 500
San Francisco, CA 94111
415-296-2519

International Venture Capital Institute (IVCI)
P.O. Box 1333
Stamford, CT 06904
203-323-3143

The Investment Exchange
Box 131
234-5149 Country Hills Blvd., N.W.
Calgary, Alberta, Canada T3A 5K8
403-208-2964/800-563-5448

Michiana Investment Network (MIN)
300 N. Michigan
South Bend, IN 46601
219-282-4350

National Association of Investment Companies (NAIC)
1111 14th Street, N.W., Suite 700
Washington, D.C. 20005
202-289-4336

National Venture Capital Association (NVCA)
1655 North Fort Myer Drive, Suite 700
Arlington, VA 22209
703-524-2549

Oklahoma Investment Forum
616 South Boston, Suite 100
Tulsa, OK 74119-1298
918-585-1201

Orange County Venture Forum (OCVF)
23041 Mill Creek Drive
Laguna Hills, CA 92653
714-855-0652

Pennsylvania Private Investors Group
Technology Council of Greater Philadelphia
435 Devon Park Drive
Wayne, PA 19087-1991
610-975-9430

The Private Investors Network
Robert H. Smith School of Business
Vanmunching Hall
University of Maryland
College Park, MD 20742-1815
301-405-2144

Rockies Venture Club (RVC)
190 E. 9th Avenue, Suite 440
Denver, CO 80203
303-831-4174

Small Business Investment Companies (SBICs)
c/o Associate Administration for Investment
U.S. Small Business Administration
409 3rd Street, S.W.
Washington, DC 20416
202-205-7589

Technology Capital Network, Inc. (TCN)
290 Main Street
Bldg. E-39, Lower Level
Cambridge, MA 02142
617-253-7163

Vankirk's Venture Capital Directory
180 Linden Street, Suite 3
Wellesley, MA 02181
703-379-9200

Vencap Data Quest
AI Research Corp.
2003 St. Julien Court
Mountain View, CA 94043-5411
415-852-9140

CHAPTER 12

HOW TO CONDUCT
AN ANGEL OFFERING

C onducting an angel offering requires that you first
develop a marketing plan. The marketing plan must
identify who are your potential investors, how you intend
to solicit them, and what is your investor's appetite for
common stock, preferred stock, or high-yield notes (with
or without warrants). Your marketing plan should also
specify the total amount you wish to raise and your
company's planned use of the proceeds.

Most angel offerings today are conducted under Rule
506 of Regulation D of the Securities Act of 1933 ("1933
Act") if the marketing plan contemplates soliciting wealthy
"accredited investors" (defined under Rule 506) and other
sophisticated investors with whom you (or any broker
helping you) have a preexisting relationship. If your marketing plan contemplates solicitation of strangers or any
form of advertising or seminars to attract investors, then
you cannot use Rule 506, which prohibits these forms of
solicitation. Likewise, you will not qualify for Rule 505 or

any of the "private placement" exemptions contained in the 1933 Act if your marketing plan contemplates the soliciting strangers, advertising, or conducting seminars.

Instead, your angel offering will have to be conducted as a public offering under Rule 504 and in compliance with the Small Corporate Offering Registration (SCOR) state rules, assuming that you intend to raise no more than $1 million over a 12-month period. If you do intend to raise more than $1 million over a 12-month period, you will have to comply with Regulation A of the 1933 Act or register your offering with the SEC.

Each of these SEC rules and forms are discussed in greater detail later in this chapter.

A "general solicitation" is defined in SEC Regulation D as follows:

> *Limitation on manner of offering.* Except as provided in Rule 504, neither the issuer nor any person acting on its behalf shall offer or sell the securities by any form of general solicitation or general advertising, including, but not limited to, the following:
>
> - Any advertisement, article, notice, or other communication published in any newspaper, magazine, or similar media or broadcast over television or radio; and
>
> - Any seminar or meeting whose attendees have been invited by any general solicitation or general advertising (subject to a minor exception).

In general, you should, if possible, tailor your marketing plan to comply with Rule 506 to avoid the hassle and delay of dealing with federal or state regulatory agencies. Unlike Rules 504 and 505, an offering under Rule 506 avoids the necessity of complying with the registration provisions of state securities laws (as will be discussed), and the amount of capital you can raise is not limited.

If you cannot comply with Rule 506 because you intend to engage in a general solicitation or intend to sell to more than 35 unsophisticated investors (as permitted by Rule 505) or more than 35 non-accredited investors, the next best choice is the Rule 504/SCOR offering exemption, which was designed as a "do-it-yourself" offering to facilitate raising small amounts of capital.

Securities Act of 1933

The offer and sale of both debt and equity securities is a highly regulated transaction. The states adopted securities laws in the late-nineteenth century. These laws are also called "blue sky" laws because they were an attempt to regulate promoters who were promising investors the "blue sky."

The 1933 Act was the first federal securities law. Congress adopted this law in response to the Depression (which it considered the result of the 1929 stock market crash) and various abusive and fraudulent securities practices that had occurred during the 1920s.

Until 1996, the 1933 Act did not preempt state blue-sky laws. Thus, any offer or sale of a security had to satisfy the applicable state law as well as the 1933 Act. In 1996, Congress amended the 1933 Act to preempt the registration provisions (but not the antifraud provisions) of state blue-sky laws for transactions under Rule 506 as well as certain other transactions in publicly traded securities. However, even after the 1996 law, the antifraud provisions of state blue-sky laws still apply and notice of Rule 506 transactions still may be required to be filed with the appropriate states.

Most federal and state securities laws can be divided into two main sections:

- Registration provisions
- Antifraud provisions

Although compliance with Rule 506 (as well as Rules 504 and 505) exempts the angel offering from the registration provisions of federal and (in the case of Rule 506) state securities laws, the antifraud provisions of these laws still apply. To comply with these antifraud provisions, a full-disclosure document should be furnished to your angel investors prior to your receiving any money from them or legally binding them. Such a disclosure document should contain a frank discussion of the "risk factors" of your business.

The Private Placement Choices

In the following offerings, no general solicitation is permitted and marketing is limited to qualified investors with whom there is a preexisting relationship with the company or broker soliciting the sale:

- Rule 505

  Primary Advantages: Can sell to 35 unsophisticated persons and unlimited number of accredited investors; no federal review required.

  Primary Disadvantages: Limited to $5 million over a rolling 12-month period; no general solicitation permitted; professional investors may extract onerous terms because of illiquidity; must comply with state securities laws.

- Rule 506

  Primary Advantages: Unlimited dollar amount can be sold to 35 sophisticated and experienced investors in financial and business matters and an *unlimited* number of accredited investors; no federal review is required and registration provisions of state securities laws are preempted, provided notice is given (if required by state).

Primary Disadvantages: No general solicitation is permitted; professional investors may extract onerous terms because of illiquidity.

According to SEC Rule 501, adopted under the 1933 Act, an "accredited investor" includes, among others, the following individual investors:

- Any natural person whose individual net worth, or joint net worth with that person's spouse, at the time of his purchase exceeds $1,000,000; and

- Any natural person who had an individual income in excess of $200,000 in each of the two most recent years or joint income with that person's spouse in excess of $300,000 in each of those years and has a reasonable expectation of reaching the same income level in the current year.

The following other requirements must be satisfied under both Rule 505 and 506:

- Disclosure of certain information (unless all purchasers are accredited investors)
- Restrictions on resale of the securities
- Notice filed with SEC and state blue-sky regulators

Antifraud provisions of the securities laws will require disclosure even in an all accredited investor offering.

Private placements may also be effectuated under the judge-made case law decided under Section 4(2) of the 1933 Act and also under Section 4(6) of that law (dealing with sales solely to accredited investors). Angel offerings to individuals under the case law of Section 4(2) are infrequent because of the conflicting court decisions and the lack of any preemption of state securities law. Section 4(6) of the 1933 Act is likewise infrequently used because it is more restrictive than Rule 506.

THE PUBLIC OFFERING CHOICES

General solicitation is permitted and there is no investor qualification for these public offerings:

1. Public Offerings Registered with SEC

   Primary Advantages: Better terms for founder than private placements. Unlimited marketing where blue-skied; no investor qualification.

   Primary Disadvantage: Cost (typical range: firm commitment underwriting, $350,000 to $500,000; self-underwritten, $100,000 to $250,000, plus underwriting discount and commissions, and expense allowance). Audited financials required.

2. Public Intrastate Offerings Registered in One State (exempt from federal but not state registration)

   Primary Advantages: Same as above. No federal review required.

   Primary Disadvantages: Can only be marketed in one state. Must comply with state registration requirements.

3. Public Regulation A Offerings (exempt from federal registration, but federal review required)

   Primary Advantages: Can "test the waters" before filing in some but not all states. Audited financial statements not required for federal review, unless otherwise available (however, states may still require audited financials); less disclosure required than in SEC registered offerings; can use question-and-answer format; unlimited marketing where blue-skied.

Primary Disadvantages: Limited to $5 million in rolling 12 months, including no more than $1.5 million in non-issuer resales; still must be reviewed by both federal and state regulators; professional help required; cost in excess of $50,000 (typical range: $75,000 to $150,000).

4. Public Rule 504/SCOR Offerings

Primary Advantages: Same as Regulation A, except no federal review required, and unaudited financial statements permitted in most states; can be completed without professional help and is therefore least expensive of all offering forms.

Primary Disadvantages: Limited to $1 million in 12 months; still must be reviewed by state regulators; higher risk of defective disclosure and personal liability if prepared without professional help.

TYPE OF OFFERING

The type of offering you choose depends on the following factors:

- How much money do you wish to raise?
- Does your marketing plan require that you generally solicit potential customers?
- Where do you wish to sell the securities?

The most important factor in choosing the type of offering is the method of marketing the offering to customers. If you want to be able to approach strangers or to advertise in newspapers, you cannot use offerings that prohibit general solicitation, as noted above. In private offerings, the SEC prohibits any solicitation of any investor with whom the company or its broker does not have a preexisting relationship.

If you need to generally solicit strangers and the investors are located in more than one state, then an intrastate public offering—an offering limited to one state, which is exempt from 1933 Act registration—is inappropriate for your company. Consequently, you must register your offering with the SEC or use a Regulation A offering.

Most self-underwritten and best-efforts public angel offerings are for less than $5 million. Accordingly, your practical choices are to use a Regulation A or an intrastate offering registered with one state. If the offering is for $1 million or less (measured over a rolling 12-month period), the SCOR offering may permit you to avoid federal registration and to file a question-and-answer SCOR form with the states in which it is to be made.

CONTROL PERSONAL LIABILITY

If you violate either the registration or antifraud provisions of federal securities laws, you may be personally liable. This is true even though you have formed a corporation or other limited liability entity and that entity received all of the sale proceeds. This is because of provisions in federal securities laws (and some state securities laws), that impose personal liability on control persons. The only defense to such control personal liability is to prove that you acted in good faith and after reasonable investigation you nevertheless still could not prevent the violation.

CHAPTER 13

JUNK-BOND FINANCING

"**J**unk bonds" is a colloquial expression referring to high-yield debt securities. Whether your business is early stage or late stage, junk bonds should be explored as a financing alternative to equity if your business has the cash flow to pay interest and principal.

The advantage of junk bonds is that the investors do not dilute your equity interest in the business. Indeed, some late-stage companies are using junk-bond financing as an alternative to an IPO or a follow-on public offering. Junk-bond financing can postpone your need for equity financing until your business can obtain a higher market valuation, thereby reducing your equity dilution at such time as equity financing is required.

Although junk-bond financing can be used by both early-stage and late-stage companies, only late-stage companies can qualify for investment banker–sponsored junk bonds, including the so-called Rule 144A financings discussed hereafter.

Although junk bonds were popularized in the 1980s, they had been used by entrepreneurs to finance their projects long before the 1980s. Notes with high interest rates have been used since the dawn of commerce. Even the Bible complains about the "usurers."

Junk bonds, by definition, pay a significantly higher interest rate than safer debt securities. For example, if a bank certificate of deposit (insured by the FDIC) for a five-year maturity has a 6 percent yield, a junk bond would pay a minimum of 9 percent to 15 percent per annum or more, depending upon the risk level.

Entrepreneurs should be willing to pay as high as 15 percent per annum interest only if they are reasonably certain that they can earn significantly more than 15 percent per annum on the incremental dollars. To the extent this is possible, entrepreneurs can grow their business without sacrificing equity.

There are two distinct markets for junk bonds:

- Retail or angel market
- Institutional market

The retail or angel market can be accessed by direct private or public offerings without using an investment banker. Even early-stage companies with a reasonable prospect of cash flow can access this market. On the other hand, the institutional market can generally be accessed only by late-stage companies, most of which will need the sponsorship of an investment banker.

Retail or Angel Market

Many investors are not interested in purchasing common stock or preferred stock in your business. These investors want some current cash flow on their investment. This is particularly true for investors who are using funds they obtain from bank CDs or other safe-debt securities to invest in your business.

The typical investor is motivated by the high interest return he can receive on your high-yield notes, as opposed to his current investment. These investors are willing to assume more risk to obtain high current cash flow from their money.

Although high-yield investors have no single profile, they are typically individuals who are 55 years of age or older and have accumulated a significant amount of savings. They are willing to risk a small portion of their savings to obtain a high yield for themselves.

Finance companies have for decades been financing their operations with junk bonds. Just read the financial pages of the newspaper in our major cities for their advertisements. However, start-up companies have also used this method for financing operations. In many cases, the start-up companies have to couple a small equity warrant with the high-yield note to induce the investment.

Even if a warrant or other "equity kicker" is required by the investor, the equity kicker is typically limited to a smaller percentage of the equity than if the financing were structured solely as a sale of common or preferred stock.

In some cases, the high-yield notes are specifically subordinated to bank and other institutional debt. Bankers view subordinated debt as equity for loan purposes, particularly when the subordination agreement prevents payment of the junk-bond principal or interest in the event of a default on the bank loan.

In some cases, particularly with start-up companies, investors may require the personal guarantee of the entrepreneur and, in some cases, his or her spouse. Obviously, such guarantees should be avoided when possible. In situations in which a personal guarantee is necessary, the guaranty should, if possible, have the following limitations:

- The entrepreneur's home should be exempted.
- The guarantee should be limited in time.
- Spousal guarantees should be avoided.

In limited circumstances, entrepreneurs may be able to convince investors to accept so-called "cash-flow notes." These notes do not require any payment of interest or principal except out of a percentage of the business's cash flow. Most investors who would be willing to accept cash-flow notes require a fixed maturity date for the ultimate payment of principal without regard to the cash flow of the company. If investors can be convinced to accept a three-year or five-year ultimate maturity date for the principal of the cash-flow note, these notes can serve to provide the capital to start up the business.

Examples of Retail or Angel Junk-Bond Offerings

Following are three examples of retail or angel financings with high-yield notes in which the author has been involved; the first was offered privately and the second and third publicly:

Example: A start-up commodity manufacturer in a start-up mode needed additional working capital and equipment to make the operation profitable. The operation was producing revenues, but not sufficient revenues to cover fixed overhead costs. The entrepreneur determined that potential investors had no interest in a purely common stock offering, and he preferred not to dilute his own equity interest by such an offering.

Instead, a private offering of 15 percent notes and warrants to purchase the common stock was structured and sold pursuant to Rule 506 under the 1933 Act to accredited investors (see chapter 12). The notes were unsecured but were not specifically subordinated. The minimum note size was $50,000. The note paid interest monthly at the rate of 15 percent per annum and the principal was due in one year or two years. If a two-year note was selected by the investor, the accompanying warrant covered more common stock than if the one-year note maturity was selected. Approximately $1.5 million was raised in this offering.

Example: A Pennsylvania racetrack needed in excess of $4 million to construct an off-track betting facility. The banks would lend a maximum of $2.5 million to fund the construction and would impose significant operational restrictions on the borrower. The entrepreneur rejected the bank financing and instead constructed with the author a $4.5-million junk-bond financing. The junk bonds were registered in a public intrastate offering in Pennsylvania under the Pennsylvania Securities Act of 1972. The junk bonds were notes that bore an approximately 9 percent per annum interest rate, with some inflation protection that could take the interest rate as high as 11 percent, and had a five-year bullet maturity (meaning the principal was due and payable at the date of maturity of the notes).

At the time, the going rate for a bank CD with a five-year maturity was slightly over 6 percent per annum. Thus investors obtained approximately an additional 3 percent over what banks were offering. The minimum unit amount that could be purchased was $5,000, thereby permitting a wide range of investors. The notes were unsecured but were not specifically subordinated. The offering was advertised at the racetrack and in the newspapers and an "800" telephone number was established. The $4.5-million offering was oversubscribed.

Example: A finance company registered a $100-million note offering with the Securities and Exchange

Commission, offering notes ranged in maturity from demand notes to five-year notes. The interest rates started at approximately 5 percent per annum and rose as high as 11 percent per annum for the five-year bullet maturity. The notes were unsecured and were specifically subordinated to senior debt. The notes were sold primarily through advertisements in the newspaper and to repeat investors (that is, upon the maturity of their existing note, investors rolled their money into a new note).

INSTITUTIONAL MARKET

Debt securities can be classified into two categories: investment grade and all others. Investment grade corporate debt securities are typically issued by large corporations and are rated by various rating agencies, such as Moody's and Standard & Poor's. These ratings vary according to the quality of the issuer and help establish the interest rate and yield on the securities. Some experts have estimated that prior to the 1980s, only approximately 1,000 corporations were large enough to issue unsecured investment grade debt securities.

Prior to the 1980s, corporations that could not qualify for rated debt securities had difficulty obtaining long-term debt financing for their operations. Banks were their initial source for debt financing. However, banks typically have low-risk thresholds. Once their bank lines were exhausted, these corporations generally had to issue convertible debt or sell their non-convertible debt to a small group of institutional investors, typically insurance companies, which were very selective as to which companies they financed.

During the 1980s, Drexel Burnham Lambert Incorporated ("Drexel") and, in particular, Michael E. Milken, developed a market for so-called "high yield" securities, also known as "junk bonds." Although these high-yield securities were called "junk bonds," many of them are not collateralized and, hence, are more accurately called notes or debentures.

High-yield mutual funds were formed to invest in junk bonds. Savings and loan corporations, insurance companies, and other institutional investors developed an appetite for these high-yield securities, since it increased the earnings of these institutions. In addition, junk-bond funding was used to finance hostile takeovers and so-called leveraged buy-outs by management and others.

Mr. Milken developed institutional markets for these securities and financed high-profile projects with their proceeds. For example, the Mirage Casino in Las Vegas was financed primarily with junk bonds.

The late 1980s and early 1990s saw the realization of the risks inherent in these securities as many issuers went bankrupt. Junk bonds are still very popular today, but the market is extremely quality-conscious.

RATING SYSTEM

The popularity of junk bonds in the 1980s forced the credit rating agencies to revise their rating system to include a junk-bond category.

Institutional investors generally will purchase junk bonds that are rated "CCC" or higher, and most institutional investors prefer a rating of "B" or higher. This contrasts with retail or angel investors, who do not demand a rated bond.

Standard & Poor's definition of "B" and "CCC" ratings are:

> **'B'** An obligation rated 'B' is MORE VULNER-ABLE to nonpayment than obligations rated 'BB,' but the obligor currently has the capacity to meet

its financial commitment on the obligation. Adverse business, financial, or economic conditions will likely impair the obligor's capacity or willingness to meet its financial commitment on the obligation.

'CCC' An obligation rated 'CCC' is CURRENTLY VULNERABLE to nonpayment, and is dependent upon favorable business, financial, and economic conditions for the obligor to meet its financial commitment on the obligation. In the event of adverse business, financial, or economic conditions, the obligor is not likely to have the capacity to meet its financial commitment on the obligation.

Plus (+) or minus (-) The ratings from 'AA' to 'CCC' may be modified by the addition of a plus or minus sign to show relative standing within the major rating categories.

RULE 144A FOR LATE-STAGE COMPANIES

If your company is large enough to permit at least a $75-million rated high-yield debt security, you can access the institutional markets for investors through an investment banker–sponsored Rule 144A offering. These offerings are typically structured as a private placement sale to an investment banking firm, which simultaneously resells the securities pursuant to Rule 144A under the Securities Act of 1993 to so-called qualified institutional buyers (QIBs). QIBs are typically professionally managed institutions that in the aggregate own and invest on a discretionary basis at least $100 million in the securities of nonaffiliated issuers. These Rule 144A offerings are typically structured similarly to IPOs, including road shows.

The author's law firm has recently been involved in offerings ranging from $75 million to $250 million, bearing interest rates ranging from approximately 10 percent to 11 percent per annum and a bullet maturity in ten years. These notes are partly subordinated and are unsecured. In one recent case, a privately held company sold junk bonds in a Rule 144A offering and used a portion of the proceeds to repurchase the equity interest of a venture capitalist. The offering permitted the founding family of the company to resume ownership of 100 percent of the stock and postponed any need for an IPO indefinitely.

The following covenants typically apply to these Rule 144A offerings:

- A fixed-charge coverage ratio of two-to-one (that is, in general you will not be able to incur other indebtedness on money borrowed unless your pre-tax consolidated cash flow is more than twice the total interest charges inclusive of the new indebtedness)

- Restrictions on dividends, repurchases of stock, and other forms of investments

- A restriction on asset sales requiring that proceeds of the asset sales be used to pay down junk-bond indebtedness (with certain exceptions)

- Restriction on mergers and other acquisitions so that certain requirements must be satisfied before you can make an acquisition

While you have some negotiating room with regard to each of these covenants and the many others that appear in a very complex indenture, the final negotiation must ultimately be acceptable to the QIBs. Therefore, your range of negotiation is very narrow.

Following in Table 13.1 are some of the major investment bankers in the Rule 144A market during 1997:

TABLE 13.1   RULE 144A HIGH-YIELD
PRIVATE-PLACEMENTS DEBT*
(Excluding CDs and Deposit Notes)
January 1, 1997–December 31, 1997

Managers	Proceeds ($Millions)	Rank	Market Share	No. of Issues
Salomon Smith Barney	8,096.6	1	8.3	117
Chase Manhattan Corp.	7,670.7	2	7.8	115
Donaldson, Lufkin & Jenrette	7,651.9	3	7.8	102
Bear, Stearns	6,983.5	4	7.1	93
Merrill Lynch & Co.	6,762.2	5	6.9	113
Morgan Stanley Dean Witter	6,417.7	6	6.5	86
Bankers Trust	6,285.9	7	6.4	91
Credit Suisse First Boston	5,059.1	8	5.2	110
Goldman, Sachs & Co.	4,402.3	9	4.5	64
NationsBank	3,977.4	10	4.1	67
Jeffries & Co.	3,675.7	11	3.7	39
CIBC Wood Gundy Securities	3,267.4	12	3.3	47
JP Morgan & Co.	2,987.4	13	3.0	62
Lehman Brothers	2,374.3	14	2.4	38
BankAmerica	2,057.6	15	2.1	29
Industry Totals	**98,140.5**	**—**	**100.0**	**668**

*Reprinted with permission of Securities Data Publishing: New York.

Chapter 14

What You Should Know About Investment Bankers

I nvestment banking firms vary enormously in both size and prestige. They range in size from one-person boutique firms to large wire houses, such as Merrill Lynch, which have several hundred investment bankers.

Each investment banking firm has its own minimum size standards for raising capital privately and publicly. Typically, the minimum size standard for private placements is significantly lower than the minimum size standard for public offerings. This is primarily because the costs associated with public offerings are much greater.

It is important that you understand these minimum size standards prior to selecting an investment banker to raise outside capital. Otherwise, you will waste a lot of time and money.

Minimum IPO Size Standards

For initial public offerings, the rule of thumb is:

- Determine your company's valuation prior to the IPO.
- Be aware that the maximum amount an investment banker will typically raise is 50 percent of your pre-IPO valuation (although, occasionally 100 percent or more is possible).

For example, if your company has a pre-IPO valuation of $30 million, the most that will typically be raised in an IPO will be 50 percent of that amount or $15 million. It would be a waste of your time and energy to approach Merrill Lynch to handle a $15 million IPO. The minimum IPO level normally handled by a top-tier investment banker is $50 million.

The minimum IPO dollar level handled by investment bankers primarily depends upon the size and prestige of the investment banker.

The rule-of-thumb formula recited above is derived from the fact that most underwriters do not want to sell more than 33 percent of your outstanding stock in an IPO. Thus, if your company has two million shares of common stock outstanding before the IPO, the underwriter typically will not want to sell to the public more than one million shares. When the one million public shares are added to the two million shares already outstanding, the public shares would constitute one-third of your outstanding stock.

If Merrill Lynch has a $50 million minimum for IPOs, your company would have to have a pre-IPO valuation of $100 million in order to permit the $50 million to constitute not more than one-third of the outstanding stock. The ratio of the public stock to the total outstanding stock is derived from the following fraction:

> *Numerator:* amount raised for company in IPO
>
> *Denominator:* pre-IPO valuation plus amount raised for company in IPO

Thus, if the minimum of $50 million must be raised in the IPO, the company must have a pre-IPO valuation of $100 million.

An easier way of expressing this concept is to say that the company's pre-IPO valuation must always be equal to at least twice the underwriter's minimum IPO amount. If your company has a pre-IPO valuation of $30 million, you must look for an investment banker willing to float an IPO of $15 million or less. These underwriters can include regional investment banking firms such as Pennsylvania Merchants Group and Janney Montgomery Scott & Company, among others. However, such underwriters would likely not include B. T. Alex Brown, which has a minimum IPO dollar amount of $25 million.

The minimum private placement dollar amount of investment bankers is usually significantly lower than their minimum IPO dollar amount. This is because private placements are less costly and less risky than IPOs for the investment banker; therefore they can justify a lower dollar threshold.

Thus, even though Merrill Lynch may have a minimum IPO level of $50 million, its minimum private placement threshold can be significantly less.

PRIVATE PLACEMENT SPONSORED BY INVESTMENT BANKER

Most major investment banker firms have placement divisions or units. These units raise capital from outside investors in so-called "private placements" for promising growth companies. Many of the growth companies are a year or two away from an IPO. Therefore, the capital raised can be viewed as "bridge capital."

However, occasionally even earlier-stage companies can qualify for investment banker–sponsored private placements if their management and growth potential are extremely attractive.

More investment bankers prefer private placements over IPOs because of the higher profitability, shorter time frame, and lower risks of private placements. It is not unusual for investment bankers to point to their IPO capabilities when marketing entrepreneurs for private placements. However, if your business is unlikely to grow after the private placement to a valuation sufficient to satisfy the minimum IPO dollar amount of that investment banker, you should ignore their IPO capabilities in deciding who to retain for your private placement.

Most investment bankers serve as intermediaries in private placements. They are not investing for their own account, but rather serve as agents by assisting you in marketing the private placement. Although investment bankers do not typically invest their own funds in these private placements, they may permit investments by some of their key officers and managers.

The investment banker's sponsorship of the investment may give credibility to the possibilities of its underwriting the eventual IPO and is therefore helpful in attracting investors to the offering.

The typical investors in these offerings are institutional investors. However, many private placements are marketed to very wealthy individuals. Witness the following advertisement from Bessemer Trust in *The New York Times:*

Why Private Investments?

Our 90-year history has taught us that individuals and families with substantial fortunes find it advantageous to have a portion of their assets invested for significant capital appreciation periods. With the erosion of wealth due to taxes and inflation, we believe private investments in buyouts, venture capital and other private investment opportunities should be a key part of a well designed, long term investment program. . . . *We believe clients should typically commit 10 percent to 25 percent of their assets to private investments.*

April 5, 1998

The New York Times, advertisement for Bessemer Trust

One of the best examples of superior investment returns through these private placements is the story of the Yale University endowment. The December 1997 Harvard Business School case study stated, "Yale has developed a rather different approach to endowment management, including substantial investments in less 'efficient' markets, such as private equity (venture capital, buyouts, nature resources, etc.), real estate and 'absolute return' investing. This approach has generated successful, indeed, enviable returns."

Table 14.1 compares Yale's return to the average of U.S. university endowment funds for the last five years.

TABLE 14.1   YALE ENDOWMENT RETURNS VS. ALL UNIVERSITY ENDOWMENTS*

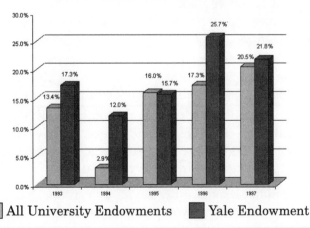

☐ All University Endowments   ■ Yale Endowment

*Selected data from Exhibit 5 of Josh Lerner and Jay Light, Yale University Investments Office: November 1997, case 298-077. Boston: Harvard Business School, 1997. Excerpted and reprinted by permission.

OPERATION OF INVESTMENT BANKER–SPONSORED PRIVATE PLACEMENT

Investment banker–sponsored private placements are prepared much the same way as an IPO, using a private-placement memorandum that looks like an IPO prospectus. Similarly to an IPO, investment banker private placements usually involve "road shows" in various cities. However, the marketing is limited to institutional investors to satisfy the requirements for a private placement.

A typical commission to the investment banker will be in the 6 percent to 9 percent range. In addition, warrants to purchase additional preferred stock or common stock of the company are sometimes required by the investment banker.

The term sheet contained in Appendix 2 illustrates an investment banker–sponsored private placement.

The major advantages of these investment banker–sponsored private placements are:

- The sponsorship of the investment banker lends credibility to the offering, particularly if the investment banker has a reputation as an IPO underwriter.
- The higher-tier investment banker performs his own due diligence on the company, thereby reducing the burden on investors in performing this task and reducing the transaction cost to the investor.
- The higher-tier investment banker will help structure the transaction and offer it to investors on a virtual take-it-or-leave-it basis, thereby eliminating most of the investor negotiation.

The major disadvantage of an investment banker private placement is that your company's valuation, although higher than in a typical venture capital transaction, can be significantly lower than in an IPO. In addition, unlike in an IPO, significant covenants and veto rights may be imposed on your company.

Chapter 15

Going Public

The primary advantage of going public is to obtain lower-cost capital. In effect, you give up less equity for the same number of dollars because of the higher valuation given to your business by the public market. Higher valuations are given to public companies than private companies because of the liquidity available to investors. Private company valuations are subjected to a substantial illiquidity discount.

A second advantage of going public is that you gain the ability to have your cake and eat it too. You can sell a portion of your company while still retaining control. Your personal liquid wealth will increase at the time of the IPO to the extent that the underwriter permits you to withdraw previously taxed subchapter S earnings (assuming your corporation was subchapter S). Even if you cannot withdraw funds at the time of the IPO, you may be permitted to sell a significant portion of your stock in the next public offering.

A complete list of the advantages and disadvantages of going public, which are set forth in my book entitled *Going Public* (Prima, 1997), are outlined as follows:

Advantages

- Lower cost of capital
- Personal wealth
- Competitive position
- Prestige (helpful in attracting key employees and in marketing)
- Ability to take advantage of market price fluctuations
- Enhanced ability to grow through acquisitions
- Enhanced ability to borrow; no personal guarantees
- Enhanced ability to raise equity
- Attracting and retaining key employees (e.g., stock options)
- Enhanced personal liquidity at higher valuations
- Ability to pay estate taxes without selling company

Disadvantages

- Expense, both of initially going public (typically $350,000 to $500,000, excluding underwriter discounts and commissions) and remaining public (typically $50,000 to $100,000 per year)
- Pressure to maintain growth pattern from stock analysts and shareholders
- Disclosure of sensitive information
- Potential loss of control
- Shareholder lawsuits, particularly class-action lawsuits
- Higher valuation for estate tax purposes

QUALIFYING FOR NASDAQ AND THE MAJOR EXCHANGES

Tables 15.1 and 15.2 illustrate the current requirements (as of July 1, 1998) for listing your stock with The NASDAQ National Market and The NASDAQ SmallCap Market—the market for companies with relatively small total capitalization. Table 15.3 shows a comparison of the listing requirements (as of July 1, 1998) of the American Stock Exchange, the New York Stock Exchange, and NASDAQ. (As of July 1, 1998, proposed changes were being considered to the New York Stock Exchange listing requirements.)

GOING PUBLIC VS. PRIVATE EQUITY CAPITAL

Many companies are too small to qualify for a public offering with a major bracket underwriter. Using the rules of thumb from the prior chapter, your company would generally need a minimum pre-IPO valuation of approximately $67 million to qualify for an IPO of approximately $33 million with major bracket underwriters, such as B. T. Alex Brown.

Suppose your company has a pre-IPO valuation of $20 to $40 million. You can still go public with a very reputable underwriter, but not necessarily the top tier. Alternatively, you can raise private equity capital through a private placement with a major bracket underwriter to bridge an IPO with them.

A pre-IPO valuation ranging from $20 to $40 million will obtain a significantly better valuation by using a second-tier underwriter rather than by raising private equity capital. Private placement investors typically discount pre-IPO valuations by as much as 33 percent. In addition, if you choose an IPO, you will escape the restrictions and controls typically imposed by private placement investors.

SUMMARY OF FINANCIAL REQUIREMENTS FOR INITIAL LISTING

TABLE 15.1   NASDAQ NATIONAL MARKET

Requirements	Listing Standard 1	Listing Standard 2	Listing Standard 3
Net Tangible Assets[1]	$6 million	$18 million	N/A
Market Capitalization[2]	N/A	N/A	$75 million or
Total Assets			$75 million and
Total Revenue			$75 million
Pretax Income (in latest fiscal year or 2 of last 3 fiscal years)	$1 million	N/A	N/A
Public Float (shares)[3]	1.1 million	1.1 million	1.1 million
Operating History	N/A	2 years	N/A
Market Value of Public Float	$8 million	$18 million	$20 million
Minimum Bid Price	$5	$5	$5
Shareholders (round lot holders)[4]	400	400	400
Market Makers	3	3	4
Corporate Governance	Yes	Yes	Yes

1. Net tangible assets means total assets (excluding goodwill) minus total liabilities.

2. For initial or continued listing under option 3, a company must satisfy one of the following to be in compliance: the market capitalization requirement or the total assets *and* the total revenue requirements.

3. Public float is defined as shares that are not held directly or indirectly by any officer or director of the issuer or by any other person who is the beneficial owner of more than 10 percent of the total shares outstanding.

4. Round lot holders are considered holders of 100 shares or more.

SUMMARY OF FINANCIAL REQUIREMENTS
FOR INITIAL LISTING

TABLE 15.2 THE NASDAQ SMALLCAP MARKET

Requirements	Listing Standard
Net Tangible Assets[1]	$4 million
	or
Market Capitalization	$50 million
	or
Net Income (in latest fiscal year or 2 of last 3 fiscal years)	$750,000
Public Float (shares)[2]	1 million
Market Value of Public Float	$5 million
Minimum Bid Price	$4
Market Makers	3
Shareholders (round lot holders)[3]	300
Operating History[4]	1 year
	or
Market Capitalization	$50 million
Corporate Governance	Yes

1. For initial or continued listing, a company must satisfy one of the following to be in compliance: the net tangible asset requirement (net tangible assets means total assets, excluding goodwill, minus total liabilities), the market capitalization requirement, or the net income requirement.

2. Public float is defined as shares that are not held directly or indirectly by any officer or director of the issuer or by any other person who is the beneficial owner of more than 10 percent of the total shares outstanding.

3. Round lot holders are considered holders of 100 shares or more.

4. If operating history is less than one year, initial listing requires market capitalization of at least $50 million.

TABLE 15.3   COMPARISON OF LISTING REQUIREMENTS AMONG AMEX, NYSE, AND NASDAQ

The following are general minimum guidelines for listing of domestic common stock. The fact that an applicant may meet the guidelines does not necessarily mean that the applicant will be approved for listing. In certain circumstances, an application for the AMEX or NASDAQ may be approved even though the applicant may not meet all guidelines.

	AMEX Regular	AMEX Alternate	NYSE Regular	NYSE Alternate	NASDAQ National Market Alternate 1	NASDAQ National Market Alternate 2	NASDAQ National Market Alternate 3	SmallCap
Net Tangible Assets[1]			$40,000,000[2]		$6,000,000	$18,000,000		Standard 1: $4,000,000
Market Capitalization				$500,000,000			$75,000,000 or	Standard 2: $50,000,000
Total Assets							($75,000,000) and	
Total Revenue				$200,000,000			($75,000,000)	
Stockholders' Equity	$4,000,000							
Net Income (in last FY [fiscal year] or 2 of the last 3 FYs)				$25,000,000[3]				
Pre-Tax Earnings (in last FY or 2 of the last 3 FYs)	$750,000		$2,500,000 in last FY and $2,000,000 in each of the 2 preceding FYs or $6,500,000 total over last 3 FYs and $4,500,000 in last FY (all 3 years must be profitable)		$1,000,000			

Public Float (Shares)	Standard 1: 500,000 Standard 2: 1,000,000 Standard 3: 500,000	1,100,000	1,100,000	1,100,000	1,100,000	1,100,000
Market Value of Public Float	Standard 1: $3,000,000 Standard 3: $15,000,000	$40,000,000[4]	$8,000,000	$18,000,000	$20,000,000	$5,000,000
Bid Price	$3.00				$5.00	$4.00
Market Makers			3	3	4	3
Shareholders	Standard 1: 800 Standard 2: 400 Standard 3: 400	Standard 1: 2,000 round lot holders Standard 2: 2,200 total holders Standard 3: 500 total holders			400	300
Average Daily Volume	Standard 3: 2,000					
Average Monthly Volume Last 6 Months		Standard 2: 100,000 Standard 3: 1,000,000[5]				
Operating History (years)	3				2	1[6]

1. Net Tangible Assets equals Total Assets less Total Liabilities & Goodwill.

2. Greater emphasis is placed on aggregate market value.

3. Before preferred dividends, adjusted to remove the effects of all items whose cash effects are "investing" or "functioning" cash flows as determined pursuant to paragraph 28(b) of the Financial Accounting Standards Board's Statement of Financial Accounting Standards No. 95, "Statement of Cash Flows" (Depreciation, amortization of goodwill, gains or losses on sales of property, plant, and equipment, etc., are examples of such items). The adjustment to net income with respect to the cash effects of (1) discounted operations, (2) the cumulative effect of an accounting change, (3) an extraordinary item or (4) the gain or loss on extinguishment of debt will be limited to the amount charged or credited in determining net income for the period.

4. Value subject to adjustments depending on market conditions.

5. Latest 12 months.

6. Market Capitalization must be at least $50 million if Operating History is less than 1 year.

The higher the pre-IPO valuation the more bargaining power you have with private placement investors. For example, with a pre-IPO valuation of $30 million or above, you can likely negotiate either no or minimal restrictions and controls. In addition, the higher your pre-IPO valuation, the greater the likelihood of any IPO and the smaller the discount valuation that you can negotiate with private placement investors.

PRE-IPO VALUATION BELOW $10 TO $20 MILLION

Suppose your company has a pre-IPO valuation below $20 million. You can still find lower-tier underwriters to take you public. Indeed, IPOs can be accomplished with pre-IPO valuations well below $10 million.

The problems with IPOs with pre-IPO valuations below $10 million are that you are limited to a small group of third-tier underwriters and the benefits associated with going public are reduced.

NASDAQ, in recent years, has been cracking down on third-tier underwriters, some of whom have investigations pending against them. In numerous situations NASDAQ refuses to list the stocks of companies they underwrite. You must carefully review with NASDAQ the records on any proposed underwriter to ascertain whether there are any pending investigations of alleged infractions by the underwriter that could adversely affect your IPO. The very existence of those investigations may prevent your company from obtaining a NASDAQ listing.

Even if the third-tier underwriter has obtained NASDAQ listings for other companies, you have no assurances that new developments will not occur and cause NASDAQ to change its mind just when your company's registration statement has been cleared by the SEC. In general, the other exchanges will follow NASDAQ's lead and similarly refuse your listing. Your due diligence in this area is critical.

Since NASDAQ does not normally provide you an advance ruling about its attitude toward a particular underwriter, you are at risk in using third-tier underwriters.

The advantage of a third-tier underwriter-sponsored IPO over private equity financing is that you obtain a much higher valuation as well as some degree of liquidity. Therefore, you suffer less equity dilution. In one recent case with which I am familiar, the pre-money valuation for private equity financing was $4 million and $8 to $10 million for the IPO.

The second major advantage of a third-tier underwriter IPO over private equity is the lack of any restriction on your company in an IPO. By contrast, private placement investors will seek to impose numerous restrictions on your operations, your compensation, and your control of your company. These are detailed in chapters 8 and 9 of this book. In addition, many times private placement investors purchase preferred stock that is in reality quasi debt, since, as an exit strategy, the private placement investor usually requires redemption rights after five years if you are not then public.

Following are the major disadvantages of a third-tier underwriter-sponsored IPO:

- Cost can exceed $300,000 even after negotiated discounts if the offering is unsuccessful and the failure occurs late in the IPO process. Third-tier underwriters have a higher record of failure than higher-tier underwriters in successfully completing IPOs. If the IPO is unsuccessful, you can be stuck with substantial accounting, legal, and printing costs.

- Third-tier underwriters typically take high fees for their services in proportion to the amount raised and require the public sale of not only common stock but a large number of warrants as well. The warrants typically have an exercise price that is set at a small premium over the IPO price; and the market overhang from a large number of warrants held by the public (and usually the third-tier underwriter) may prevent your stock price from rising in the after-market.

- An IPO can cost $200,000 to $500,000, or more, whereas a private equity transaction can usually be accomplished for less than $150,000.

- There is usually limited interest in the IPO among institutional investors because of its small size; this decreases the liquidity of the stock in the after-market.

- Third-tier underwriters typically do a poor job in supporting the stock after the IPO (this is also sometimes true of first-tier underwriters). Therefore, you will need to employ a financial public relations firm, and even its activity may not be effective. Consequently your stock price may flounder despite good earnings growth.

- Your stock price will be at the mercy of only a few market makers because of the lack of institutional investor interest and the small float. This makes your stock more susceptible to being manipulated and will result in a greater spread between the "bid" and "asked" price.

- It is more likely that your IPO stock will be sold to "investors" who will hold it only a short time, even as little as one day, to profit from an after-market price increase.

- All the above factors can result in your post-IPO stock price falling below the IPO price, resulting in unhappy investors. This may temporarily sully the reputation of your company.

- Your company will be subject to the ongoing costs of being public, which generally range from $50,000 to $100,000 per year (inclusive of the cost of directors' and officers' liability insurance).

- Even if your company grows nicely with the IPO proceeds, some first-tier underwriters may not be willing to underwrite a follow-on issue (an issue after the IPO) because of the taint of the third-tier underwriter. This attitude changes with the passage of time. (The author believes that these disadvantages, particularly the last one, can be exaggerated. The exaggeration is usually made by first-tier underwriters who prefer that you use their private placement group.)

The decision as to whether to use a third-tier underwriter or private equity is a difficult one. Even after considering all the disadvantages of a third-tier underwriter IPO, some of the author's clients have nevertheless decided to use that route, primarily because of the higher IPO valuation and fewer restrictions for the company.

The author's clients who were pleased with their choice were usually those who experienced a successful capital raise. The unhappy clients were typically those in situations where the third-tier underwriter never completed the IPO and the client had to pay the costs of the unsuccessful IPO. There is nothing to prevent you from proceeding with an IPO with a third-tier underwriter and then switching to a private placement if the IPO is unsuccessful. In this situation much of the legal and accounting work can be reused.

DIRECT IPOs OVER THE INTERNET

Direct IPOs over the Internet are becoming increasingly popular for small growth companies as vehicles for raising capital. These offerings generally fall under Regulation

A, which allows small companies with offerings under $5 million to conduct a public offering that is exempt from registration requirements under Section 3(b) of the Securities Act. Using the Internet for such offerings provides several advantages. First, companies seeking to raise capital over the Internet may be able to avoid expensive brokerage fees that they otherwise would have to pay to underwriters. Second, companies may reach wider audiences of potential investors than they otherwise could reach through paper-based offerings. Finally, the time and costs involved in the delivery of offering materials may be reduced by electronic transmission.

In March 1995, the New York–based Spring Street Brewing Company (Spring Street), a microbrewer, successfully used the Internet to raise $1.6 million from 3,500 investors in a direct IPO pursuant to Regulation A. In its IPO, Spring Street sold over 870,000 shares at $1.85 a share. Spring Street opted for this route of raising capital mainly because of the high costs associated with conducting a traditional IPO with the help of underwriters. Spring Street was the first company to publicly sell shares of common stock through the Internet. In doing so, Spring Street paved the way for other small companies that may similarly wish to attempt to raise capital directly via the Internet.

IPO TIMETABLES

Table 15.4 is a typical timetable for an IPO once a letter of intent with an underwriter has been signed.

However, the chart is misleading because Phase 1 does not begin until a letter of intent is signed, and obtaining an executed letter of intent can take several months to several years. During this period, you must put your corporate house in order and market your company to

TABLE 15.4   KEY STEPS IN THE IPO PROCESS

Stages		Week												
		1	2	3	4	5	6	7	8	9	10	11	12	13	14
Phase 1	Due diligence	x	x	x											
	Draft registration statement	x	x	x	x										
Phase 2	Initial filing with SEC				x										
	Preparation of road show and marketing materials					x	x								
Phase 3	Receiving of comments from SEC							x	x	x	x				
	Printing and distributing of red herrings									x	x				
	Road show presentations										x	x			
Phase 4	Pricing of IPO													x	
	Filing of final prospectus with SEC													x	
	Closing of IPO														x

potential underwriters. You should implement the advance planning steps outlined in chapter 4, resolve shareholder issues, and prepare a marketing plan. Underwriters will typically take several months before entering into a letter of intent to better understand the company.

Therefore, your IPO planning should normally assume that a minimum period of approximately nine months will elapse between your deciding to go public and actually receiving the funds.

CHAPTER 16

ROLL-UPS AND ACQUISITIONS

A "roll-up" is a consolidation of a previously fragmented industry. The purpose of the consolidation is to create economies of scale. In many cases, professional management is installed.

Today, roll-ups come in three flavors:

- Roll-ups before an IPO
- Roll-ups after an IPO
- Roll-ups simultaneously with an IPO

The third category, also known as "poof" roll-ups, involves the merger or other consolidation of a group of companies in the same industry, which will be funded with the proceeds from an IPO. If the IPO occurs, the transactions are closed, and "poof," we have a public company. The advent of the "poof" roll-up is a 1990s' phenomenon.

Examples of recent "poof" roll-ups are as follows in Table 16.1:

TABLE 16.1   ROLL-UPS FUNDED WITH IPO PROCEEDS

Company	Line of Business	Companies Acquired	Offering ($Millions)
UniCapital	Equipment leasing	12	$532.0
United Auto Group	Auto dealerships	7	187.5
Advanced Communications	Local exchange carrier	6	128.8
Group MAC	HVAC, plumbing	13	105.0
Integrated Electrical	Electrical contracting	15	91.0
Dispatch Management	Point-to-point delivery	41	79.5
Comfort Systems USA	HVAC services	12	79.3
Condor Technology	IT services	8	76.7
Medical Management	Physician management	5	66.0
USA Floral	Distribution of flowers	8	65.0
Metals USA	Processor of metals	9	59.0
Group 1 Automobile	Auto dealerships	30	57.6
Quanta	Electrical contracting	4	45.0
Compass International	Out-sourced services	5	43.0
ImageMax	Document management	11	37.2

Appendix 4 contains an article on roll-ups in the industrial distribution field and additional contractor and distribution-related IPO roll-ups.

American business has a long history of entrepreneurs and financiers consolidating previously fragmented industries. For example in the 1980s, large public companies emerged from previously fragmented industries as diverse as solid-waste disposal, funeral services, and video rentals. Companies that emerged from this earlier phase of consolidation include: Paging Network Inc. (paging systems); WMX Technologies Inc. (formerly Waste Management, Inc.) and USA Waste Services, Inc. (solid-waste disposal); Service Corporation International (funeral services); and Blockbuster Entertainment Corporation (video rentals).

The roll-up phenomenon is not recent. More than 100 years ago, John D. Rockefeller did something similar when he founded Standard Oil. By 1882, Rockefeller had rolled 41 companies into the Standard Oil trust, which ultimately resulted in Standard Oil of New Jersey and related companies.

THE STRATEGY OF ROLL-UPS

A roll-up is a method of increasing the valuation of your business by combining it with other businesses in the same industry. A roll-up is designed to increase the valuation of your business by:

- permitting your business to grow large enough to qualify for an IPO, thereby achieving higher public company valuations;
- creating cost-saving efficiencies, which further increases your combined income and further enhances the IPO valuation; and
- increasing market penetration.

Roll-ups permit greater market penetration, particularly in industries in which customers have multiple locations and prefer their suppliers to have the ability to service these multiple locations. Roll-ups of customers tend to beget roll-ups of their suppliers, since the consolidated customers tend to have central purchasing and prefer dealing with single suppliers who can service multiple facilities.

Roll-ups can even be useful in industries selling to retail customers or to business customers who do not have multiple locations. All other things being equal, these customers prefer dealing with larger well-capitalized suppliers who will stand behind their product or service. Suppliers that are publicly traded companies with national operations have greater prestige, which may assist them in marketing customers.

PRIVATE COMPANY ROLL-UPS

A publicly traded company can effectuate a roll-up either using cash or its own marketable stock, or some combination.

However, it is difficult for a private company to effectuate a roll-up without cash. It is hard to induce someone to sell their business in exchange for stock of a privately held company, which provides no liquidity to the seller. Even if the privately held buyer agrees to repurchase its stock after five years if there is no IPO or sale, there is a risk that the privately held company may not be able to afford the repurchase after five years.

Since cash is typically required to effectuate private company roll-ups, it is not unusual for private companies to seek out venture capital to supply these funds. Venture capitalists, in turn, are attracted to the roll-up strategy since it may afford an excellent growth strategy if the roll-up is successful, with an exit of either an IPO or a sale.

Some privately held companies are able to effectuate their roll-up strategy using internally generated funds and normal bank financing. However, the minimum IPO size requirements discussed hereafter make it difficult for most privately held companies to ramp up their size sufficiently to qualify for a higher-tier IPO underwriter without seeking outside capital.

Technically, a "poof" roll-up can be effectuated without a substantial amount of outside capital, since the mergers are completed with the cash proceeds from the IPO. However, a "poof" roll-up will typically require more than $1 million to cover the legal, accounting, and printing costs of these complicated transactions. Therefore, it is not unusual in these roll-ups to have the promoter fund these transaction costs and to either be reimbursed for these costs from the IPO or to receive a small equity percentage of the consolidated company to compensate for the risk, or some combination of cash and stock.

The recent tendency of higher-tier underwriters of "poof" roll-ups to raise the minimum IPO size level for these transactions has further increased the transaction cost and encouraged the use of promoters with outside risk capital.

Meeting IPO Size Requirements

Small to medium-sized privately held businesses tend to have a valuation of four to seven times EBITDA (less debt). The inability of these businesses to qualify for an IPO prevents them from achieving public company valuations, which can run ten or more times EBITDA.

One primary reason that small to medium-sized companies cannot qualify for an IPO is their size. To interest a higher-tier underwriter, the IPO must be sufficiently large to attract significant institutional interest. Most institutional investors want minimum public company valuations, after the IPO is completed, of anywhere from $50 million to $100 million or more.

To achieve a minimum valuation after the IPO of $100 million, your business would need to have a minimum value before the IPO of $66 ⅔ million—that is, 66 ⅔ percent of the pre-IPO valuation.

The 66 ⅔ percent rule of thumb results from the desire of underwriters not to sell more than 33 ⅓ percent of the outstanding common stock (as adjusted for the new IPO stock) to the public. Thus, as noted in chapter 15, if your company has two million shares of common stock outstanding before the IPO, the underwriter typically would not want to sell more than one million new shares of common stock in the IPO.

After the IPO, the pre-IPO shareholders would own 66 ⅔ percent of the outstanding common stock (two million divided by three million) and the public would own 33 ⅓ percent (one million divided by three million). To achieve a pre-IPO valuation of $66 ⅔ percent million, most small and medium-sized businesses must grow; a roll-up is one method of growing.

COST EFFICIENCIES

A well-structured roll-up permits cost savings for the combined enterprise. The cost-savings efficiency results from:

- Reducing back-office staff
- Increasing purchasing power

- Advertising efficiencies
- Eliminating duplicate locations
- Eliminating duplicate car and truck fleets
- Efficiencies in purchasing insurance, employee benefits, and administrative expenses
- Eliminating duplicate executives

The reduction in the administrative back-office staff is usually the primary cost-saving efficiency in a roll-up. It is usually not necessary to grow your back-office staff in the exact same proportion as an increase in sales or revenues. As a result, your net income should rise after the IPO from these cost savings alone.

THE MULTIPLIER EFFECT

A well-structured roll-up into an IPO increases your company's valuation disproportionately to the actual revenue and income growth. Thus, if your company was worth five times EBITDA before the roll-up, it could be worth ten times EBITDA in an IPO. This is true even though the combined income of the rolled-up companies has increased only slightly after the roll-up. The higher public company multiplier versus the lower privately held company multiplier plays the major role in this phenomenon.

In addition, your actual EBITDA should be disproportionately higher than the percentage increase in your pre–roll-up revenues as a result of your cost savings. These cost savings are then multiplied by the higher IPO valuation to increase your valuation.

The combined effect of the higher public company multiplier, plus the increased earnings due to cost savings, can have a dramatic overall effect on the post roll-up valuations—way out of proportion to the actual EBITDA increase achieved in the roll-up. This disproportionate or multiplier effect is what is driving the roll-up phenomenon.

SUPPOSE YOU JUST WANT TO SELL YOUR BUSINESS

Many businesspeople do not want the hassle of an IPO. They just want to sell their business at a higher valuation than it currently enjoys.

The roll-up strategy is an equally valuable strategy for those who wish only to sell their businesses. By building up your business through roll-up acquisitions, you can make your company extremely attractive to buyers who are interested in IPO roll-ups. This is particularly true if your business is large enough to permit the buyer to qualify for an IPO or to accelerate the IPO of the buyer.

If your company is large enough to permit the buyer to qualify for an IPO or to accelerate the buyer's IPO, you should be able to achieve a higher valuation when you sell to that buyer. This is because the acquisition of your business permits the buyer a higher multiple of EBITDA for the buyer's business through an IPO and increases the buyer's post-closing EBITDA through cost savings.

Growing your business through a roll-up also permits you access to a larger group of potential buyers. Today, a large number of financial buyers are attempting their own roll-ups as a strategy. They are looking for a "platform" company to achieve an industry roll-up. Once they acquire a platform company, they enlarge the platform company through acquisitions.

However, most financial buyers are typically not interested in businesses worth less than $10 million to $20 million. By rolling up your business to increase its value to over $20 million, you may be able to attract these financial buyers by becoming either their platform company or accelerating the IPO of their existing platform company.

Increasing your valuation also facilitates the sale of your company through an auction. In general, auctions produce the high sales prices (see my book *How Much Is Your Business Worth?* Prima, 1996). These auctions are typically conducted by an investment banker. To interest top-tier investment bankers, such as Merrill Lynch or Dillon Read, your business should typically be worth between at least $50 to $100 million. However, a number of smaller investment bankers will handle auctions of companies worth $20 to $50 million.

SIMULTANEOUS OR "POOF" ROLL-UPS

A recent phenomenon discussed below is the simultaneous or "poof" roll-up. There are many roll-up promoters who finance these roll-ups and obtain 10 percent to 15 percent of the total IPO shares as consideration. The earliest of these promoters are Jonathan Ledecky and Notre Capital Ventures, II (Houston, Texas), but numerous other promoters have joined the business.

Mr. Ledecky created one of the earliest and largest roll-ups in U.S. Office Products Co. and has since created three more, including USA Floral Products, Inc., a flower distributor. Steven Harter, chairman of Notre Capital Ventures II, has completed a number of "poof" roll-ups, including Coach USA, Inc., a roll-up in the motor-coach industry; Comfort Systems, USA, Inc., which is consolidating the HVAC services industry; and Home USA, Inc., a consolidator of mobile home retailers.

These promoters typically interest a number of companies in the same industry into combining at the same time that an IPO occurs. If the IPO occurs, the merger closes and "poof," there is a public company.

These promoters will typically offer each of the combining companies a combination of cash and stock in the public company. The rates vary with transactions and each promoter. A typical Notre transaction is 30 percent cash and 70 percent stock of the publicly held company. The stock of the publicly held company is not liquid and typically cannot be sold until at least one year (or in some cases, an even longer time period) has passed or until certain performance goals are satisfied by the publicly held company. Some businesspeople have difficulty in selling their company into a poof roll-up, thereby losing control of their business to a potentially untested management team and receiving only 30 percent of the purchase price in cash.

The percentage of stock and cash received by each of the rolled-up companies is usually negotiable, depending on the promoter. It is not unheard of to have as much as 70 percent or more of the consideration payable in cash.

A chief executive officer from outside the combining companies will typically be hired to run the combined publicly held company. The key to a successful "poof" roll-up is the ability of the new management team to pull together the diverse businesses and cultures of the constituent companies after the IPO.

Protect Yourself from Unsuccessful Acquisitions

A significant percentage of all acquisitions are unsuccessful. A study by a New York University professor has indicated that 65 percent fail. Roll-ups are not exempted from the risk of failure.

In some cases the failure is the result of bad timing, changes in the marketplace, bad luck, or other unforeseeable events. In other cases the failure was foreseeable.

As a general rule, the best acquisitions are made by one of two methods:

- Buying a small division of a very large company
- Buying a business in bankruptcy or on the verge of bankruptcy

A small division of a very large company is typically sold by large company personnel who have no motivation other than to prevent an accounting loss on the sale. As a result, a sale of assets at the book value of the assets, with no goodwill, is quite feasible. The book value of the assets may be substantially less than their real economic value.

Troubled company acquisitions are very difficult and complicated to complete, but can prove to be the best values. The key is to have an experienced bankruptcy attorney who can protect you from unwanted liabilities and claims.

COMMON MISTAKES IN ROLL-UPS AND OTHER ACQUISITIONS

There is general agreement that the most common reason that roll-ups fail is because they lack an experienced management team to operate the combined companies, particularly in "poof" roll-ups after the IPO has been completed. However, many mistakes occur in the roll-up process prior to the IPO.

Following are a few common mistakes made in roll-ups and other acquisitions, which are within the control of the acquiring entity.

Common Mistake No. 1: Failing to perform sufficient due diligence on the roll-up or acquisition target.

This is the most common cause of foreseeable failure. If you do not regularly make acquisitions, you will need to assemble a sophisticated due-diligence team to be certain that you are not overpaying for the target. There is no such thing as overdoing your due diligence.

The most common mistake in performing due diligence is the buyer's failure to understand the needs of the target's customers and their existing relations with the target's employees. At a minimum, the buyer should call upon the top five customers and have representatives personally visit them.

The buyer's representatives must thoroughly explore with the customers any existing personal relationships they have with the target's key employees. If they find that such relationships exist, buyers should give key employees positive incentives to remain with the buyer and negative incentives to discourage them from leaving the buyer (for example, a covenant not to compete).

To the extent possible, a buyer should understand the seller's motivations for selling. Many sellers decide to exit when they foresee problems ahead for the business.

Common Mistake No. 2: Rolling-up or acquiring a company whose financial statements will not satisfy the SEC, resulting in the postponement of your IPO.

In order to go public, you will normally need audited financial statements for three full fiscal years prior to IPO filing. If your acquisition target does not have audited financial statements for the three-year period, you may have to hold up your IPO until you can obtain such audits. It is not always possible to obtain such audits retroactively, particularly if the acquisition target maintains inadequate records or primarily sells from inventory.

Therefore, you must bring your auditors into the acquisition process at an early stage to make certain that the target's financial statements can satisfy SEC requirements. If the target acquisition's financial statements cannot pass muster, you may be required to postpone your IPO for as many as three years, unless the target acquisition falls below certain materiality thresholds established by the SEC.

> **Common Mistake No. 3:** Relying too heavily on the target's audited financial statements.

When the target provides audited financial statements to the buyer, buyers tend to have their accountants review them and to rely upon the review to detect any issues that would affect the valuation of the target's business. The more prestigious the auditing firm for the target, the greater the tendency of the buyer to rely upon them.

Such reliance brings three problems:

- In many states the auditor has no liability whatsoever to the buyer if the target's financial statements are in error, unless the target's auditors have specifically authorized the buyer to so rely.

- Generally accepted accounting principles are extremely elastic and it is not possible to ferret out all the actual accounting principles and practices just by reviewing the target's audited financial statement; instead a thorough review by your own auditor is essential.

- The auditor for the target's financial statements is generally entitled to rely upon the target management's representation letter to the auditor; therefore, even if you purchase the stock of the target, the target's outside auditor can defend the buyer's lawsuit by claiming that the buyer was misled by the fraud of the target's management.

Common Mistake No. 4: Obtaining an inadequate escrow or hold-back (such as notes) of the purchase price.

Possession of an escrow or hold-back of the purchase price places the buyer in the driver's seat. If the buyer has a post-closing claim, the buyer can just refuse to pay the escrow or hold-back amount.

Many sophisticated acquirers refuse to pay the target or its shareholders more cash than the book value of the target's net assets. The balance of the purchase price consists of notes. If the buyer has post-closing claims against the target or its shareholders, these notes can be offset by the claim amount.

If the escrow or hold-back is nonexistent or inadequate, collecting on claims against the target or its shareholders can be extremely expensive, time-consuming, and frustrating. In some cases, after the target, or its shareholders, pays its taxes on your purchase price and its own attorney's fees, very little is left for the buyers to collect even when they win their lawsuits. An arbitration provision in the purchase contract can sometimes be helpful in this regard by reducing litigation discovery expenses and avoiding the cost and delay of endless appeals. To be fully effective, the arbitration provision should prevent or severely limit pre-arbitration discovery and make the arbitrator's award non-appealable to the extent possible.

Common Mistake No. 5: Paying the same earnings multiplier that you expect to receive in an IPO for significantly smaller companies in your industry, if your company is the lead company in a roll-up.

For example, if you expect to receive a multiplier of ten times your next twelve-month earnings projection in an IPO, a much smaller company in the roll-up should be priced at a reasonable discount from this multiplier (8, for example). Otherwise, your only leverage from the consolidation results from the cost savings and efficiencies you can achieve. In some situations, it is not possible to realize these savings and efficiencies, at least initially. As a result, your post-IPO earnings may be flat, resulting in the marketplace punishing your post-IPO trading price.

CHAPTER 17

WITHDRAWING EQUITY FROM YOUR BUSINESS

The strategy of growing your business with outside capital has one major downside to many entrepreneurs. If their growth strategy fails, and the business ultimately fails, they have risked their entire business in which a substantial portion of their net worth is invested. As a result, many businesspeople prefer not to accept outside capital because of their fear of losing their entire business.

On the other hand, refusing to accept outside capital to fund a growth strategy has a major disadvantage. This major disadvantage is the inability to obtain a sufficient sale price for the business to fund the retirement plans of the entrepreneur. For example, if the entrepreneur wishes to retire with a tax-free income equal to $500,000 per year, he will need to sell his business for an amount in excess of $13 million. This is because taxes and transaction costs will probably absorb $3 million of the sale proceeds, leaving the entrepreneur approximately $10 million on which he might earn a tax-free return of approximately 5 percent per annum.

One method of resolving the dilemma of desiring to grow, versus not wishing to risk what you already have, is to withdraw equity from your business before undertaking the growth strategy. This can be accomplished by removing excess capital from the business and by engaging in what is called a "leveraged recapitalization."

LEVERAGED RECAPITALIZATION

Leveraged recapitalizations come in two types:

- Borrowing funds from a bank or other senior lender without providing the lender with any equity kicker or personal loan guarantees
- Borrowing funds from a combination of senior and mezzanine lenders/investors with equity kickers and with no personal loan guarantees

The advantage of borrowing funds without equity kickers is that you retain 100 percent of the equity of your business. The disadvantage is that this form of borrowing limits the total amount of the loan and therefore limits the amount you can withdraw from the business.

A leveraged recapitalization with an equity kicker typically involves having your company borrow money from a combination of senior lenders and mezzanine investors, who receive debt securities (for example, one a senior debt security and the other a subordinated debt security) together with warrants to purchase your company's stock. Your company then uses the money to recapitalize your company, and you receive cash in the recapitalization for a portion of your stock. You wind up with a significant stock position in your company (but not 100 percent), plus the cash.

Many companies cannot qualify for a leveraged recapitalization. They do not have either the assets or the cash flow to support a leveraged recapitalization or the growth prospects necessary to attract mezzanine lenders or an equity fund. Some companies are already so heavily leveraged that further leverage is not feasible.

Leveraged recapitalizations work only if your company can attract an asset-based lender or a cash-flow lender or has such a high growth potential that you can attract a mezzanine or equity investor.

To attract an asset-based lender, you will need substantial asset values, particularly liquidation values. The following are the normal requirements for asset-based lenders:

- *Accounts receivable:* 70 percent to 85 percent
- *Inventory:* 40 percent to 65 percent
- *Machinery and equipment:* 75 percent to 80 percent of orderly liquidation value
- *Real estate:* the lesser of 50 percent of fair-market value or 75 percent of quick-auction value
- Senior-term debt (fixed or adjusted rate; three-to-seven-year term)
- Working capital revolver (floating rate; one-to-three-year term)

To attract a cash-flow lender, your company needs cash flow sufficient to cover 2.5 times the debt service on senior debt and at least 2.0 times all debt service. If your business does not have this kind of cash flow, a leveraged recapitalization will not work.

Following are the normal requirements for a cash-flow lender:

- Based on cash-flow coverages (cash flow divided by total interest cost)

- 2.0 times total coverage typical (2.5 times senior interest coverage)
- Senior revolving credit facility (floating rate; one-to-three-year term)
- Senior term debt (fixed or floating rate; three-to-seven-year term)
- Mezzanine debt (fixed rate; five-to-ten-year term; "equity kicker")

Leveraged recapitalizations do not require any personal guarantee by you for the debt of the institutional investor.

A leveraged recapitalization does not require significant growth prospects. Your company must have only sufficient assets to attract an asset-based lender or sufficient cash flow to cover the senior debt service and other debt service until their maturity.

If you cannot qualify for a senior debt recapitalization but have significant growth prospects, and you are not ready to go public, you may still be able to effect a leveraged recapitalization.

Some providers of so-called mezzanine financing will lend your company money in exchange for debt plus an equity kicker if they can project a return of at least 22 percent to 28 percent per annum. This does not mean that you have to pay 22 percent to 28 percent interest per year. It means that the potential growth in value of the equity kicker, plus the interest, must equal at least 22 percent to 28 percent per year.

Assume that your business has explosive growth potential, but you are not ready to go public and your current cash flow cannot support much more debt service than you already have. You should consider a private equity fund as an investor. They typically are interested only if they can expect a return of 35 percent to 45 percent per year.

The problem with any leveraged recapitalization is that you will have to provide an exit for your lenders/investors. The exit for the senior and mezzanine debt is obviously the maturity date of that debt. However, the exit for the equity must usually occur in three to seven years through any of the following:

- Going public
- Selling the business
- Repurchasing the lender/investor equity

The primary advantages of the leveraged recapitalization are:

- You receive some cash from the company, thereby achieving a degree of liquidity.
- You retain control of the company, subject to the restriction imposed by the lender or investors.

The primary disadvantages are:

- Your company is highly leveraged, and you must operate in that environment.
- The institutional lenders/investors have some equity in your business, so you have minority shareholders with whom to contend.
- The institutional lenders/investors will impose restrictions on the operation of your company until they exit.

If you engage in a leveraged recapitalization, consider making family gifts of stock immediately thereafter, since your stock valuation will be depressed.

A leveraged recapitalization could be followed by a public offering after an appropriate growth period.

Chapter 18

Financing Your Business with Credit Cards

According to a recent study by the Arthur Andersen Enterprise Group, credit cards were a significant form of financing for smaller companies. Their 1997 survey of smaller companies indicated that 34 percent of companies with less than nineteen employees used credit card financing. Table 18.1 shows the results of their survey.

Types of Financing by Size of Company

Table 18.1 shows the percentage of respondents that used various types of financing to meet their capital needs during the twelve months prior to the Arthur Andersen survey.

The larger businesses in the Arthur Andersen survey were significantly more likely to use commercial bank loans, leasing, and asset-based financing than their smaller counterparts.

TABLE 18.1 TYPES OF FINANCING USED
BY NUMBER OF EMPLOYEES IN COMPANY*

	Up to 19 Employees	20 to 99 Employees	100 to 499 Employees
Commercial bank loan	34 %	62 %	67 %
Credit cards	34	27	22
Vendor credit	19	28	27
Private loans	17	10	8
Leasing	13	34	40
Personal or home-equity bank loan	16	8	5
Selling/pledging accounts receivable	4	8	8
SBA-guaranteed loan	4	5	5
Asset-based, inventory as collateral	3	8	20
Private placement of stock	3	3	2
Venture capital	2	1	3
Public issuance of stock	1	0	2

*Reprinted with permission of Arthur Andersen.

Smaller companies were more likely to use credit cards, private loans, personal bank loans, or home-equity loans.

Table 18.2 displays even more revealing findings in the Arthur Andersen survey, focusing on the growing trend of the use of credit cards as a source of financing for companies.

LEGAL REVIEW

Before anyone uses a credit card for business financing, you should have your lawyer carefully review the fine print

TABLE 18.2   CREDIT CARDS REPLACING COMMERCIAL BANK LOANS?*

Percentage of respondents that used the following types of financing in the past 12 months:

Credit cards continue to grow in popularity as a form of financing. When we first asked this question in 1993, only 17 percent of companies indicated they used credit cards as a source of financing. Today that number has doubled to 34 percent. At the same time, the number of companies that have used commercial bank loans has declined from 49 percent in 1993 to 38 percent in 1997.

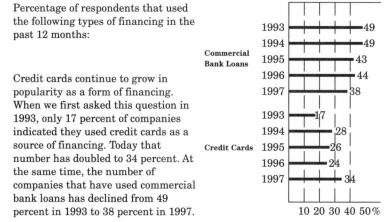

Commercial Bank Loans
1993 — 49
1994 — 49
1995 — 43
1996 — 44
1997 — 38

Credit Cards
1993 — 17
1994 — 28
1995 — 26
1996 — 24
1997 — 34

10 20 30 40 50%

*Reprinted with permission of Arthur Andersen.

on the credit card agreement to determine whether this violates your contract with the credit card company.

INTEREST RATES AND REPAYMENT TERMS

Since interest rates on credit cards vary widely and are usually extremely high, you should select carefully the credit cards you intend to use as financing vehicles so as to provide you with the lowest interest financing cost. In general, American Express provides a low interest cost to its cardholders. However, interest costs from some banks on VISA cards can be comparable, or even lower, than the American Express interest charges.

Repayment terms also vary among the various credit cards and the sponsoring financial institutions. Generally, credit cards with the longest repayment period are the more desirable, assuming that there is no prepayment penalty. A careful review of the credit card repayment agreement is crucial.

HAZARDS OF CREDIT-CARD FINANCING

The following article from *The Wall Street Journal* illustrates some of the hazards of trying to finance your business with credit cards.

BANKING ON PLASTIC: TO FINANCE A DREAM, MANY ENTREPRENEURS BINGE ON CREDIT CARDS*

Mr. Murdock, the Inventor, Has Unique Golf Clubs and a Mountain of Debt

'Failure Is Not an Option'

by Rodney Ho, staff reporter of *The Wall Street Journal*

    Wilbert Murdock's "untouchable-debt box" sits taped shut in the corner of his bedroom closet.

    Inside are his demons: statements and receipts from more than $25,000 in credit-card bills he built up the past two years developing his latest entrepreneurial product, a computerized golf club. On the outside of the box, he has attached his personal fighting words: "Succeed or Die." He'll open the box, he says, only when he can pay back the money.

    For now, the Bronx, N.Y., former professor sits in the dimly lighted basement of his mother's apartment, avoiding weekly calls and letters from American Express Co. and other creditors. Instead, Mr. Murdock, 39 years old, tries to focus on his vision: turning the golf club, which

---

uses sensors to teach duffers how to correct their swings, into a successful business—especially one that will create jobs in the inner city, where Mr. Murdock grew up.

Mr. Murdock's predicament of essentially financing his business with credit cards is becoming more common. One-third of businesses with 19 or fewer employees use credit cards as a way to fund themselves—nearly double the number in 1993, according to a recent study by accounting firm Arthur Andersen and trade group National Small Business United. Teaser introductory rates as low as 5.9 percent and the crush of card offers have made credit cards a convenient, no-questions-asked option for many small businesses.

Credit cards are "the best means for financing a start-up like mine [because] the credit-card companies don't care how the money is spent," Mr. Murdock says.

But the risks are clear. Over the years, the credit woes of the plastic-laden American consumer have been well-chronicled. Now, that problem increasingly is spilling over into the small-business environment.

While credit-card companies don't publicly break out their business delinquencies, vs. those for individuals, about 40 percent of small-business credit-card users in the Arthur Andersen survey say they revolve their balances. And at least one-third of personal bankruptcies stem from failed small-business start-ups, notes Paul Richard, executive vice president of the non-profit National Center for Financial education in San Diego.

Personal Liability

"Credit cards are addictive," Mr. Murdock says. "You feel like you're not spending money, but you are." Mr. Murdock says he never tried to get a corporate card under his company's name, which would have protected him from personal liability if, for example, the company filed for bankruptcy. "Instead, it's hanging over my head," he says.

For Mr. Murdock, there is virtually no consumerism in his minimalist lifestyle. His wood-paneled basement apartment in his mother's home consists of little more than a few warping bookshelves, stacks of kung-fu videos, and a twin bed that doubles as a couch. He has no desk—his 486 computer sits on an end table, forcing him to balance his keyboard on his lap. To save on electricity bills, he keeps his incandescent lights off during the day, leaving only a depressing, yellowish hue of the fluorescent lights in the nearby kitchen. His 1986 Nissan Pulsar has sat idle in the driveway for more than a year, in need of repairs.

Like many tinkerers, Mr. Murdock is obsessed with his vision. There's always the "breakthrough opportunity" or the "temporary setback" that moves his golf device one step forward or one step back.

And occasionally, of course, there is the debt thing.

Mom's Financing

In addition to the $25,000 he owes the card companies, Mr. Murdock also is on the hook for $40,000 to his mother. His partners, including former New York Knicks basketball great Earl "the Pearl" Monroe, have ponied up at least $32,000 in exchange for their stake of about 10 percent of the company.

For more than a year now, the credit-card companies have been grinding him with phone calls, asking when or if payment is coming. Citicorp's Diners Club sued him last summer, and the two sides put together a repayment plan, Mr. Murdock says. "It was the worst feeling in my life being sued, but I knew sacrifices had to be made," he says. "My partners don't even know it happened." An embarrassed Mr. Murdock promised to repay the debts as soon as possible. But he hasn't yet. (Diners Club declined to comment.)

Instead, Mr. Murdock funnels what money he gets into the business and has learned ways to avoid pestering questions. He filters calls through his phone's Caller ID. If a collection-agency operator tries to be folksy with him by using his first name, Wilbert, he hangs up, since his friends and business associates know he normally goes by Will or his middle name, Quincy. Credit-related letters go straight into the garbage unopened, now that the debt box in his closet has been sealed. "I don't need the aggravation," he says. Still, he has no animus toward the credit-card companies: "They're just doing their jobs."

Though the credit-card companies decline to comment about Mr. Murdock's specific situation, they say that in general they have little recourse when a person has minimal assets to chase. Mr. Murdock has practically nothing of worth to a creditor. American Express says it tries to work with small businesses on a case-by-case basis, creating repayment plans if possible, even waiving interest. Eventually, though, the companies will write off the debt.

Mr. Murdock insists he isn't going to let that happen and has no intention or need to file for bankruptcy.

It hasn't always been this way for Mr. Murdock. For years, he avoided debt, adhering to his parents' aversion to it and his modest upbringing. Growing up in the Baruch Houses, a Manhattan high-rise housing project that in its early days was filled with mostly African-American middle-class families like his, he watched his parents toil long hours at a grocery store they owned in Brooklyn. In the early 1970s, after being robbed at his store, his father switched to a more stable job as an engineer at International Business Machines Corp. But he kept his entrepreneurial juices flowing by selling Amway products on the side.

As a teenager, Mr. Murdock helped out, delivering Amway cleansers to neighbors. He also trolled the streets of Manhattan's financial district as a messenger. A nearly fatal traffic accident caused permanent injuries to his back and knee, but helped trigger an interest in technology and body mechanics. He received a bachelor's degree in electrical engineering and a master's in bioengineering from Polytechnic Institute in Brooklyn.

Failed Products

After a short stint as an engineer, he taught computer science and engineering at various New York City colleges. But his real goal was outside the classroom, where his mind was constantly focused on invention. Still using no debt, he worked through his savings, as well as loans from about 20 family members and friends.

He had a string of products that fell short. His first firm in 1983 used real-time wireless motion analysis as a diagnostic medical tool. After raising $40,000 with a dozen partners, he ran out of money within 18 months. Soon after, Mr. Murdock dabbled in ideas to eradicate carpal-tunnel syndrome, prevent people from falling asleep while driving, and customize sneakers, among others.

He sometimes spent his wages on his company rather than food. "I didn't understand being hungry until I became an entrepreneur," he says. Combining teaching with his business efforts took a toll on Mr. Murdock, who physically collapsed for a week in 1986 from exhaustion. This gave him time to reassess his priorities, and he soon quit teaching and moved back to his parents' home to take care of his ailing dad and pursue his entrepreneurial dream full time.

But the same problems cropped up again and again. Ronald Johnson, a fellow Polytechnic student and investor of $23,000 in Mr. Murdock's projects over the years, says that in each case, Mr. Murdock had good ideas but was hamstrung by a lack of financing and business experience. Banks rebuffed him because of his lack of collateral. He never got far enough along to attract venture capital. And partnership talks with his father's old employer, IBM, didn't go beyond talk.

He did attract Mr. Monroe, whom Mr. Murdock met while designing a computerized shadow-boxing system in the early 1990s. "Something about his persistence and sincerity drew me to him," says Mr. Monroe, an owner of a building subcontracting business who continues to provide Mr. Murdock with business advice and a dose of credibility.

Dream Company

Mr. Murdock's current venture, Internet Golf Multimedia Inc., came to him in a dream, he says. While he doesn't play golf often, he understands players' obsession with self-improvement. His idea: a club that provides instant feedback by tracking a golfer's stroke. With sensors attached to its head, the club emits beeps based on whether a golfer hits the "sweet spot." Via a wireless signal, it creates a database of swings on a laptop computer.

In the summer of 1995, focused on making that dream into a real product, Mr. Murdock let debt into his life. "It's all or nothing," he recalls thinking at the time. So he applied for an American Express green card, which requires full payment each month. He tried to maintain payments early on, but quickly fell behind, choosing to use investment money on an outside engineer to develop the software that would communicate with the golf club. By the end of 1995, he owed American Express $5,000; the company shut off the spigot.

Needing more cash to refine the software program, Mr. Murdock spied a Diners Club magazine ad and took advantage of its two-month, interest-free, grace period. Over a year, he amassed $15,000 in debt on software and hardware before Diners Club closed his account in late 1996. Early the next year, he procured a revolving MasterCard with a $4,000 credit line. (Mr. Murdock says he can't remember the bank issuer and refuses to open his debt box to find out.)

Putter Prototype

To save cash, Mr. Murdock also tapped students to help design the clubs and tweak the software. Two Internet Golf Multimedia board members also took out *their* credit cards and charged $32,000 on his behalf with promises of future equity stakes. The influx of cash helped him finish the putter prototype, including the sensors.

Nonetheless, Mr. Murdock exhausted his MasterCard credit by midsummer, not even paying the minimums. As efforts to get grants fell short, one reliable source of funding, his mother, kept coming through.

Rosa El-Amin has contributed more than $40,000 to her son's cause in the past two years, juggling balances among six credit cards. "Every time they raise my credit limit, I take it," she says. "They even sometimes let you skip a month." When new cards come along, she grabs them.

This is a departure for her. Ms. El-Amin, whose own discipline stems from her teen years when she managed finances on the family farm in South Carolina, says she views the money less as debt and more as an investment. To this day, she gives frequent pep talks to lift her son's spirits, telling him that what he's doing is important not just for him, but for the nation's future. And then, she jokes, "I say, 'Hurry up and make the money and get me out of here!'"

Last year, as she was helping out, Mr. Murdock cut up his own credit cards, which were probably useless by then, and vowed to himself, "Failure is not an option."

All the while, he continued preparing to take his golf clubs to market. The picture is brightening. In November, a Taiwanese company—whose name he won't disclose— agreed to manufacture the clubs, he says, and absorb some development costs. His first production models of the putters, he says, arrived in February and are being tested.

Paranoia lurks beneath his sunny exterior. "One obstacle is he's worried that if he reveals too much to these big guys, they'll take his technology and run with it," says Mr. Monroe, the former basketball star. Mr. Murdock says "paranoia is well-founded" because intellectual property is so easy to steal.

"Small Market"

Competitors in the swing-analyzing field, which range from modest $100 clubhead speed readers to elaborate $10,000 computer systems, have no idea who he is. "It's a small market," says Alan Kaechele, vice president of marketing for Astar Inc., a San Diego maker of a video-golf system, "and requiring someone to swing a special golf club is a tough sell."

Mr. Murdock dismisses such talk. His technology, he insists, is far ahead of theirs at an affordable price (he estimates $300 for the putter). "If someone builds a better golf club, I'll retire and work in a grocery store," he says.

Despite his dismal financial situation, he says he still receives credit-card solicitations in the mail through his business, though he doesn't bother to fill out the applications. And he won't hesitate to use credit cards if his business takes off.

For now, though, the debt burden can be crushing. He keeps the debt box untouched in the closet, he says, "to protect my mind and focus on the future." But on a recent day, suffering from a head cold, his wall of optimism crumbles for a moment and he breaks down sobbing. "It's a shameful thing to have this debt," he says.

Later, his spirit is resuscitated. In a moment of levity, he muses: "Maybe after I pay off my debts, I can do an Amex commercial."

APPENDIX 1

SAMPLE TERM SHEET
FOR AN EARLY-STAGE PROFESSIONALLY MANAGED VENTURE CAPITAL TRANSACTION

T he following is a term sheet provided by Stephen M. Sammut, a biotech venture capitalist, and used in the course Mr. Sammut and the author teach in the MBA program at the Wharton School of Business of the University of Pennsylvania. XYZ Technologies is a company that was in a product development stage for about two years prior to approaching venture capitalists for financing. Up to this time, the company was wholly owned by the two founders who had put in personal financial resources and a full-time, non-compensated effort. The founders, in their own name, had developed and patented a sophisticated system that permitted on-site generation of a chemical that is used widely in a variety of industrial and medical settings. Installation and operation of these systems would provide significant economies for XYZ's customers. The patent position was very strong, the management credible, and the business strategy sound. On the basis of company's status, a venture capital fund that managed several pools of capital, including funds from a state economic development organization, made an offer designed to capitalize the company and have it relocate to the venture fund's home state. The fund, ACT Partners, assisted in securing a factory site, at highly favorable terms, in a nearby city from the local government.

ACT also wanted to syndicate the deal with another local venture fund, ACORN, and a state agency, STATE. The facility was financed by the Council on Economic Development (CED).

The venture capitalists were confident of XYZ's future, but did not want to have management's time occupied with future fund raising. Based on the company's operating plan, capital needs were forecasted to breakeven and positive cash flow. The total required investment would be committed, but would be made available to the company in a series of four tranches. After months of negotiation, the following term sheet was accepted by both sides, and legal counsel directed to draft appropriate documents.

Issuer

XYZ Technologies Corporation ("XYZ" or the "Company")

Securities

Convertible Preferred Stock (the "Preferred")

Offering Size

$3.5 million to be allocated among the investors as follows:

> ACT: $1.1 million
> STATE: $0.375 million
> ACORN: $2.025 million

Takedowns or tranches will be as follows:

> $1.0 million at closing.

Prior to the initial closing, the investors and management must have agreed on a final operating budget for the first 12 months, the use of proceeds for the initial takedown, and an allocation of the initial equity among management [non-founders]. In addition, (a) all the intellectual property owned by the Founders (and/or related entities) that are (or potentially are) related to XYZ's business must have been transferred to XYZ, and (b) a "not to exceed" contract for the renovation of the Bridgeport facility should be in place.

$750,000 upon completion of a [Beta Test] unit to the satisfaction of the investors.

$1.0 million upon the satisfactory completion of the following milestones:

3.1 Sale of 250 units, including 150 to ABC Company;

3.2 Signing of one other North American distribution agreement, which will project a minimum of $1 million of sales within 12 months of signing;

3.3 Hiring of a CFO acceptable to the Board.

$750,000 upon the satisfactory completion of the following milestones:

4.1 Cumulative revenues of $2.5 million;

4.2 Positive cash flow (net income + depreciation) in the aggregate for the previous three months of at least $500,000;

4.3 Five revenue-generating customers in place.

In addition, the Council on Economic Development (CED) will fund on a pro-rata basis to the Preferred an aggregate of $3.5 million from a $1.75 million CED grant and a $1.75 million 10-year loan from CED whose terms and conditions will be satisfactory to the Investors (approximately a 10-year loan with a non-cumulative interest rate of no more than 2 percent; interest payments deferred for at least 5 years). The loan will be entitled to security in the fixed assets (not including A/R0 of XYZ) and will have attached 5-year warrants to purchase a number of shares equal to 1 percent of the pro forma shares outstanding after the takedown of the Preferred.

Price

The pre-money value including all outstanding warrants and options, any authorized but unissued warrants and options (including a reasonable pool of a number of shares for future hires), all common and Preferred shares and any other outstanding equity equivalents will be $4.75 million. The pre-money value for the third closing will be 20 percent higher on a per-share basis and the value for the fourth closing 20 percent higher than the per-share closing on the third closing. In addition, the Investors will receive on a pro-rata basis to each closing, warrants to purchase a number of Preferred shares equal to 30 percent of the Preferred Shares so purchased at an exercise price equal to 125 percent of the Preferred price per share. The exercise may be by cash or on a cashless basis at the sole option of the holder.

Use of Proceeds

The proceeds from the sale of the Preferred Stock will be used for working capital, sales expenditures, and further product research and development as more fully set forth on the Sources and Uses table to be approved by both the Company and Investors and appended to the financing document.

Dividends

Four percent (4%) per year, payable in stock or cash on a cumulative basis at the option of the Company beginning six (6) quarters after closing.

Redemption

The Preferred shall be redeemed at a cost in equal annual installments at the end of the years five to eight unless the stock shall have been previously converted into Common Stock.

Liquidation Rights

The holders of the Preferred will be entitled to a liquidation preference over the Common Stock. The liquidation preference will also apply in the event of a sale of all or substantially all the assets of the Company or a merger or consolidation of the Company. First, the Preferred will receive a return of capital.

Any remaining proceeds shall be allocated between the Common and Preferred stockholders on a pro-rata basis, treating the Preferred on an as-if-converted basis.

Optional Conversion

At any time at the holder's option, the Preferred may be converted into Common Stock on a one-for-one basis or at such rates as result from the application of anti-dilution (see below).

Mandatory Conversion

The Preferred will be converted at the Company's option concurrently with the closing of the initial public offering of the Company's Common Stock so long as the aggregate amount raised by such offering equals or exceeds a Common share price of at least three times the conversion price of the Preferred.

Voting Rights

The Preferred will have full voting rights equal to the number of shares of Common Stock into which the Preferred may be converted. A vote of 51 percent of the Preferred (such vote not to be unreasonably withheld) will be required for the Company to engage in an extraordinary act including (exceptions to be decided by the Board will be so noted):

> Adoption of the annual budget by the Board of Directors by less than a two-thirds affirmative vote;
>
> Incurring third-party indebtedness above $250,000 in any one year will be subject to Board approval;
>
> Incurring any capital expenditure above $250,000 in any one year will be subject to Board approval;
>
> Sale of any material asset or the sale, merger, or consolidation of the Company into or with any other entity;
>
> Purchase or redemption of any Company securities or any cash distributions to equity holders (other than the repurchase of shares of terminating employees);

Issuance or sale of Company securities with rights, preferences, and privileges senior to or a parity with the Preferred;

Changing the nature of the business in any material way or any material change to the Company's Business Plan;

Transactions with affiliates except as approved by the Board of Directors by a two-thirds or greater affirmative vote;

The amendment of the Company's articles of incorporation or bylaws which adversely affects the Preferred shareholders or any rights, preferences, or privileges granted to Investors therein or herein;

A change in the number of authorized directors; and/or

A liquidation or dissolution of the Company, or a reclassification of its outstanding capital stock.

Anti-Dilution Adjustments

Conversion ratio adjusted on a standard weighted average basis. "Dilutive issuance" shall not include Common Stock issued or issuable to employees, directors, and consultants pursuant to the option plan currently in existence or any other plan or amendment approved by holders of 50 percent of the Preferred.

Proportional adjustments for stock splits and stock dividends will not trigger anti-dilution adjustments.*

Board

The Preferred holders will be entitled to elect two (2) Board positions out of a five-person Board. AIPLP and ACORN are each entitled to designate one member. For serving on the Board, the Venture representatives will receive options to purchase 1,000 shares of Preferred (at the initial purchase price per share) for each meeting attended. The other Board members will include

---

*To accommodate this provision, legal counsel essentially had to create a separate series of Preferred Stock for each takedown or tranche because of the different prices negotiated for shares that would be issued in each tranche.

the Founder (assuming the Founder owns greater than 20 percent of the Company), a management representative, and a mutually acceptable outsider. If the Founder owns less than 20 percent, the seat will be represented by management.

Non-Disclosure and Proprietary Information Agreement

The Founders and key employees of the Company will enter into Non-Disclosure and Proprietary Information Agreements with the Company in a form reasonably acceptable to the Company and the investors.

Vesting of Common Stock

Management Common Stock (including Founder's stock) and options to buy Common Stock will vest over a five-year period. Founder's stock will be 40 percent vested on the day of closing. The remaining stock (60 percent) will vest over five years. In the event of voluntary or "with cause" involuntary termination, unvested stock will be forfeited to the Company. "With cause" refers to behavior or actions by management that are illegal, immoral, etc., and a continuing association as management of the Company will have a detrimental influence on the Company. The continued vesting of Founder's stock for Founder will be based on Company's performance relative to the final approved budget at closing. Vesting will proceed as defined above as long as the Company achieves 80 percent of its operating income budget, and if the Company sells X # of systems by month 10 after closing, with at least half sold in the USA.

In the event that the Company does not achieve 80 percent of its operating budget in any six-month period, there will be six months to remedy the cumulative shortfall. If the cumulative shortfall is not remedied to be 80 percent of operating income of operating income budget after this period, the Board has the authority to remove Founder as CEO, and terminate his employment by a majority vote of the Board of Directors.

Each holder of the Preferred will be furnished by the Company with an annual budget and annual audited financial statements within 90 days following the end of each fiscal year as well as monthly financials. In addition, the Company must deliver an operating plan no later than 60 days prior to the end of each fiscal year.

Shareholders' Agreement

A Shareholders' Agreement will be entered into among significant equity holders of the Company's Common Stock. Such agreement shall include, among others, the following Provision:

Transfer of Interests: No party may sell, transfer, or otherwise dispose of any equity interest (except in case of the sale of the entire Company as approved by the Company's Board and the holders of a majority of Preferred) other than as permitted in the Shareholders' Agreement.

Right of First Refusal

Investors shall be afforded a right of first refusal to participate in any sale of company securities upon the same terms and conditions as proposed by the Company. The participation rights will be in proportion to the investors' ownership position prior to the offering. In the event of such proposed sale and issuance, investors shall be given a 30-day notice and period in which to act upon such proposal.

Tag-Along

Investors shall be afforded a "tag-along" right that will provide that in the event the Company or the Company's Shareholders receive a solicited or unsolicited proposal from a third party to acquire all or some of their equity securities, the offeree(s) shall be required to make such proposal available to all the Company's equity holders on a pro-rata basis.

Registration Rights Agreement

Investors and the Company shall enter into a Registration Rights Agreement providing for the registration of shares of Common Stock issued upon conversion of the Preferred upon the following terms:

Company Registration: The investors shall be entitled to "piggyback" registration rights on all registrations of the Company subject to the right, however, of the Company and its underwriters in good faith to reduce the number of shares proposed to be registered pro rata among all investors in view of market conditions.

S-3 Rights: Investors shall be entitled to two (2) demand registrations on Form S-3 (if available to the Company) so long as such registered offerings are not less than $500,000.

Expenses: The Company shall bear registration expenses (exclusive of underwriting discounts and commissions) of all such piggybacks and S-3 registrations (including the expense of a single counsel to the selling shareholders not to exceed $10,000).

Standoff Provisions: If requested by the underwriters no investor or any other shareholder will sell shares of the Company's stock for up to 180 days following a public offering by the Company of its stock.

Termination of Rights: The registration rights shall terminate on the date three years after the Company's initial public offering, or with respect to each investor, at such time as (1) the Company's shares are publicly traded and (2) the investor is entitled to sell all of its shares in any 90-day period pursuant to Securities Act Rule 144.

Directors' and Officers' Indemnification

The Company will represent that it has provisions in its articles or bylaws for the indemnification of officers and directors to the full extent permitted by law and will covenant to keep such indemnification in place for so long as any representative of the investors serves on the Board of Directors.

Directors' and Officers' Liability Insurance

The Company will use its best efforts to obtain and keep directors' and officers' liability insurance in the minimum amount of $1 million if such coverage is available at commercially acceptable rates.

Other

The company will obtain key-man insurance in the amount of $2 million.

All applicable issued patents, patent applications, patent applications in progress, and any future inventions associated with the Company, in any jurisdiction, shall be assigned to the Company, regardless of field of use.

Prior to the initial closing, the Company will have entered into employment agreements with: [key management] acceptable to investors.

Reimbursement to the investors of: (a) legal expenses up to a maximum of $25,000 for preparing the documents associated with the financing, and (b) consultants' fees incurred in connection with "due diligence" up to a maximum of $5,000.

Representations and Warranties

Standard representations and warranties.

Signatures

The undersigned acknowledge that this term sheet represents a non-binding agreement in principle. All parties maintain the right to withdraw any offer herein contained, or further negotiate terms and conditions.

XYZ Founders	Date	XYZ Founders	Date
ACT	Date	ACORN	Date
STATE	Date	CED	Date

APPENDIX 2

SAMPLE TERM SHEET

FOR AN INVESTMENT BANKER–SPONSORED PRIVATE PLACEMENT

Summary of Preliminary Proposed Terms

I. The Offering

Issuer:	ABC Holdings, Inc. (the "Company").
Issue:	Private Placement of Series B Convertible Preferred Stock (the "Series B Preferred Stock") offered to accredited investors only pursuant to Regulation D.
Amount:	Minimum of $2.5 million and maximum of $7.5 million, exclusive of an over-allotment option of up to $2.5 million to be issued by the Company (the "Greenshoe").
Pre-Offering Valuation (Fully Diluted):	$7.0 million
Use of Proceeds:	Acquisitions

Purchase
Agreement: The Series B Preferred Stock shall be
                    purchased pursuant to a Stock Purchase
                    Agreement which shall contain representa-
                    tions, warranties, and covenants of the
                    Company and conditions to closing custom-
                    ary for a transaction of this kind.

Estimated
Closing Date: Within three months from the date of the
                    Placement Agent Agreement.

II. Summary of Preferred Stock Terms

Right of
Conversion: Each share of Series B Preferred Stock is
                    convertible at any time (at the option of the
                    holder) initially on a share-for-share basis
                    into the Company's Common Stock (the
                    "Common Stock").

Automatic
Conversion: Each share of Series B Preferred Stock
                    shall automatically be converted into
                    shares of Common Stock at the closing of
                    an initial public offering in which the gross
                    proceeds to the Company are not less than
                    $10 million and the investors of the Series
                    B Preferred Stock realize an annual aver-
                    age rate of return of 40 percent (a
                    "Qualified Public Offering").

Dividend
Provisions: The holders of the Series B Preferred Stock
                    shall be entitled to receive cumulative
                    dividends at the rate of 8 percent per
                    annum when, and if, declared by the Board
                    of Directors.

Seniority: Any future issue of Preferred Stock shall
                    not be senior to the Series B Preferred
                    Stock, except upon the consent of at least

67 percent of the then outstanding shares
of the Series B Preferred Stock.

Liquidation
Preference:

The holders of the Series B Preferred Stock
shall be entitled to receive, prior and in
preference to any distribution of any of the
assets of the Company or proceeds thereof
to the holders of Common Stock (the
"Liquidation Preference").

Merger,
Consolidation,
or Sale:

Upon the consolidation or merger of the
Company in which stockholders of the
Company own less than 50 percent of the
voting securities of the resulting or surviving corporation, or the sale or transfer of
all or substantially all the assets of the
Company, the holders of the Series B
Preferred Stock shall have the option to (i)
receive the Liquidation Preference plus
accrued and unpaid dividends, or (ii)
participate with the holders of Common
Stock on an as-converted basis.

Voting Rights:

The holders of Series B Preferred Stock
shall be entitled to vote with the Common
Stock of the Company as a single class on
the basis of one vote per share of Series B
Preferred Stock.

Registration
Rights:

The holders of the Series B Preferred Stock
will be entitled to certain demand and
piggyback registration rights for the
Common Stock to be received upon conversion of the Series B Preferred Stock
following an initial public offering.

Mandatory
Redemption:

On or after the earlier of (i) five years from
the date of the closing hereunder or (ii) the

date at which any other series of Preferred
Stock is entitled to mandatory redemption,
the holders of the Series B Preferred Stock
shall have the option of "putting" their
Series B Preferred Stock back to the
Company for the Liquidation Preference
plus any accrued and unpaid dividends.

Anti-Dilution
Provisions: The holders of the Series B Preferred Stock
shall have certain anti-dilution provisions,
which shall be calculated on a weighted-
average basis.

Preemptive
Right (Right of
First Refusal):   Holders of the Series B Preferred Stock
shall have the same right of first refusal
providing for the purchase of shares of
future private offerings of equity securities
(or warrants or other securities convertible
into equity securities) of the Company that
will enable them to maintain their fully
diluted percentage ownership of the Company. This right shall terminate upon a
Qualified Public Offering.

Tag-Along
Provision
(Co-Sale Rights):   In the event that an offer is made to
purchase shares of Common Stock owned
by any officers, directors, or 5 percent
holders of the Company, the holders of the
Series B Preferred Stock shall have the
right to sell a pro-rata portion of their
shares to such purchaser.

Board of
Directors: The holders of the Series B Preferred
Stock, as a class, will be entitled to desig-
nate one (1) member of the Board of
Directors which shall consist of no more
than five (5) members of which three (3)
shall be outsiders.

Information
Rights
and Access: The holders of the Series B Preferred Stock
and Darren Keith & Company, Inc. shall
have the right to promptly receive: (i)
quarterly unaudited financial statements
within 45 days after the end of each quarter; (ii) annual audited financial
statements within 90 days after the end of
each year; (iii) a budget and operating plan
for each year at least 45 days prior to the
start of each year; (iv) copies of all reports
sent to stockholders or filed with the SEC;
(v) notification of material litigation; and
(vi) other information as reasonably requested.

Amendments
and Waivers
of Rights: Amendments to and waivers of the rights
of the holders of the Series B Preferred
Stock must be approved by the holders of
67 percent of the Series B Preferred Stock.

III.   **Placement Agent Compensation**

Exclusive
Placement
Agent: Darren Keith & Company, Inc.

Placement
Agent Fee: Eight percent (8%) of the total amount
raised. The Company shall receive a credit
of three percent (3%) for any amount raised
from officers, directors, and predetermined
friends of the Company.

Expense
Allowance: Fifty thousand dollars ($50,000), twenty-
five thousand ($25,000) of which is payable
upon the signing of a Placement Agent
Agreement.

Warrants:

Five-year warrants to purchase Common Stock equal to 10 percent of the number of as-converted shares of the Series B Preferred Stock sold hereunder at a 10 percent premium to the conversion price.

Other:

Upon closing of the Offering, Darren Keith & Company, Inc. shall have a right of first refusal for all investment banking activities of the Company for a period of two years from the final closing of this Offering and shall have observer rights to meetings of the Board of Directors until the Company's initial public offering. The Darren Keith & Company, Inc. observer shall be promptly reimbursed for reasonable out-of-pocket expenses incurred in attending such meetings.

EXHIBIT TO APPENDIX 2

April 8, 1998

Darren Keith & Company, Inc.
123 Avenue of the Americas
New York, New York 10004

Attention: Darren Alexander
               Senior Vice President

Gentlemen:

In connection with our engagement of Darren Keith & Company, Inc. ("Darren Keith") as our financial advisor and investment banker, we hereby agree to indemnify and hold harmless Darren Keith and its affiliates, and the respective directors, officers, shareholders, agents, and employees of any of the foregoing (collectively the "Indemnified Persons") from and against any and all claims, actions, suits, proceedings (including those of shareholders), damages, liabilities, and expenses incurred by any of them (including the fees and expenses of counsel), which are (a) related to or arise out of (i) any actions taken or omitted to be taken (including any untrue statements made or any statements omitted to be made) by the Company or (ii) any actions taken or omitted to be taken by any Indemnified Person in connection with our engagement of Darren Keith or (b) otherwise relate to or arise out of Darren Keith's activities on our behalf under Darren Keith's engagement. We shall reimburse any Indemnified Person for all expenses (including the fees and expenses of counsel) incurred by such Indemnified Person in connection with investigating, preparing, or defending any such claim, action, suit, or proceeding (collectively a "Claim"), whether or not in connection with pending or threatened litigation in which any Indemnified Person is a party. We will not, however, be responsible for any Claim that is finally judicially determined to have resulted exclusively from the gross negligence or willful misconduct of any person seeking indemnification hereunder. We further agree that no Indemnified Person shall have any liability to us for or in connection with our engagement of Darren Keith except for any Claim incurred by us solely as a direct result of any Indemnified Person's gross negligence or willful misconduct.

We further agree that we will not, without the prior written consent of Darren Keith, settle, compromise, or consent to the entry of any judgment in any pending or threatened Claim in respect of which indemnification may be sought hereunder (whether or not any Indemnified Person is an actual or potential party to such Claim), unless such settlement, compromise, or consent includes an unconditional, irrevocable release of each Indemnified Person hereunder from any and all liability arising out of such Claim.

Promptly upon receipt by an Indemnified Person of notice of any complaint or the assertion or institution of any Claim with respect to which indemnification is being sought hereunder, such Indemnified Person shall notify us in writing of such complaint or of such assertion or institution. Failure to so notify us shall not relieve us from any obligation we may have hereunder, unless and only to the extent such failure results in the forfeiture by us of substantial rights and defenses, and will not in any event relieve us from any other obligation or liability we may have to any Indemnified Person otherwise than under this Agreement. If we so elect or are requested by such Indemnified Person, we will assume the defense of such Claim, including the employment of counsel reasonably satisfactory to such Indemnified Person and the payment of the fees and expenses of such counsel. In the event, however, that such Indemnified Person reasonably determines in its sole judgment that having common counsel would present such counsel with a conflict of interest or if the defendant in, or target of, any such Claim, includes an Indemnified Person and us, and such Indemnified Person reasonably concludes that there may be legal defenses available to it or other Indemnified Persons different from or in addition to those available to us, then such Indemnified Person may employ its own separate counsel to represent or defend it in any such Claim and we shall pay the fees and expenses of such counsel. Notwithstanding anything herein to the contrary, if we fail timely or diligently to defend, contest, or otherwise protect against any Claim, the relevant Indemnified Party shall have the right, but not the obligation, to defend, contest, compromise, settle, assert cross claims or counterclaims, or otherwise protect against the same, and shall be fully indemnified by us therefor, including without limitation, for the fees and expenses of its counsel and all amounts paid as a result of such Claim or the compromise or settlement thereof. In any Claim in which we assume the defense, the Indemnified Person shall have the right to participate in such Claim and to retain its own counsel therefor at its own expense.

We agree that if any indemnity sought by an Indemnified Person hereunder is held by a court to be unavailable for any reason (whether or not Darren Keith is the Indemnified Person), we and Darren Keith shall contribute to the Claim for which such indemnity is held unavailable in such proportion as is appropriate to reflect the relative benefits to us, on the one hand, and Darren Keith on the other, in connection with Darren Keith's engagement referred to above, subject to the limitation that in no event shall the amount of Darren Keith's contribution to such Claim exceed the amount of fees actually received by Darren Keith from us pursuant to Darren Keith's engagement. We hereby agree that the relative benefits to us, on the one hand, and Darren Keith on the other, with respect to Darren Keith's engagement shall be deemed to be in the same proportion as (a) the total value paid or proposed to be paid or received by us or our stockholders as the case may be, pursuant to the transaction (whether or not consummated) for which you are engaged to render services bears to or (b) the commission fee paid or proposed to be paid to Darren Keith in connection with such engagement.

Our indemnify, reimbursement, and contribution obligations under this Agreement shall be in addition to, and shall in no way limit or otherwise adversely affect any rights that any Indemnified Party may have at law or at equity.

We hereby consent to personal jurisdiction and service of process and venue in any court in which any claim for indemnity is brought by any Indemnified Person.

It is understood that, in connection with Darren Keith's engagement, Darren Keith may be engaged to act in one or more additional capacities and that the terms of the original engagement or any such additional engagement may be embodied in one or more separate written agreements. The provisions of this Agreement shall apply to the original engagement, any such additional engagement and any modification of the original engagement or such additional engagement and shall remain in full force and effect following the completion or termination of Darren Keith's engagement(s).

Very truly yours,

ABC Holdings, Inc.

By: _____

Kimberly Lageman,
President

Confirmed and agreed to:

Darren Keith & Company, Inc.

By: _____

Darren Alexander
Senior Vice President

Date: _____

APPENDIX 3

SAMPLE VENTURE CAPITAL AGREEMENT

STOCK PURCHASE AGREEMENT*
RELATING TO 50,000 SHARES OF
SERIES A CONVERTIBLE PREFERRED STOCK OF
ABC, INC.

DATED: _____

TABLE OF CONTENTS

*This is a first draft of a venture capital agreement for a $1 million financing of a start-up software company, as drafted by counsel for the venture capitalist. See chapter 10 for a summary and analysis of this document.

---

*These schedules were omitted from the initial draft agreement, but would be prepared prior to execution of the final agreement.

ABC, INC.   1
STOCK PURCHASE AGREEMENT   2
                                                              3
THIS STOCK PURCHASE AGREEMENT is made as of   4
_____ by and between ABC, INC., a Pennsylvania corpo-   5
ration (the "Company"), and the investors listed on Schedule I   6
hereto, each of which is herein referred to as an "Investor."   7
THE PARTIES HEREBY AGREE AS FOLLOWS: 8
                                                              9
1.   *Purchase and Sale of Stock.*   10
                                                             11
1.1   *Sale and Issuance of Series A Preferred Stock.*   12
                                                             13
(a)   The Company shall adopt and file with the Secretary   14
of Pennsylvania on or before the Closing (as defined below) the   15
Amended and Restated Articles of Incorporation in the form   16
attached hereto as Exhibit A.   17
                                                             18
(b)   Subject to the terms and conditions of this Agreement   19
and in reliance upon the representations and warranties and   20
covenants contained herein, each Investor agrees, severally but   21
not jointly, to purchase at the Closing, and the Company agrees   22
to sell and issue to each Investor at the Closing, that number   23
of shares of the Company's Series A Convertible Preferred Stock,   24
without par value, stated value $20.00 per share (the "Series A   25
Preferred Stock"), set forth opposite such Investor's name on   26
Schedule I hereto for the aggregate purchase price set forth   27
thereon payable in accordance with Section 1.2 hereof.   28
                                                             29
1.2   *Closing.* The purchase and sale of the Series A Preferred   30
Stock shall take place at the offices of Lipman, Lipman, and   31
Lipman, Philadelphia, Pennsylvania 19103, at 9:00 A.M., on the   32
fifth business day following the satisfaction or waiver of the   33
conditions set forth in Section 4 hereof, or at such other time   34
and place as the Company and Investors acquiring in the ag-   35
gregate more than 50 percent of the shares of Series A Preferred   36
Stock sold pursuant hereto agree upon orally or in writing   37
(which time and place are designated as the "Closing"). At the   38
Closing the Company shall deliver to each Investor a certifi-   39
cate representing the Series A Preferred Stock which such   40

Investor is purchasing against delivery to the Company by such Investor of the full purchase price therefor, one-half of which shall be paid by check payable to the Company's order or by wire transfer to such account as the Company shall designate, at the option of such Investor, and the other one-half of which shall be paid by the execution and delivery of a promissory note of the investor in the form set forth in Exhibit F hereto. No Investor shall be obligated to purchase any shares of Series A Preferred Stock at the Closing unless an aggregate of at least 90 percent of the total number of shares of Series A Preferred Stock to be sold hereunder pursuant to Section 1.1(b) are purchased concurrently therewith. If the Closing has not been consummated by _____, any Investor, by notice to the Company may terminate this Agreement without liability hereunder.

1.3   *Subsequent Sale of Series A Preferred Stock.*

(a)   To the extent that any Investor does not comply with its obligations hereunder, until the 30th day immediately following the Closing, the Company may sell, to any Investor or to any other person approved by the Board of Directors of the Company, up to the balance of the shares of Series A Preferred Stock to be sold hereunder pursuant to Section 1.1(b) hereof but which are not purchased by such Investors at the Closing, at a price not less than the price per share paid by the Investors herein.

(b)   No purchase of any shares of Series A Preferred Stock hereof shall be deemed to have been made pursuant to this Agreement and no rights hereunder shall inure to any such purchaser, unless such purchase is made at the Closing pursuant to Section 1.1(b) hereof or thereafter in accordance with Section 1.3(a) hereof.

2.   *Representations and Warranties of the Company.* The Company hereby represents and warrants to each Investor that, except as set forth on a Schedule of Exceptions attached as Schedule II hereto, each of which exceptions shall specifically identify the relevant subparagraph hereof to which it relates

and shall be deemed to be representations and warranties as if   1
made hereunder: 2

3

2.1   *Organization, Good Standing, and Qualification.* The   4
Company is a corporation duly organized, validly existing, and   5
in good standing under the laws of Pennsylvania and has all   6
requisite corporate power and authority to carry on its busi-   7
ness as now conducted and as proposed to be conducted in the   8
ABC, Inc. _____ Business Plan (the "Placement Memo-   9
randum") heretofore furnished to the Investors. The Company   10
is duly qualified to transact business and is in good standing in   11
each jurisdiction in which the failure so to qualify would have   12
a material adverse effect on its business or properties.   13

14

2.2   *Capitalization.* The authorized capital of the Company   15
consists, or will consist at or prior to the Closing taking into   16
account the transactions contemplated by Sections 4.11, 4.12,   17
and 4.15, of: 18

19

(a)   *Preferred Stock:* 150,000 shares of Preferred Stock (the   20
"Preferred Stock"), of which 50,000 shares have been designated   21
Series A Preferred Stock. No shares of Preferred Stock, includ-   22
ing without limitation any shares of Series A Preferred Stock,   23
are presently issued and outstanding, although up to 50,000   24
shares of Series A Preferred Stock will be sold pursuant to this   25
Agreement. The rights, privileges, and preferences of the Se-   26
ries A Preferred Stock will be as stated in the Company's   27
Amended and Restated Articles of Incorporation attached hereto   28
as Exhibit A.   29

30

(b)   *Common Stock:* 500,000 shares of Common Stock, par   31
value $.10 per share ("Common Stock"), of which 108,134 shares   32
are issued and outstanding and are owned by the persons and   33
in the amounts specified in Schedule III hereto.   34

35

(c)   Except for the conversion privileges of the Series A Pre-   36
ferred Stock to be issued under this Agreement, the rights of   37
Investors under Section 7.4 hereof, and 15,813 shares of Com-   38
mon Stock reserved for issuance upon the exercise of options   39
granted to employees, directors, or consultants, there are not   40

outstanding any options, warrants, rights (including conversion or preemptive rights), or agreements for the purchase or acquisition from the Company or, to the knowledge of the Company from any Shareholder, of any shares of the capital stock of the Company.

2.3   *Subsidiaries.* The Company does not presently own or control, directly or indirectly, any interest in any other corporation, association, or other business entity.

2.4   *Authorization.* All corporate action on the part of the Company, its officers, directors, and shareholders necessary for the authorization, execution, and delivery of this Agreement and the agreements attached as exhibits hereto (such agreements being herein referred to as the "Ancillary Agreements"), the performance of all obligations of the Company under each of the Agreement and the Ancillary Agreements, and the authorization, issuance (or reservation for issuance), and delivery of the Series A Preferred Stock being sold hereunder and the Common Stock issuable upon conversion of the Series A Preferred Stock has been taken or will be taken prior to the Closing, and this Agreement and the Ancillary Agreements constitute (or will constitute upon the execution thereof) the valid and legally binding obligations of the Company and each of the other parties thereto (other than the Investors), enforceable in accordance with their respective terms.

2.5   *Valid Issuance of Preferred and Common Stock.*

(a)   The Series A Preferred Stock which is being purchased by the Investors hereunder, when issued, sold, and delivered in accordance with the terms hereof or thereof, will be duly and validly issued, fully paid and nonassessable and, assuming the accuracy of the representations of the Investors in this Agreement, will be issued in compliance with all applicable federal and state securities laws. The Common Stock issuable upon conversion of the Series A Preferred Stock purchased under this Agreement has been duly and validly reserved for issuance and, upon issuance in accordance with the terms of the Amended and Restated Articles of Incorporation of the Company, shall be duly

and validly issued, fully paid and nonassessable, and issued in   1
compliance with all applicable securities laws, as presently in   2
effect, of the United States and each of the states whose securi-   3
ties laws govern the issuance of any of the Series A Preferred   4
Stock hereunder.   5
                                                                  6
  (b)   The outstanding shares of Common Stock are all duly   7
and validly authorized and issued, fully paid and nonassess-   8
able, were not issued in violation of the terms of any contract   9
binding upon the Company, and were issued in compliance with   10
all applicable federal and state securities laws.   11
                                                                  12
2.6   *Governmental Consents.* No consent, approval, order, or   13
authorization of, or registration, qualification, designation, dec-   14
laration, or filing with, any federal, state, local, or provincial   15
governmental authority on the part of the Company is required   16
in connection with the execution of this Agreement and the con-   17
summation of the transactions contemplated hereby or thereby.   18
                                                                  19
2.7   *Litigation.* There is no action, suit, proceeding, or inves-   20
tigation pending or currently threatened against the Company   21
of any nature whatsoever, including without limitation any ac-   22
tion, suit, proceeding or investigation which questions the validity   23
of this Agreement or the right of the Company to enter into it or   24
to consummate the transactions contemplated hereby, nor is the   25
Company aware that there is any basis for the foregoing. The   26
foregoing also includes, without limitation, actions pending or   27
threatened (or any basis therefor known to the Company) in-   28
volving the prior employment of any of the Company's employees,   29
their use in connection with the Company's business of any in-   30
formation or techniques allegedly proprietary to any of their   31
former employers, or their obligations under any agreements   32
with prior employers. The Company is not a party or subject to   33
the provisions of any order, writ, injunction, judgment, or decree   34
of any court or government agency or instrumentality. There is   35
no action, suit, proceeding, or investigation by the Company cur-   36
rently pending or which the Company intends to initiate.   37
                                                                  38
2.8   *Proprietary Information Agreements.* The employees of the   39
Company identified on the Schedule of Exceptions constitute all   40

1 of the officers and key employees of the Company, and each of
2 them have executed a proprietary information nondisclosure and
3 invention assignment agreement in the form attached hereto as
4 Exhibit B. The Company, after reasonable investigation, is not
5 aware that any of its employees are in violation thereof, and the
6 Company will use its best efforts to prevent any such violation.
7
8 2.9   *Intellectual Property.*
9
10   (a)   The Company has sole and exclusive title and owner-
11 ship of all patents, trademarks, service marks, trade names,
12 copyrights, trade secrets, information, proprietary rights and
13 processes (the foregoing, "Intellectual Property") necessary for
14 its business as now conducted and as proposed to be conducted
15 as described in the placement memorandum without any con-
16 flict with or infringement of the rights of others. A list of all
17 patents, patent applications, trademarks, service marks, trade
18 names, and copyrights owned by the Company is set forth in
19 the Schedule of Exceptions. There are no outstanding options,
20 licenses, or agreements of any kind to which the Company is a
21 party or by which it is bound relating to any Intellectual Prop-
22 erty, whether owned by the Company or another person or
23 entity. The Company has not received any communications al-
24 leging that the Company has violated or, by conducting its
25 business as proposed, would violate any of the Intellectual Prop-
26 erty or other proprietary rights of any other person or entity.
27 The Company is not aware that any of its employees are obli-
28 gated under any contract (including licenses, covenants, or
29 commitments of any nature) or other agreement, or subject to
30 any judgment, decree, or order of any court or administrative
31 agency, that would interfere with the use of such employee's
32 best efforts to promote the interests of the Company or that
33 would conflict with the Company's business proposed to be con-
34 ducted. Neither the execution nor delivery of this Agreement
35 nor the carrying on of the Company's business by the em-
36 ployees of the Company, nor the conduct of the Company's
37 business as proposed, will conflict with or result in a breach
38 of the terms, condition, or provisions of, or constitute a de-
39 fault under, any contract, covenant, or instrument under
40 which any of such employees is now obligated. The Com-

pany does not believe it is or will be necessary to utilize any 1
inventions of any of its employees (or people it currently in- 2
tends to hire) made prior to their employment by the 3
Company. 4

5

(b) The Company's computer software and the other soft- 6
ware owned by the Company as described in the Placement 7
Memorandum (including all related source and object code, 8
data input, text and screen graphics, manuals and docu- 9
ments, the "Software") performs as described in the 10
Placement Memorandum and in accordance with the docu- 11
mentation and other written material used in connection 12
with the Software and is free of defects in programming and 13
operation, is in machine-readable form, contains all current 14
revisions of such Software, and includes all computer pro- 15
grams, materials, tapes, know-how, object and source codes, 16
other written materials, know-how and processes related to 17
the Software. In particular, the Software W software prod- 18
uct will run on the following personal computers: IBM PCs, 19
PC XTs, PC ATs, PS 2s or compatibles that have at least 20
512K of random access memory and any of the following 21
graphics capabilities: CGA, EGA, or VGA. All right, title, 22
and interest in and to the Software are owned exclusively 23
by the Company, free and clear of all liens, claims, charges, 24
or encumbrances, and no party other than the Company has 25
any interest in the Software, including without limitation, 26
any security interest, license, contingent interest, or other- 27
wise. The Company's development, use, sale, or exploitation 28
of the Software does not violate any rights of any other per- 29
son or entity and the Company has not received any 30
communication alleging such a violation. The Company does 31
not have any obligation to compensate any person for the 32
development, use, sale, or exploitation of the Software nor 33
has the Seller granted to any other person or entity any li- 34
cense, option, or other rights to develop, use, sell, or exploit 35
in any manner the Software, whether requiring the payment 36
of royalties or not. There have been no patents applied for 37
and no copyrights registered for any part of the Software. 38
There are no trademark rights of any person or entity in the 39
name "Software W" or "Software A." 40

1 2.10 *Compliance with Other Instruments.*

3 (a) The Company is in compliance with each, and is not in vio-
4 lation or default of any, provision of its charter documents or bylaws,
5 or judgment, order, writ, or decree, or any material contract, agree-
6 ment, instrument, or commitment to which it is a party or by which
7 it is bound, or provision of any statute, rule, or regulation appli-
8 cable to the Company, its assets, or its business. There is no term or
9 provision in any of the foregoing documents and instruments which
10 materially adversely affects the business (as now conducted or as
11 proposed to be conducted in the Placement Memorandum), assets
12 or financial condition of the Company. The execution, delivery, and
13 performance of this Agreement or any of the Ancillary Agreements
14 and the consummation of the transactions contemplated hereby and
15 thereby will not result in any such violation or be in conflict with or
16 constitute, with or without the passage of time or giving of notice,
17 either a default under any such provision, instrument, judgment,
18 order, writ, decree, or contract or an event that results in the cre-
19 ation or any lien, charge, or encumbrance upon any assets of the
20 Company.

22 (b) The Company has avoided every condition, and has not
23 performed any act, the occurrence of which would result in the
24 Company's loss of any right granted under any license, distribu-
25 tion, or other agreement.

27 2.11 *Agreements.*

29 (a) Except for agreements explicitly contemplated hereby, there
30 are no binding agreements between the Company and any of its of-
31 ficers, directors, affiliates, employees, or shareholders.

33 (b) There are no binding agreements to which the Company is
34 a party or by which it is bound which involve obligations of, or pay-
35 ments to, the Company in excess of $5,000.

37 2.12 *Placement Memorandum.* The Placement Memorandum has
38 been prepared in good faith by the senior management of the Com-
39 pany and does not contain any untrue statement of a material fact
40 nor does it omit to state a material fact necessary to make the state-

ments made therein not misleading in light of the circumstances in 1
which they are made, except that with respect to projections con- 2
tained in the Placement Memorandum, the Company represents 3
only that such projections were prepared in good faith and that the 4
Company reasonably believes the assumptions upon which such pro- 5
jections are based are reasonably likely to occur. 6
                                                                     7
2.13   *Registration Rights.* Except as provided in Section 6 of 8
this Agreement, the Company has not granted or agreed to grant 9
any registration rights, including without-limitation demand 10
or piggyback rights, to any person or entity. 11
                                                                     12
2.14   *Title to Property and Assets.* The Company has good 13
and marketable title to its property and assets free and clear of 14
all mortgages, liens, claims, and encumbrances, except such 15
encumbrances and liens that arise in the ordinary course of 16
business and do not materially impair the Company's owner- 17
ship or use or the value of such property or assets. With respect 18
to the property and assets it leases, the Company is in compli- 19
ance with such leases, enjoys peaceful and undisturbed 20
possession thereunder, and, holds a valid leasehold interest free 21
of any liens, claims, or encumbrances. All of the tangible assets 22
of the Company are in good operating condition and repair (sub- 23
ject only to ordinary wear and tear) and are usable in the 24
ordinary course of business. 25
                                                                     26
2.15   *Financial Statements.* The Schedule of Exceptions in- 27
cludes the audited financial statements of the Company 28
(balance sheet, profit and loss statement, and statement of op- 29
erations) at _____ and for the fiscal year then ended 30
and the unaudited financial statements of the Company at 31
_____ (together, the "Financial Statements"). The 32
Financial Statements are complete and correct in all material 33
respects and have been prepared in accordance with generally 34
accepted accounting principles applied on a consistent basis 35
throughout the periods indicated and with each other. The Fi- 36
nancial Statements accurately set out and describe the financial 37
condition of the Company as of the dates, and for the periods, 38
indicated therein. Except as set forth in the Financial State- 39
ments, the Company has no liabilities, fixed, contingent, 40

asserted, unasserted, known, unknown, or otherwise, other than liabilities incurred in the ordinary course of business subsequent to_____ and obligations under contracts and commitments incurred in the ordinary course of business and not required under generally accepted accounting principles to be reflected in the Financial Statements, which, individually or in the aggregate, are not material to the financial condition of the Company. The Company maintains and will continue to maintain a standard system of accounting established and administered in accordance with generally accepted accounting principles.

2.16   *Changes.* Since _____, there has not been:

(a)   any change in the assets, liabilities, financial condition, or operating results of the Company from that reflected in the Financial Statements, except changes in the ordinary course of business that have not been, in the aggregate, materially adverse;

(b)   any declaration or payment of any dividend, or any authorization or payment of any distribution, on any of the capital stock of the Company, or any redemption or repurchase of any capital stock of the Company;

(c)   any damage, destruction, or loss, whether or not covered by insurance, materially and adversely affecting the assets, properties, financial condition, operating results, prospects, or business of the Company (as such business is presently conducted and as it is proposed to be conducted);

(d)   any waiver by the Company of a valuable right or of a material debt owed to it;

(e)   any satisfaction or discharge of any lien, claim, or encumbrance or payment of any obligation by the Company, except in the ordinary course of business and which is not material to the assets, properties, financial condition, operating results, or business of the Company (as such business is presently conducted and as it is proposed to be conducted);

(f)   any change or amendment to a material contract or arrangement by which the Company or any of its assets or properties is bound or subject;

(g)   any material change in any compensation arrangement or agreement with any employee; or

(h)   to the Company's knowledge, any other event or condition of any character that might materially and adversely affect the assets, properties, financial condition, operating results, or business of the Company (as such business is presently conducted and as it is proposed to be conducted).

2.17   *Employee Benefit Plans.* The Company does not have any employee benefit plan as defined in the Employee Retirement Income Security Act of 1974, as amended ("ERISA").

2.18   *Tax Returns, Payments, and Elections.* The Company has timely filed all tax returns and reports as required by law. These returns and reports are true and correct in all material respects. The Company has paid all taxes and other assessments due, except those contested by it in good faith, which are listed in the Schedule of Exceptions, and has duly made all deposits required to be made by law with respect to employees' withholding taxes. The provision for taxes of the Company as shown in the Financial Statements is adequate for taxes due or accrued as of the date thereof.

2.19   *Insurance.* The Company has in full force and effect (i) fire and casualty insurance policies, with extended coverage, sufficient in amount (subject to reasonable deductibles) to allow it to replace any of its properties that might be damaged or destroyed; and (ii) such other insurance policies as are listed in the Schedule of Exceptions.

2.20   *Minute Books.* The minute books of the Company contain a complete summary of all meetings of directors and stockholders or partners since the time of incorporation or creation and reflect all transactions referred to in such minutes or records accurately in all material respects.

2.21 *Labor Agreements and Actions.* The Company is not bound by or subject to (and none of its assets or properties is bound by or subject to) any written or oral, express or implied contract, commitment, or arrangement with any labor union, and no labor union has requested or, to the knowledge of the Company, has sought to represent any of the employees, representatives, or agents of the Company. There is no strike or other labor dispute involving the Company pending, or to the knowledge of the Company threatened, which could have a material adverse effect on the assets, properties, financial condition, operating results, or business of the Company (as such business is presently conducted and as it is proposed to be conducted), nor is the Company aware of any labor organization activity involving its employees. The Company is not aware that any officer or key employee, or that any group of key employees, intends to terminate their employment with the Company, nor does the Company have a present intention to terminate the employment of any of the foregoing. The employment of each employee of the Company is terminable at the will of the Company without further liability of the Company to such employee except for the payment of such employee's normal salary accrued but not paid through the date of such termination.

2.22 *Disclosure.* The Company has fully provided each Investor with all the information that such Investor has requested for deciding whether to purchase the Series A Preferred Stock and all information which the Company believes is reasonably necessary to enable such Investor to make such decision. Neither this Agreement, nor any other agreement, document, certificate, or written statement furnished to the Investors or Lipman, Lipman, and Lipman by or on behalf of the Company in connection with the transactions contemplated hereby (including without limitation, the Financial Statements) contains any untrue statement of a material fact or omits to state a material fact necessary in order to make the statements contained herein or therein not misleading. There is no fact within the knowledge of the Company or any of its officers that has not been disclosed herein or in writing by them to the Investors and which materially adversely affects, or in the future in their

opinion may, insofar as they can now foresee, materially ad- 1
versely affect the business, properties, assets, or condition, 2
financial or otherwise, of the Company. Without limiting the 3
foregoing, the Company has no knowledge or belief that there 4
exists, or is pending or planned, any patent, invention, de- 5
vice, application, or principle or any statute, rule, law, 6
regulation, standard, or condition that would materially ad- 7
versely affect the condition, financial or other, or the operations 8
of the Company. 9
10

3.   *Representations and Warranties of the Investors.* Each 11
Investor, severally with respect to such Investor but not jointly 12
nor with respect to any other Investor, hereby represents and 13
warrants that: 14
15

3.1   *Authorization.* This Agreement constitutes its valid and 16
legally binding obligation, enforceable in accordance with its terms. 17
18

3.2   *Purchase Entirely for Own Account.* This Agreement is 19
made with each Investor in reliance upon such Investor's rep- 20
resentation to the Company, which by such Investor's execution 21
of this Agreement such Investor hereby confirms, that the Se- 22
ries A Preferred Stock to be received by such Investor and the 23
Common Stock issuable upon conversion thereof (collectively, 24
the "Securities") will be acquired for investment for such 25
Investor's own account, not as a nominee or agent, and not with 26
a view to the resale or distribution of any part thereof, and 27
that such Investor has no present intention of selling, granting 28
any participation in, or otherwise distributing the same, but 29
subject to the ability of such of the Investors as may be part- 30
nerships to distribute its assets to its partners. By executing 31
this Agreement, each Investor further represents that such 32
Investor does not have any contract, undertaking, agreement, 33
or arrangement with any person to sell, transfer, or grant par- 34
ticipation to such person or to any third person, with respect to 35
any of the Securities. Each Investor represents that it has full 36
power and authority to enter into this Agreement. 37
38

3.3   *Disclosure of Information.* It believes it has received 39
all the information it considers necessary or appropriate for 40

deciding whether to purchase the Series A Preferred Stock. Each Investor further represents that it has had an opportunity to ask questions and receive answers from the Company regarding the terms and conditions of the offering of the Series A Preferred Stock. The foregoing, however, does not limit or modify the representations and warranties of the Company in Section 2 of this Agreement or the right of the Investors to rely thereon.

3.4   *Investment Experience.* Each Investor is an investor in securities or companies in the development stage and acknowledges that it is able to fend for itself, can bear the economic risk of its investment, and has such knowledge and experience in financial or business matters that it is capable of evaluating the merits and risks of the investment in the Series A Preferred Stock. Each Investor also represents it has not been organized for the purpose of acquiring the Series A Preferred Stock.

3.5   *Restricted Securities.* It understands that the shares of Series A Preferred Stock it is purchasing are characterized as "restricted securities" under the federal securities laws inasmuch as they are being acquired from the Company in a transaction not involving a public offering and that under such laws and applicable regulations such securities may not be resold without registration under the Securities Act of 1933, as amended (Act), except in certain limited circumstances. In this connection, each Investor represents that it is familiar with Rule 144 under the Act, as presently in effect, and understands the resale limitations imposed thereby and by the Act.

3.6   *Further Limitations on Disposition.* Without in any way limiting the representations set forth above, each Investor further agrees not to make any disposition of all or any portion of the Securities unless and until:

(a)   there is then in effect a Registration Statement under the Act covering such proposed disposition and such disposition is made in accordance with such Registration Statement; or

(b)   (i) such Investor shall have notified the Company of the proposed disposition and shall have furnished the Company with

a detailed statement of the circumstances surrounding the pro- 1
posed disposition, and (ii) if reasonably requested by the 2
Company, such Investor shall have furnished the Company with 3
an opinion of counsel, reasonably satisfactory to the Company, 4
that such disposition will not require registration of such shares 5
under the Act. It is agreed that the Company will not require 6
opinions of counsel for transactions made pursuant to Rule 144 7
by an Investor except in unusual circumstances. 8

9

(c) Notwithstanding the provisions of paragraphs (a) and 10
(b) no such registration statement or opinion of counsel shall 11
be necessary for a transfer by an Investor (i) that is a partner- 12
ship to a partner of such partnership or a retired partner of 13
such partnership who retires after the date hereof, or to the 14
estate of any such partner or retired partner or the transfer by 15
gift, will, or intestate succession of any partner to his spouse or 16
lineal descendants or ancestors, if the transferee agrees in writ- 17
ing to be subject to the terms hereof to the same extent as if he 18
were an original Investor hereunder; or (ii) at any time after 19
the provisions of Subparagraph (k) of Rule 144 are applicable 20
to such Investor. 21

22

3.7　　*Legends.* It is understood that the certificates evidenc- 23
ing the Series A Preferred Stock (and the Common Stock issuable 24
upon conversion thereof) may bear the following legend: 25

26

These securities have not been registered under the Se- 27
curities Act of 1933. They may not be sold, offered for 28
sale, pledged, or hypothecated in the absence of a regis- 29
tration statement in effect with respect to the securities 30
under such Act or an opinion of counsel satisfactory to 31
the Company that such registration is not required or 32
unless sold pursuant to Rule 144 of such Act. 33

34

4.　　*Conditions of Investor's Obligations at Closing.* The ob- 35
ligations of each Investor under Section 1.1(b) of this Agreement 36
are subject to the fulfillment on or before the Closing of each of 37
the following conditions, the waiver of which shall not be effec- 38
tive against any Investor who does not consent in writing 39
thereto: 40

4.1   *Representations and Warranties.* The representations and warranties of the Company contained in Section 2 shall be true on and as of the Closing with the same effect as though such representations and warranties had been made on and as of the date of such Closing.

4.2   *Performance.* The Company shall have performed and complied with all agreements, obligations, and conditions contained in this Agreement that are required to be performed or complied with by it on or before the Closing.

4.3   *Compliance Certificate.* The President of the Company shall deliver to each Investor at the Closing an accurate certificate certifying that the conditions specified in Sections 4.1 and 4.2 have been fulfilled and stating that there shall have been no adverse change in the business, affairs, prospects, operations, properties, assets, or condition of the Company since _____.

4.4   *Proceedings and Documents.* All corporate and other proceedings in connection with the transactions contemplated at the Closing and all documents incident thereto shall be reasonably satisfactory in form and substance to each Investor and Lipman, Lipman, and Lipman, and they shall have received all such counterpart original and certified or other copies of such documents as they may reasonably request.

4.5   *Board of Directors.* The directors of the Company shall consist of the following persons:_____

4.6   *Due Diligence Review.* The Investors and Lipman, Lipman, and Lipman shall have completed a due diligence and business review of the Company, which may include a patent and other proprietary information review, which meets with their satisfaction.

4.7   *Certain Ancillary Agreements.* Stock Restriction Agreements in the form attached as Exhibit C, and a Stockholders' Agreement in the form attached as Exhibit D, and Employment Agreements in the form attached hereto as Exhibit E,

shall have been executed by the respective parties identified
on such Exhibits.

4.8   *Key-Man Insurance.* The Company shall have obtained,
and shall have furnished to the Investors copies of, term insurance (or binders with respect thereto) on the lives of each of
Entrepreneur 1 and Entrepreneur 2 in the amount of at least
$3,000,000, in each case with the proceeds payable solely to
the Company.

4.9   *Opinion of Company Counsel.* Each Investor shall have
received from counsel for the Company, an opinion, dated as of
the Closing, in form and substance reasonably satisfactory to
the Investors and Lipman, Lipman, and Lipman.

4.10   *Blue-Sky Compliance.* The Company shall have com-
plied with all requirements of federal and state securities or
"Blue Sky" laws with respect to the issuance of the Series A
Preferred Stock to the Investors hereunder.

4.11   *Modification of Prior Investor Corp. Arrangements.* The
Prior Investor Corp. ("Prior Investor Corp.") shall have entered
into the following arrangements in form and substance reasonably satisfactory to the Investors:

(a)   The Note of the Company, dated, in the outstanding
principal amount $79,142 as of _____ shall have been
converted into Common Stock of the Company on the basis of
one share of Common Stock for each $20.00 of outstanding prin-
cipal and accrued interest.

(b)   One half of the outstanding short-term debt of the Company to Prior Investor Corp. shall have been converted into
Common Stock of the Company on the basis of one share of
Common Stock for each $20.00 of outstanding principal and
accrued interest. The remainder of such short-term debt shall
be repaid to Prior Investor Corp. by the Company immediately
following the Closing.

(c)   The Company shall have made arrangements to cause

1   Bank to release its security interest in all Prior Investor Corp.
2   assets pledged as collateral to secure a line of credit and term
3   loan of the Company from Bank and to release the Company
4   from all obligations under any guarantee by the Company of
5   any obligations of Prior Investor Corp.
6
7   4.12   *Accrued Salaries.* Up to $34,000 of accrued but unpaid
8   salaries to Entrepreneur 1 and Entrepreneur 2 at the Closing
9   Date shall have been converted into Common Stock of the Com-
10   pany on the basis of one share of Common Stock for each $20.00
11   of accrued salary. Any accrued but unpaid salaries in excess of
12   $34,000 shall be waived by Messrs. Entrepreneur 1 and 2.
13
14   4.13   *Amendment of Magazine 1 Agreement.* The Company
15   shall have obtained an amendment, in form and substance rea-
16   sonably satisfactory to the Investors, of Section 11.4 of the
17   Agreement, _____, between the Company and Maga-
18   zine 1, providing that the obligation of the Company thereunder
19   to cease certain activities upon termination of such agreement
20   shall solely relate to the use of the "Magazine 2" name in con-
21   nection with the Software W software package and does not
22   prohibit further manufacturing, marketing, and selling of the
23   Software W software package by the Company without using
24   the Magazine 2 name. The Company shall obtain Magazine 1's
25   approval, in form and substance reasonably satisfactory to the
26   Investors, of the W software product.
27
28   4.14   *Amendment of Broker Agreement.* The Company shall
29   have obtained an amendment, in form and substance reason-
30   ably satisfactory to the Investors, of the Software Agreement,
31   dated _____, between the Company and Broker dis-
32   tinguishing between the Software A and Software W products
33   and providing that the marketing and exploitation of the Soft-
34   ware W software product by the Company does not violate such
35   agreement.
36
37   4.15   *Termination of Existing Shareholder Agreements.* The
38   parties thereto shall have terminated that certain Voting Trust
39   Agreement, dated _____, among Shareholder 1, Share-
40   holder 2, Shareholder 3, and Shareholder 4 and that certain

Shareholders' Agreement, dated _____, among Share- **1**
holder 1, Shareholder 2, Shareholder 3, Shareholder 4, **2**
Shareholder 5, Shareholder 6, Shareholder 7, Shareholder 8, and **3**
Shareholder 9, and ABC, Inc., and all rights and obligations of **4**
any party thereunder shall have ceased. **5**

6

4.16   *Proprietary Information Agreements.* The following per- **7**
sons shall have executed Proprietary Information Agreements **8**
in the form set forth as Exhibit B hereto _____. **9**

10

5.   *Conditions of the Company's Obligations at Closing.* The **11**
obligations of the Company to any Investor under this Agree- **12**
ment are subject to the fulfillment on or before the Closing of **13**
each of the following conditions by such Investor: **14**

15

5.1   *Representations and Warranties.* The representations **16**
and warranties of such Investor contained in Section 3 shall be **17**
true on and as the Closing with the same effect as though such **18**
representations and warranties have been made on and as of **19**
the Closing. **20**

21

5.2   *Payment of Purchase Price.* Such Investor shall have **22**
delivered the purchase price specified in Section 1.1. **23**

24

6.   *Registration Rights.* The Company covenants and **25**
agrees as follows: **26**

27

6.1   *Definitions.* For purposes of this Section 6: **28**

29

(a)   The terms "register" and "registration" refer to a regis- **30**
tration effected by preparing and filing a registration statement **31**
or similar document in compliance with the Act, and the decla- **32**
ration or ordering of effectiveness of such registration statement **33**
or document. **34**

35

(b)   The term "Registrable Securities" means (1) the Common **36**
Stock issuable or issued upon conversion of the Series A Pre- **37**
ferred Stock which is sold to Investors hereunder, and (2) any **38**
Common Stock of the Company issued as (or issuable upon the **39**
conversion or exercise of any warrant, right, or other security **40**

which is issued as) a dividend or other distribution with respect to, or in exchange for or in replacement of, such Series A Preferred Stock or Common Stock, excluding in all cases, however, any Registrable Securities sold by a person in a transaction in which his rights under this Section 6 are not assigned.

(c) The number of shares of "Registrable Securities then outstanding" shall be determined by the number of shares of Common Stock outstanding which are, and the number of shares of Common Stock issuable pursuant to then exercisable or convertible securities which are, Registrable Securities.

(d) The term "Holder" means any person owning or having the right to acquire Registrable Securities or any assignee thereof in accordance with Section 6.13 hereof.

(e) The term "Form S-3" means such form under the Act as in effect on the date hereof or any registration form under the Act subsequently adopted by the Securities and Exchange Commission (SEC) which permits inclusion or incorporation of substantial information by reference to other documents filed by the Company with the SEC.

6.2 *Request for Registration.*

(a) If the Company shall receive at any time after the earlier of (i) the first anniversary of the date hereof or (ii) three (3) months after the effective date of the first registration statement for a public offering of securities of the Company, a written request from the Holders of a majority of the Registrable Securities then outstanding that the Company file a registration statement under the Act covering the registration of at least forty percent (40%) of the Registrable Securities then outstanding (or a lesser percent if the anticipated aggregate offering price, net of underwriting discounts and commissions, would exceed $500,000), then the Company shall, within ten (10) days of the receipt thereof, give written notice of such request to all Holders, and shall, subject to the limitations of Subsection 6.2(b), effect as soon as practicable, and in any event within ninety (90) days of the receipt of such request, the registration

under the Act of all Registrable Securities which the Holders 1
request to be registered within twenty (20) days of the mailing 2
of such notice by the Company in accordance with Section 8.6. 3
Neither the Company nor any person other than the Holders 4
shall be entitled to include shares in the registrations made 5
under this Section 6.2. 6

7

(b) If the Holders initiating the registration request here- 8
under ("Initiating Holders") intend to distribute the Registrable 9
Securities covered by their request by means of an underwrit- 10
ing, they shall so advise the Company as a part of their request 11
made pursuant to this Section 6.2 and the Company shall in- 12
clude such information in the written notice referred to in 13
Subsection 6.2(a). In such event, the right of any Holder to in- 14
clude his Registrable Securities in such registration shall be 15
conditioned upon such Holder's participation in such under- 16
writing and the inclusion of such Holder's Registrable Securities 17
in the underwriting (unless otherwise mutually agreed by a 18
majority in interest of the Initiating Holders and such Holder) 19
to the extent provided herein. All Holders proposing to distrib- 20
ute their securities through such underwriting shall (together 21
with the Company as provided in Subsection 6.4(e)) enter into 22
an underwriting agreement in customary form with the under- 23
writer or underwriters selected for such underwriting by a 24
majority in interest of the Initiating Holders. Notwithstanding 25
any other provision of this Section 6.2, if the underwriter ad- 26
vises the Initiating Holders in writing that marketing factors 27
require a limitation of the number of shares to be underwrit- 28
ten, then the Company shall so advise all Holders of Registrable 29
Securities which would otherwise be underwritten pursuant 30
hereto, and the number of shares of Registrable Securities that 31
may be included in the underwriting shall be allocated among 32
all Holders thereof, including the Initiating Holders, in pro- 33
portion (as nearly as practicable) to the amount of Registrable 34
Securities of the Company owned by each Holder. 35

36

(c) The Company is obligated to effect only two such regis- 37
trations pursuant to this Section 6.2. 38

39

(d) Notwithstanding the foregoing, if the Company shall 40

furnish to Holders requesting a registration statement pursuant to this Section 6.2, a certificate signed by the President of
the Company stating that in the good faith judgment of the
Board of Directors of the Company, it would be seriously detrimental to the Company and its shareholders for such
registration statement to be filed and it is therefore essential
to defer the filing of such registration statement, the Company
shall have the right to defer such filing for a period of not more
than sixty (60) days after receipt of the request of the Initiating Holders; provided, however, that the Company may not
utilize this right more than once in any twelve-month period.

6.3   *Company Registration.* If (but without any obligation
to do so) the Company proposes to register (including for this
purpose a registration effected by the Company for shareholders other than the Holders) any of its Stock or other securities
under the Act in connection with the public offering of such
securities solely for cash (other than a registration relating
solely to the sale of securities to participants in a Company
stock plan, or a registration on any form that does not include
substantially the same information, other than information
related to the selling shareholders or their plan of distribution,
as would be required to be included in a registration statement
covering the sale of the Registrable Securities), the Company
shall, at such time, promptly give each Holder written notice of
such registration. Upon the written request of each Holder given
within twenty (20) days after mailing of such notice by the Company in accordance with Section 8.6, the Company shall, subject
to the provisions of Section 6.6, cause to be registered under
the Act all of the Registrable Securities that each such Holder
has requested to be registered.

6.4   *Obligations of the Company.* Whenever required under
this Section 6 to effect the registration of any Registrable Securities, the Company shall, as expeditiously as reasonably
possible:

(a)   Prepare and file with the SEC a registration statement
with respect to such Registrable Securities and use its best efforts to cause such registration statement to become effective,

and, upon the request of the Holders of a majority of the Registrable Securities registered thereunder, keep such registration statement effective for up to one hundred-twenty (120) days.

(b)   Prepare and file with the SEC such amendments and supplements to such registration statement and the prospectus used in connection with such registration statement as may be necessary to comply with the provisions of the Act with respect to the disposition of all securities covered by such registration statement.

(c)   Furnish to the Holders such numbers of copies of a prospectus, including a preliminary prospectus, in conformity with the requirements of the Act, and such other documents as they may reasonably request in order to facilitate the disposition of Registrable Securities owned by them.

(d)   Use its best efforts to register and qualify the securities covered by such registration statement under such other securities or Blue Sky laws of such jurisdictions as shall be reasonably requested by the Holders, provided that the Company shall not be required to qualify to do business or to file a general consent to service or process in any such states of jurisdictions.

(e)   In the event of any underwritten public offering, enter into and perform its obligations under an underwriting agreement, in usual and customary form, with the managing underwriter of such offering. Each Holder participating in such underwriting shall also enter into and perform its obligations under such an agreement.

(f)   Notify each Holder of Registrable Securities covered by such registration statement at any time when a prospectus relating thereto is required to be delivered under the Act of the happening of any event as a result of which the prospectus included in such registration statement, as then in effect, includes an untrue statement of a material fact or omits to state a material fact required to be stated therein or necessary to make the statements therein not misleading in the light of the circumstances then existing.

1 (g) In the case of an underwritten public offering, furnish,
2 at the request of any Holder requesting registration of Regis-
3 trable Securities pursuant to this Section 6, on the date that
4 such Registrable Securities are delivered to the underwriters
5 for sale in connection with a registration pursuant to this Sec-
6 tion 6, (i) an opinion, dated such date, of the counsel
7 representing the Company for the purposes of such registra-
8 tion, in form and substance as is customarily given to
9 underwriters in an underwritten public offering, addressed to
10 the underwriters and (ii) a letter dated such date, from the
11 independent certified public accountants of the Company, in
12 form and substance as is customarily given by independent cer-
13 tified public accountants to underwriters in an underwritten
14 public offering, addressed to the underwriters.
15
16 6.5 *Furnish Information.* It shall be a condition precedent
17 to the obligations of the Company to take any action pursuant
18 to this Section 6 with respect to the Registrable Securities of
19 any selling Holder that such Holder shall furnish to the Com-
20 pany such information regarding itself, the Registrable
21 Securities held by it, and the intended method of disposition of
22 such securities as shall be required to effect the registration of
23 such Holder's Registrable Securities.
24
25 6.6 *Expenses of Demand Registration.* All expenses other
26 than underwriting discounts and commissions incurred in con-
27 nection with registrations, filings, or qualifications pursuant
28 to Section 6.2, including (without limitation) all registration,
29 filing, and qualification fees, printers' and accounting fees, fees
30 and disbursements of counsel for the Company, and the rea-
31 sonable fees and disbursements of one counsel for the selling
32 Holders shall be borne by the Company; provided, however, that
33 the Company shall not be required to pay for any expenses of
34 any registration proceeding begun pursuant to Section 6.2 if
35 the registration request is subsequently withdrawn at the re-
36 quest of the Holders of a majority of the Registrable Securities
37 to be registered (in which case all Participating Holders shall
38 bear such expenses), unless the Holders of a majority of the
39 Registrable Securities agree to forfeit their right to one demand
40 registration pursuant to Section 6.2; provided further, however,

that if at the time of such withdrawal, the Holders have learned 1
of a material adverse change in the condition, business, or pros- 2
pects of the Company from that known to the Holders at the 3
time of their request, then the Holders shall not be required to 4
pay any of such expenses and shall retain their rights pursu- 5
ant to Section 6.2. 6

7

6.7   *Expenses of Company Registration.* The Company shall 8
bear and pay all expenses incurred in connection with any reg- 9
istration, filing, or qualification of Registrable Securities with 10
respect to the registrations pursuant to Section 6.3 for each 11
Holder (which right may be assigned as provided in Section 12
6.13), including (without limitation) all registration, filing, and 13
qualification fees, printers' and accounting fees relating or al- 14
locable thereto, and the fees and disbursements of one counsel 15
for the selling Holders selected by them, but excluding under- 16
writing discounts and commissions relating to Registrable 17
Securities. 18

19

6.8   *Underwriting Requirements.* In connection with any of- 20
fering involving an underwriting of shares being issued by the 21
Company, the Company shall not be required under Section 6.3 22
to include any of the Holders' securities in such underwriting 23
unless they accept the terms of the underwriting as agreed upon 24
between the Company and the underwriters selected by it, and 25
then only in such quantity as will not, in the opinion of the un- 26
derwriters, jeopardize the success of the offering by the Company. 27
If the total amount of securities, including Registrable Securi- 28
ties, requested by shareholders to be included in such offering 29
exceeds the amount of securities sold other than by the Com- 30
pany that the underwriters reasonably believe compatible with 31
the success of the offering, then the Company shall be required 32
to include in the offering only that number of such securities, 33
including Registrable Securities, which the underwriters believe 34
will not jeopardize the success of the offering (the securities so 35
included to be apportioned pro rata among the selling share- 36
holders according to the total amount of securities entitled to be 37
included therein owned by each selling shareholder or in such 38
other proportions as shall mutually be agreed to by such selling 39
shareholders) but in no event shall (i) the amount of securities 40

1 of the selling Holders included in the offering be reduced below
2 twenty-five percent (25%) of the total amount of securities in-
3 cluded in such offering, unless such offering is the initial public
4 offering of the Company's securities in which case the selling
5 shareholders may be excluded if the underwriters make the de-
6 termination described above and no other Shareholder's
7 securities are included, or (ii) notwithstanding (i) above, any
8 shares being sold by a Shareholder exercising a demand regis-
9 tration right similar to that granted in Section 6.2 be excluded
10 from such offering. For purposes of the preceding parenthetical
11 concerning apportionment, for any selling shareholder that is a
12 Holder of Registrable Securities and which is a partnership or
13 corporation, the partners, retired partners, and shareholders of
14 such Holder, or the estates and family members of any such part-
15 ners and retired partners, and any trusts for the benefit of any
16 of the foregoing persons shall be deemed to be a single "selling
17 shareholder," and any pro-rata reduction with respect to such
18 "selling shareholder" shall be based upon the aggregate amount
19 of shares carrying registration rights owned by all entities and
20 individuals included in such "selling shareholder," as defined in
21 this sentence.
22
23 6.9   *Delay of Registration.* No Holder shall have any right
24 to obtain or seek an injunction restraining or otherwise delay-
25 ing any such registration as the result of any controversy that
26 might arise with respect to the interpretation or implementa-
27 tion of this Section 6.
28
29 6.10   *Indemnification.* In the event any Registrable Securities
30 are included in a registration statement under this Section 6:
31
32   (a)   To the extent permitted by law, the Company will in-
33 demnify and hold harmless each Holder, any underwriter (as
34 defined in the Act) for such Holder, and each person, if any, who
35 controls such Holder or underwriter within the meaning of the
36 Act or the Securities Exchange Act of 1934, as amended (the
37 "1934 Act"), against any losses, claims, damages, or liabilities
38 (joint or several) to which they may become subject under the
39 Act, the 1934 Act, or other federal or state law, insofar as such
40 losses, claims, damages, or liabilities (or actions in respect

thereof) arise out of or are based upon any of the following state- 1
ments, omissions, or violations (collectively a "Violation"): (i) 2
any untrue statement or alleged untrue statement of a mate- 3
rial fact contained in such registration statement, including 4
any preliminary prospectus (but only if such is not corrected in 5
the final prospectus) contained therein or any amendments or 6
supplements thereto, (ii) the omission or alleged omission to 7
state therein a material fact required to be stated therein, or 8
necessary to make the statements therein not misleading (but 9
only if such is not corrected in the final prospectus), or (iii) any 10
violation or alleged violation by the Company in connection with 11
the registration of Registrable Securities of the Act, the 1934 12
Act, any state securities law or any rule or regulation promul- 13
gated under the Act, the 1934 Act, or any state securities law; 14
and the Company will pay to each such Holder, underwriter, or 15
controlling person, as incurred, any legal or other expenses rea- 16
sonably incurred by them in connection with investigating or 17
defending any such loss, claim, damage, liability, or action; pro- 18
vided, however, that the indemnity agreement contained in this 19
Subsection 6.10(a) shall not apply to amounts paid in settle- 20
ment of any such loss, claim, damage, liability, or action if such 21
settlement is effected without the consent of the Company 22
(which consent shall not be unreasonably withheld); nor shall 23
the Company be liable in any such case for any such loss, claim, 24
damage, liability, or action to the extent that it arises out of or 25
is based upon a violation which occurs in reliance upon and in 26
conformity with written information furnished expressly for 27
use in connection with such registration by any such Holder, 28
underwriter, or controlling person. 29

30

(b)   To the extent permitted by law, each selling Holder will 31
indemnify and hold harmless the Company, each of its directors, 32
each of its officers who has signed the registration statement, 33
each person, if any, who controls the Company within the mean- 34
ing of the Act, any underwriter, any other Holder selling securities 35
in such registration statement, and any controlling person of 36
any such underwriter or other Holder, against any losses, 37
claims, damages, or liabilities (joint or several) to which any of 38
the foregoing persons may become subject, under the Act, the 39
1934 Act, or other federal or state law, insofar as such losses, 40

1 claims, damages, or liabilities (or actions in respect thereto)
2 arise out of or are based upon any Violation, in each case to the
3 extent (and only to the extent) that such Violation occurs in
4 reliance upon and in conformity with written information fur-
5 nished by such Holder expressly for use in connection with such
6 registration; and each such Holder will pay, as incurred, any
7 legal or other expenses reasonably incurred by any person in-
8 tended to be indemnified pursuant to this Subsection 6.10(b),
9 in connection with investigating or defending any such loss,
10 claim, damage, liability, or action; provided, however, that the
11 indemnity agreement contained in this Subsection 6.10(b) shall
12 not apply to amounts paid in settlement of any such loss, claim,
13 damage, liability, or action if such settlement is effected with-
14 out the consent of the Holder, which consent shall not be
15 unreasonably withheld; provided, that, in no event shall any
16 indemnity under this Subsection 6.10(b) exceed the gross pro-
17 ceeds from the offering received by such Holder.
18
19   (c)   Promptly after receipt by an indemnified party under
20 this Section 6.10 of notice of the commencement of any action
21 (including any governmental action), such indemnified party
22 will, if a claim in respect thereof is to be made against any
23 indemnifying party under this Section 6.10, deliver to the in-
24 demnifying party a written notice of the commencement thereof
25 and the indemnifying party shall have the right to participate
26 in, and, to the extent the indemnifying party so desires, jointly
27 with any other indemnifying party similarly noticed, to assume
28 the defense thereof with counsel mutually satisfactory to the
29 parties; provided, however, that an indemnified party shall have
30 the right to retain its own counsel, with the fees and expenses
31 to be paid by the indemnifying party, if representation of such
32 indemnified party by the counsel retained by the indemnifying
33 party would be inappropriate due to actual or potential differ-
34 ing interests between such indemnified party and any other
35 party represented by such counsel in such proceeding. The fail-
36 ure to deliver written notice to the indemnifying party within
37 a reasonable time of the commencement of any such action, if
38 prejudicial to its ability to defend such action, shall relieve such
39 indemnifying party of any liability to the indemnified party
40 under this Section 6.10, but the omission to so deliver written

notice to the indemnifying party will not relieve it of any liability that it may have to any indemnified party otherwise than
under this Section 6.10.

(d)   The obligations of the Company and Holders under this
Section 6.10 shall survive the completion of any offering of Registrable Securities in a registration statement under this Section
6 and otherwise.

6.11   *Reports Under Securities Exchange Act of 1934.* With a
view to making available to the Holders the benefits of Rule 144
promulgated under the Act and any other rule or regulation of
the SEC that may at any time permit a Holder to sell securities
of the Company to the public without registration or pursuant
to a registration on Form S-3, the Company agrees to:

(a)   make and keep public information available, as those
terms are understood and defined in SEC Rule 144, at all times
after ninety (90) days after the effective date of the first registration statement filed by the Company for the offering of its
securities to the general public;

(b)   take such action, including the voluntary registration
of its Common Stock under Section 12 of the 1934 Act, as is
necessary to enable the Holders to utilize Form S-3 for the sale
of their Registrable Securities, such action to be taken as soon
as practicable after the end of the fiscal year in which the first
registration statement filed by the Company for the offering of
its securities to the general public is declared effective;

(c)   file with the SEC in a timely manner all reports and
other documents required of the Company under the Act and
the 1934 Act; and

(d)   furnish to any Holder, so long as the Holder owns any
Registrable Securities, forthwith upon request (i) a written
statement by the Company as to its compliance with the reporting requirements of SEC Rule 144 (at any time after ninety
[90] days after the effective date of the first registration statement filed by the Company), the Act, and the 1934 Act (at any

time after it has become subject to such reporting requirements), or as to its qualification that it qualifies as a registrant
whose securities may be resold pursuant to Form S-3 (at any
time after it so qualifies); (ii) a copy of the most recent annual
or quarterly report of the Company and such other reports
and documents so filed by the Company; and (iii) such other
information as may be reasonably requested in availing any
Holder of any rule or regulation of the SEC which permits the
selling of any such securities without registration or pursuant to such form.

6.12 *Form S-3 Registration.* In case the Company shall receive from any Holder or Holders of at least five percent (5%) of
the Registrable Securities then outstanding a written request
or requests that the Company effect a registration on Form S-
3 and any related qualification or compliance with respect to
all or a part of the Registrable Securities owned by such Holder
or Holders, the Company will:

(a)   promptly give written notice of the proposed registration, and any related qualification or compliance, to all other
Holders; and

(b)   as soon as practicable, effect such registration and all
such qualifications and compliances as may be so requested
and as would permit or facilitate the sale and distribution of
all or such portion of such Holder's or Holders' Registrable Securities as are specified in such request, together with all or
such portion of the Registrable Securities of any other Holder
or Holders joining in such request as are specified in a written
request given within fifteen (15) days after receipt of such written notice from the Company; provided, however, that the
Company shall not be obligated to effect any such registration,
qualification, or compliance, pursuant to this Section 6.12: (i)
if Form S-3 is not available for such offering by the Holders; (ii)
if the Holders, together with the holders of any other securities
of the Company entitled to inclusion in such registration, propose to sell Registrable Securities and such other securities (if
any) at an aggregate price to the public (net of any underwriters' discounts or commissions) of less than $250,000; (iii) if the

Company shall furnish to the Holders a certificate signed by 1
the President of the Company stating that in the good faith 2
judgment of the Board of Directors of the Company, it would be 3
seriously detrimental to the Company and its shareholders for 4
such Form S-3 Registration to be effected at such time, in which 5
event the Company shall have the right to defer the filing of 6
the Form S-3 registration statement for a period of not more 7
than sixty (60) days after receipt of the request of the Holder or 8
Holders under this Section 6.12; provided, however, that the 9
Company shall not utilize this right more than once in any 10
twelve-month period; (iv) if the Company has, within the twelve- 11
month period preceding the date of such request, already 12
effected two registrations on Form S-3 for the Holders pursu- 13
ant to this Section 6.12; or (v) in any particular jurisdiction in 14
which the Company would be required to qualify to do busi- 15
ness or to execute a general consent to service of process in 16
effecting such registration, qualification, or compliance; and 17
                                                                18

(c)   subject to the foregoing, the Company shall file a regis- 19
tration statement covering the Registrable Securities and other 20
securities so requested to be registered as soon as practicable 21
after receipt of the request or requests of the Holders. All ex- 22
penses incurred in connection with the registrations requested 23
pursuant to Section 6.12, including (without limitation) all reg- 24
istration, filing, qualification, printer's and accounting fees and 25
the reasonable fees and disbursements of counsel for the sell- 26
ing Holder or Holders and counsel for the Company, shall be 27
borne by the Company. Any underwriters' discounts or com- 28
missions associated with Registrable Securities, and all 29
expenses incurred in connection with the third and subsequent 30
registrations requested pursuant to Section 6.12 shall be borne 31
pro rata by the Holder or Holders participating in the Form S- 32
3 Registration. Registrations effected pursuant to this Section 33
6.12 shall not be counted as demands for registration or regis- 34
trations effected pursuant to Sections 6.2. 35
                                                                36

6.13   *Assignment of Registration Rights.* The rights to cause 37
the Company to register Registrable Securities pursuant to this 38
Section 6 may be assigned by a Holder to a transferee or as- 39
signee of any Registrable Securities; provided, however, the 40

1 Company is, within a reasonable time after such transfer, fur-
2 nished with written notice of the name and address of such
3 transferee or assignee and the securities with respect to which
4 such registration rights are being assigned; and provided, fur-
5 ther, that such assignment shall be effective only if immediately
6 following such transfer the further disposition of such securi-
7 ties by the transferee or assignee is restricted under the Act;
8 and provided further that registration rights may not be trans-
9 ferred to a competitor of the Company.
10
11 6.14   *Limitations on Subsequent Registration Rights.* From
12 and after the date of this Agreement except as permitted under
13 Section 1.3 hereof, the Company shall not, without the prior
14 written consent of the Holders of a majority of the outstanding
15 Registrable Securities, enter into any agreement with any
16 Holder or prospective Holder of any securities of the Company
17 which would allow such Holder or prospective Holder (a) to in-
18 clude such securities in any registration filed under Section
19 6.2 hereof, unless under the terms of such agreement, such
20 Holder or prospective Holder may include such securities in
21 any such registration only to the extent that the inclusion of
22 his securities will not reduce the amount of the Registrable
23 Securities of the Holders which is included or (b) to make a
24 demand registration which could result in such registration
25 statement being declared effective prior to the earlier of either
26 of the dates set forth in Subsection 6.2(a) or within one hun-
27 dred-twenty (120) days of the effective date of any registration
28 effected pursuant to Section 6.2.
29
30 6.15   *Amendment of Registration Rights.* Any provision of this
31 Section 6 may be amended or the observance thereof may be
32 waived (either generally or in a particular instance and either
33 retroactively or prospectively), only with the written consent
34 of the Company and the holders of a majority of the Registrable
35 Securities then outstanding. Any amendment or waiver effected
36 in accordance with this Section 6 shall be binding upon each
37 Holder of any securities purchased under this Agreement at
38 the time outstanding (including securities into which such se-
39 curities are convertible), each future Holder of all such
40 securities, and the Company.

6.16   *"Market Stand-Off" Agreement.* Any Holder of Regis- 1
trable Securities being registered under this Section 6 agrees, 2
if requested by the Company or an underwriter of such regis- 3
tered public offering, not to sell or otherwise transfer or dispose 4
of any Common Stock (or other securities) of the Company held 5
by such Holder other than shares of Registrable Securities in- 6
cluded in the registration during a period of up to ninety (90) 7
days following the effective date of the initial registration state- 8
ment of the Company filed under the Act, provided that all other 9
persons selling securities in such underwritten public offering 10
and all officers and directors of the Company shall enter into 11
similar agreements. Such agreement shall be in writing in the 12
form satisfactory to the Company and such underwriter, and 13
may be included in the underwriting agreement. The Company 14
may impose stop-transfer instructions with respect to the se- 15
curities subject to the foregoing restriction until the end of the 16
required stand-off period. 17
                                                                          18
7.   *Covenants of the Company.* 19
                                                                          20
7.1   *Delivery of Financial Statements.* The Company shall 21
deliver to each investor: 22
                                                                          23
   (a)   as soon as practicable, but in any event within ninety 24
(90) days after the end of each fiscal year of the Company, an 25
income statement for such fiscal year, a balance sheet of the 26
Company as of the end of such year, and a schedule as to the 27
sources and applications of funds for such year, such year-end 28
financial reports to be in reasonable detail, prepared in accor- 29
dance with generally accepted accounting principles ("GAAP"), 30
and audited and certified by independent public accountants 31
of nationally recognized standing selected by the Company; 32
                                                                          33
   (b)   as soon as practicable, but in any event within forty- 34
five (45) days after the end of each of the first three (3) quarters 35
of each fiscal year of the Company, an unaudited profit or loss 36
statement and schedule as to the sources and application of 37
funds for such fiscal quarter and an unaudited balance sheet 38
as of the end of such fiscal quarter, in reasonable detail and 39
prepared in accordance with GAAP; 40

(c) within thirty (30) days of the end of each month, an unaudited income statement and schedule as to the sources and application of funds for such month and an unaudited balance sheet as of the end of such month, in reasonable detail and prepared in accordance with GAAP, together with an analysis by management of the Company's financial condition and results of operations during such period and explanation by management of any differences between such condition or results and the budget and business plan for such period;

(d) as soon as practicable, but in any event thirty (30) days prior to the end of each fiscal year, a budget and business plan for the next fiscal year, prepared on a monthly basis, including balance sheets and sources and applications of funds statements for such months and, as soon as prepared, any other budgets or revised budgets prepared by the Company;

(e) with respect to the financial statements called for in subsections (b) and (c) of this Section 7.1, an instrument executed by the Chief Financial Officer or President of the Company and certifying that such financial statements were prepared in accordance with GAAP consistently applied with prior practice for earlier periods and fairly present the financial condition of the Company and its results of operation for the period specified, subject to normal year-end audit adjustment, and certifying that such officer has reviewed the provisions of this Agreement and has no knowledge of any default by the Company in the performance or observance of any of the provisions of this Agreement or, if such officer has such knowledge, specifying such default and the nature thereof;

(f) such other information relating to the financial condition, business, prospects, or corporate affairs of the Company as the Investor may from time to time reasonably request, provided, however, that the Company shall not be obligated to provide any information which it reasonably considers to be a trade secret, the disclosure of which the Company reasonably believes may adversely affect its business.

7.2 *Inspection; Observer Rights.* The Company shall permit

each Investor, at such Investor's expense, to visit and inspect   1
the Company's properties, to examine its books of account and   2
records, and to discuss the Company's affairs, finances, and ac-   3
counts with its officers, all at such reasonable times as may be   4
requested by the Investor; provided, however, that the Company   5
shall not be obligated pursuant to this Section 7.2 to provide   6
access to any information which it reasonably considers to be a   7
trade secret, the disclosure of which the Company reasonably   8
believes may adversely affect its business. The Company will   9
give each Investor (or any representative designated by such   10
Investor) not less than two (2) days' prior written notice of each   11
meeting of the Board of Directors of the Company and of any   12
other committee or group exercising responsibilities comparable   13
to those exercised by the Board of Directors, specifying the time   14
and place of such meeting and, to the extent then known, the   15
matters to be discussed thereat and inviting each such Investor   16
(or such representative) to attend and participate therein (with-   17
out, however, a right to vote thereat in such capacity). The right   18
provided hereunder shall be deemed to be revived and such   19
Shares shall not be offered unless first re-offered to the Eligible   20
Investors in accordance herewith.   21
   22
7.3   *Employee Stock Issuances.* The Company covenants and   23
agrees that (i) after the date hereof it shall not issue, or grant   24
options with respect to, more than 15,813 shares of Common   25
Stock to employees (adjusted to reflect subsequent stock divi-   26
dends, stock splits, or recapitalizations), and (ii) it shall not   27
issue, or grant options with respect to, any securities to em-   28
ployees unless the amount and terms of each such issuance or   29
grant shall first have been approved by the Compensation Com-   30
mittee contemplated by Section 7.7(k) hereof.   31
   32
7.4   *Right of First Offer.* Subject to the terms and conditions   33
specified in this Section 7.4, the Company hereby grants to each   34
Investor (so long as such Investor holds at least 5 percent of the   35
aggregate number of shares of Series A Preferred Stock purchased   36
hereunder by all Investors and Common Stock issued upon con-   37
version thereof ["Eligible Investors"], adjusted to reflect   38
subsequent changes after the date hereof in the number of shares   39
of Common Stock outstanding by reason of stock dividends, stock   40

splits, or recapitalizations, or the like), a right of first offer with respect to future sales by the Company of its Shares (as hereinafter defined). Each time the Company proposes to offer any shares of, or securities convertible into or exercisable for any shares of, any class of its capital stock ("Shares"), the Company shall first make an offering of such Shares to each Investor in accordance with the following provisions:

(a) The Company shall deliver a notice pursuant to Section 8.6 ("Notice") to each of the Investors stating (i) its bona fide intention to offer such Shares, (ii) the number of such Shares to be offered, and (iii) the price, if any, for which it proposes to offer such Shares.

(b) Within fifteen (15) calendar days after mailing of the Notice, each Eligible Investor may elect to purchase, at the price and on the terms specified in the Notice, all but not less than all of that portion of such Shares which equals (such number of Shares, the "First Offer Shares") the proportion that (x) the number of shares of Common Stock issued and held or issuable upon conversion of the Series A Preferred Stock then held by such Eligible Investor bears to (y) the aggregate number of shares of Common Stock into which the shares of Series A Preferred Stock purchased hereunder by all Eligible Investors on the date hereof, without regard to any subsequent conversions or retirements of such Series A Preferred Stock, would then be convertible.

(c) The Company may, during the 120-day period following the expiration of the period provided in Subsection 7.4(b) hereof, offer any Shares which have not been subscribed for pursuant to Subparagraph (b) hereof to any person or persons at a price not less than, and upon terms no more favorable to the offeree than, those specified in the Notice. If the Company does not consummate the proposed sale of the Shares within such period, the right provided hereunder shall be deemed to be revived and such Shares shall not be offered unless first reoffered to the Eligible Investors in accordance herewith.

(d) The right of first offer in this Section 7.4 shall not be applicable (i) to the issuance or sale of up to 15,813 shares of

Common Stock (or options therefor) (adjusted to reflect subsequent stock dividends, stock splits, or recapitalization) issued
after the date hereof to employees, directors, or consultants for
the primary purpose of soliciting or retaining their employment;
(ii) to shares issued or issuable by the Company in connection
with any merger or reorganization transaction in which the
Company is the surviving company; or (iii) to or after consummation of the Company's sale of its Common Stock in a bona
fide, firm commitment underwriting pursuant to a registration statement on Form S-1 under the Act (or any equivalent
successor form), the public offering price of which was not less
than $120.00 per share (adjusted to reflect subsequent stock
dividends, stock splits, or recapitalization) and the net proceeds
to the Company of which was not less than $5,000,000 (such an
offering, a "Qualified Public Offering").

7.5   *Insurance.* Until the fifth anniversary of the Closing, the
Company shall maintain term insurance on the lives of each of
Entrepreneur 1 and Entrepreneur 2, each in the amount of at
least $3,000,000, with the proceeds payable solely to the Company.

7.6   *Board of Directors.* The Company shall use its best efforts to maintain a Board of Directors consisting of not more
than six persons and to cause and maintain the election to the
Board of Directors of (i) two designees of the holders of a majority of the outstanding Series A Preferred Stock, (ii) two designees
of the holders of a majority of the outstanding Common Stock,
and (iii) two persons who are officers of the Company and who
are approved as directors by the Holders of a majority of the
outstanding Common Stock and the Holders of a majority of
the outstanding Series A Preferred Stock. The Company shall
promptly reimburse such directors for any expenses incurred
by them in connection with their activities as directors of the
Company. The Company shall indemnify each of such directors
against liability to the fullest extent permitted by applicable
law. The Company shall hold meetings of its Board of Directors
not less than once every three months.

7.7   *Other Affirmative Covenants.* Without limiting any
other covenants and provisions hereof, the Company covenants

1 and agrees that it will perform and observe, and cause each of
2 its subsidiaries in existence from time to time to observe and
3 perform, the following covenants and provisions, unless, with
4 respect to a specific transaction, a waiver of certain specified
5 provisions of this Section 7.7 in connection solely with such
6 transaction is given by the affirmative vote of the holders of no
7 less than a majority of the outstanding shares of Series A Pre-
8 ferred Stock voting as a separate class:
9
10 (a) *Payment of Taxes and Trade Debt.* Pay and discharge
11 all taxes, assessments, and governmental charges or levies im-
12 posed upon it or upon its income, profits, or business, or upon
13 any properties belonging to it, prior to the date on which pen-
14 alties attach thereto, and all lawful claims which, if unpaid,
15 might become a lien or charge upon any properties of the Com-
16 pany, provided that the Company shall not be required to pay
17 any such tax, assessment, charge, levy, or claim which is being
18 contested in good faith and by appropriate proceedings if the
19 Company shall have set aside on its books sufficient reserves,
20 if any, with respect thereto. Pay, when due, or in conformity
21 with customary trade terms but not later than ninety (90) days
22 from the due date, all lease obligations, all trade debt, and all
23 other indebtedness incident to the operations of the Company,
24 except such as are being contested in good faith and by proper
25 proceedings if the Company shall have set aside on its books
26 sufficient reserves, if any, with respect thereto.
27
28 (b) *Maintenance of Insurance.* Maintain insurance with re-
29 sponsible and reputable insurance companies or associations
30 in such amounts and covering such risks as is customarily car-
31 ried by companies engaged in similar businesses and owning
32 similar properties in the same general areas in which the Com-
33 pany operates, but in any event in amounts sufficient to prevent
34 the Company from becoming a co-insurer.
35
36 (c) *Preservation of Corporate Existence.* Preserve and main-
37 tain its corporate existence, rights, franchises, and privileges in
38 the jurisdiction of its incorporation, and qualify and remain quali-
39 fied as a foreign corporation in each jurisdiction in which such
40 qualification is necessary or desirable in view of its business and

operations or the ownership or lease of its properties. Preserve 1
and maintain all licenses and other rights to use Intellectual 2
Property owned or possessed by it and deemed by the Company 3
to be necessary or useful to the conduct of its business. 4
5
(d) *Compliance with Laws.* Comply with the requirements 6
of all applicable laws, rules, regulations, and orders of any gov- 7
ernmental authority, noncompliance with which could 8
materially adversely affect its business or condition, financial 9
or otherwise. 10
11
(e) *Keeping of Records and Books of Account.* Keep ad- 12
equate records and books of account in which complete entries 13
will be made in accordance with generally accepted accounting 14
principles consistently applied, reflecting all financial transac- 15
tions of the Company and in which, for each fiscal year, all 16
proper reserves for depreciation, depletion, obsolescence, am- 17
ortization, taxes, bad debts, and other purposes in connection 18
with its business shall be made. 19
20
(f) *Maintenance of Properties.* Maintain and preserve all 21
of its properties and assets, necessary or useful in the proper 22
conduct of its business, in good repair, working order, and con- 23
dition, ordinary wear and tear excepted. 24
25
(g) *Compliance with ERISA.* Comply with all minimum 26
funding requirements applicable to any pension, employee ben- 27
efit plans, or employee contribution plans which are subject to 28
ERISA or to the Code, and comply in all other material respects 29
with the provisions of ERISA and the Code, and the rules and 30
regulations thereunder, which are applicable to any such plan. 31
The Company shall not permit any event or condition to exist 32
which could permit any such plan to be terminated under cir- 33
cumstances which would cause the lien provided for in Section 34
4068 of ERISA to attach to the assets of the Company. 35
36
(h) *Budgets Approval.* Prior to the commencement of each 37
fiscal year commencing after the date hereof, prepare and sub- 38
mit to, and obtain the approval of the holders of no less than a 39
majority of the outstanding shares of Series A Preferred Stock 40

1 voting as a separate class of, monthly capital and operating
2 expense budgets, cash-flow projections, profit and loss projec-
3 tions, and a business plan. The Company shall not enter into
4 any activity or make any expenditure not envisioned by the
5 budget and business plan.
6
7   (i) *Financings*. Promptly, fully, and in detail, inform the
8 Board of Directors of any discussions, offers, or contracts relat-
9 ing to possible financings of any nature for the Company,
10 whether initiated by the Company or any other person, except
11 for minor financings of less than $25,000 which do not include
12 as a feature thereof any right to acquire any of the equity secu-
13 rities of the Company.
14
15   (j) *New Developments*. Cause all technological develop-
16 ments, inventions, discoveries, or improvements by the
17 Company's employees or agents to be fully documented in ac-
18 cordance with the Company's existing practices, cause all key
19 employees and consultants of the Company to execute appro-
20 priate patent assignment agreements to the Company and,
21 where possible and appropriate, to file and prosecute United
22 States and foreign patent applications relating to and protect-
23 ing such developments on behalf of the Company.
24
25   (k) *Compensation*. Prepare and submit to, and obtain the
26 approval of, the Compensation Committee of the Board of Direc-
27 tors (which shall consist of three members of the Board of
28 Directors of which at least two members shall be directors elected
29 pursuant to Section 7.6(i) hereof) of a compensation policy for its
30 officers, which shall contain guidelines for reasonable levels of
31 salary and other employment benefits, and which shall be peri-
32 odically updated, and comply with such compensation policy in
33 making all compensation offers to new officers and compensa-
34 tion changes to existing officers, of which all cash compensation
35 and equity compensation offers or changes shall be subject to
36 the approval of the Board of Directors.
37
38 7.8   *Certain Negative Covenants*. Without limiting any
39 other covenants and provisions hereof, the Company covenants
40 and agrees that it will comply with and observe the following

negative covenants and provisions and will not, unless, with
respect to a specific transaction, a waiver of certain specified
provisions of this Section 7.8 in connection solely with such
transaction is given by the affirmative vote of the holders of no
less than a majority of the outstanding shares of Series A Preferred Stock voting as a separate class:

(a) *Merger or Sale of Assets.* Merge or consolidate with, or
sell, assign, lease, or otherwise dispose of or voluntarily part
with the control of (whether in one transaction or in a series of
transactions) a material portion of its assets to any person
(whether now owned or hereinafter acquired) or sell, assign, or
otherwise dispose of (whether in one transaction or in a series
of transactions) any of its accounts receivable (whether now in
existence or hereinafter created) at a discount or with recourse,
to any person, except for sales or other dispositions of assets in
the ordinary course of business.

(b) *Dealings with Affiliates.* Enter into any transaction, including, without limitation, any loans or extensions of credit or
royalty agreements with any officer or director of the Company
or Holder of any class of capital stock of the Company, or any
member of their respective immediate families or any corporation or other entity directly or indirectly controlled by one or
more of such officers, directors, or stockholders or members of
their immediate families except in the ordinary course of business and on terms not less favorable to the Company than it
would obtain in a transaction between unrelated parties.

(c) *Change in Nature of Business.* Make, or permit, any
material change in the nature of its business as carried on at
the date hereof or as contemplated in the Placement Memorandum prior to the date hereof.

(d) *Acquisition of Shares by the Company.* Redeem, purchase,
or otherwise acquire for value (or pay into or set aside for a sink-
ing fund for such purchase), any share or shares of any equity
security of the Company, except for shares of stock of employees
who are leaving the Company to the extent that such repurchase
is required under the terms of an agreement disclosed herein.

(e) *Amendment to Charter.* Make any amendment to its Articles of Incorporation or bylaws which limits its legal capacity or ability to perform its obligations under this Agreement, the Securities or any other instrument or agreement executed or to be executed pursuant to the provisions hereof or thereof or which may materially adversely affect the rights of the Investors.

7.9 *Termination of Certain Covenants.* The covenants set forth in Subsections 7.1(c), (d), (e), and (f), and Sections 7.2, 7.3, 7.4, 7.6, 7.7, and 7.8 shall terminate as to Investors and be of no further force or effect upon the consummation of a Qualified Public Offering.

8. *Miscellaneous.*

8.1 *Survival of Warranties.* The warranties, representations, and covenants of the Company and Investors contained in or made pursuant to this Agreement shall survive the execution and delivery of this Agreement and the Closing and shall in no way be affected by any investigation of the subject matter thereof made by or on behalf of the Investors or the Company.

8.2 *Successors and Assigns.* The terms and conditions of this Agreement shall inure to the benefit of and be binding upon the respective successors and assigns of the parties. Nothing in this Agreement, express or implied, is intended to confer upon any party other than the parties hereto or their respective successors and assigns any rights, remedies, obligations, or liabilities under or by reason of this Agreement, except as expressly provided in this Agreement. Neither this Agreement nor its rights and obligations thereunder can be assigned by the Company, and any such attempted assignment will be void. Any Investor can transfer all or any portion of its rights and obligations hereunder to any other person or entity selected by such Investor who is not a competitor of the Company.

8.3 *Governing Law.* This Agreement shall be governed by and construed under the laws of the Commonwealth of Pennsylvania as applied to agreements entered into and to be performed entirely within Pennsylvania.

8.4   *Counterparts.* This Agreement may be executed in two 1
or more counterparts, each of which shall be deemed an origi- 2
nal, but all of which together shall constitute one and the same 3
instrument.   4
                                                               5
8.5   *Titles and Subtitles.* The titles and subtitles used in 6
this Agreement are used for convenience only and are not to be 7
considered in construing or interpreting this Agreement.   8
                                                               9
8.6   *Notices.* Unless otherwise provided, any notice required 10
or permitted under this Agreement shall be given in writing   11
and shall be deemed effectively given upon personal delivery   12
to the party to be notified or upon deposit with the United States 13
Post Office, by registered or certified mail, postage prepaid and 14
addressed to the party to be notified at the address indicated 15
for such party on the signature page hereof, or at such other 16
address as such party may designate by ten (10) days' advance 17
written notice to the other parties.   18
                                                               19
8.7   *Finder's Fee.* Each party represents that it neither is 20
nor will be obligated for any finders' fee or commission in con- 21
nection with this transaction. Each Investor agrees to indemnify 22
and to hold harmless the Company from any liability for any   23
commission or compensation in the nature of a finders' fee (and 24
the costs and expenses of defending against such liability or 25
asserted liability) for which the Investor or any of its officers, 26
partners, employees, or representatives is responsible. The   27
Company agrees to indemnify and hold harmless each Inves-   28
tor from any liability for any commission or compensation in   29
the nature of a finders' fee (and the costs and expenses of de- 30
fending against such liability or asserted liability) for which 31
the Company or any of its officers, employees, or representa- 32
tives is responsible.   33
                                                               34
8.8   *Expenses.* Irrespective of whether the Closing is effected, 35
the Company shall pay up to $20,000 of all costs and expenses 36
incurred by the Investors with respect to the negotiation, ex- 37
ecution, delivery, and performance of this Agreement, including 38
without limitation, the reasonable fees and expenses of Lipman, 39
Lipman, and Lipman, special counsel for the Investors. If any 40

action at law or in equity is necessary to enforce or interpret the terms of this Agreement or the Articles of Incorporation, the prevailing party shall be entitled to reasonable attorney's fees, costs, and necessary disbursements in addition to any other relief to which such party may be entitled.

8.9   *Amendments and Waivers.* Except as specified in Section 6.15, any term of this Agreement may be amended and the observance of any term of this Agreement may be waived (either generally or in a particular instance and either retroactively or prospectively), only with the written consent of the Company and the holders of a majority of the Common Stock issued or issuable upon conversion of the Series A Preferred Stock held by the Investors. Any amendment or waiver effected in accordance with this Section 8 shall be binding upon each holders of any securities purchased under this Agreement at the time outstanding (including securities into which such securities are convertible), each future Holder of all such securities, and the Company; provided, however, that no condition set forth in Section 5 hereof may be waived with respect to any Investor who does not consent thereto.

8.10   *Severability.* If one or more provisions of this Agreement are held to be unenforceable under applicable law, such provision shall be excluded from this Agreement and the balance of the Agreement shall be interpreted as if such provision were so excluded and shall be enforceable in accordance with its terms.

8.11   *Aggregation of Stock.* All shares of the Series A Preferred Stock held or acquired by affiliated entities or persons shall be aggregated together for the purpose of determining the availability of any rights under this Agreement.

    IN WITNESS WHEREOF, the undersigned have executed,   1
or caused to be executed on their behalf by an agent there-   2
unto duly authorized, this Agreement as of the date first above   3
written.   4

  5

The Company: ABC, INC.   6

  7

  8

  9

                 By: _____   10

                 Title: 11

  12

                 Address: 13

                 Philadelphia, PA 19104   14

  15

The Investors: XYZ, LTD.   16

  17

  18

  19

                 By: _____   20

                 Title: 21

  22

                 Address: 23

  24

  25

  26

  27

  28

  29

  30

  31

  32

  33

  34

  35

  36

  37

  38

  39

  40

EXHIBIT A OF APPENDIX 3

AMENDED AND RESTATED
ARTICLES OF INCORPORATION OF ABC, INC.

FIRST: *Corporate Name.* The name of the corporation is "ABC, INC."

SECOND: *Registered Office.* The location and post office address of the registered office of the corporation in this Commonwealth is _____.

THIRD: *Corporate Purpose.* The purpose or purposes for which the corporation is incorporated under the Business Corporation Law of the Commonwealth of Pennsylvania are to engage in, and to do any lawful act concerning, any or all lawful business for which corporations may be incorporated under said Business Corporation Law.

FOURTH: *Corporate Existence.* The term of existence of the corporation is perpetual.

FIFTH: *Capital Stock.*

(A) *Classes of Stock.* The aggregate number of shares which the corporation shall have authority to issue is 650,000 shares, divided into 500,000 shares of Common Stock, par value $.10 per share, and 150,000 shares of Series Preferred Stock, without par value.

(B) *Rights, Preferences, and Restrictions of Series Preferred Stock.* The Series Preferred Stock authorized by these Articles may be issued from time to time in one or more series. The Board of Directors of the corporation shall have the full authority permitted by law to establish one or more series and the number of shares constituting each such series and to fix by resolution full, limited, multiple, or fractional, or no voting rights, and such designations, preferences, qualifications, privileges, limitations, restrictions, options, conversion rights, and other special or relative rights of any series of the Series Preferred Stock that may

be desired. Excluding the Series A Preferred Stock referred to
hereinafter and subject to the limitation on the total number of
shares of Series Preferred Stock which the corporation has authority to issue hereunder, the Board of Directors is also
authorized to increase or decrease the number of shares of any
series, subsequent to the issue of that series, but not below the
number of shares of such series then outstanding. In case the
number of shares of any series shall be so decreased, the shares
constituting such decrease shall resume the status which they
had prior to the adoption of the resolution originally fixing the
number of shares of such series.

(C)   *Designation of Series A Convertible Preferred Stock.* There
is hereby established a series of the Series Preferred Stock designated "Series A Convertible Preferred Stock" (herein referred
to as "Series A Preferred Stock"), consisting of 50,000 shares,
having a stated value per share equal to $20.00, and having the
relative rights, designations, preferences, qualifications, privileges, limitations, and restrictions applicable thereto as follows:

1.   *Dividend Provisions.*

(a)   The Holders of shares of Series A Preferred Stock shall
be entitled to receive dividends, out of any assets legally available therefor, prior and in preference to any declaration or
payment of any dividend (payable other than in Common Stock
or other securities and rights convertible into or entitling the
Holder thereof to receive, directly or indirectly, additional shares
of Common Stock of this corporation) on the Common Stock of
this corporation, in an amount per share per annum equal to the
greater of (i) $3.00 or (ii) an amount which is equal to the prod-
uct of (1) the number of shares of Common Stock into which one
share of Series A Convertible Stock is convertible at the time of
declaration of such dividend, multiplied by (2) the aggregate per
share amount of all cash dividends, and the aggregate per share
amount (payable in cash, based upon the fair market value at
the time the non-cash dividend or other distribution is declared
or paid as determined in good faith by the Board of Directors) of
all non-cash dividends or other distributions on the Common
Stock of the corporation other than a dividend payable in shares

of Common Stock or a subdivision of the outstanding shares of
Common Stock (by reclassification or otherwise), declared on the
Common Stock of the corporation. Such dividends shall be payable when, as, and if declared by the Board of Directors. Such
dividends shall be cumulative, but accumulations of dividends
shall not bear interest.

(b)   No deposit, payment, or distribution of any kind shall
be made in or to any purchase or redemption requirement applicable to any class or series of junior shares unless all
accumulations of dividends earned on the Series A Preferred
Stock as of the last day of the most recently ended year shall
have been paid. So long as any Series A Preferred Stock shall
remain outstanding, no dividend or other distribution (except
in junior shares) shall be paid or made on the Common Stock of
the corporation or on other junior shares of the corporation and
no share of Common Stock or other junior shares shall be purchased or otherwise acquired by the corporation or any
subsidiary of the corporation other than upon exercise of the
corporation's rights under any restricted stock purchase agreement or by exchange therefor of junior shares or out of the
proceeds of the substantially concurrent sale of junior shares,
unless (whether or not there shall be funds legally available
therefor) all accumulations of dividends earned on the Series A
Preferred Stock as of the last day of the most recently ended
year shall have been paid. The term "junior shares" shall mean
any class or series of stock junior to the Series A Preferred Stock
as to dividends and the distribution of assets upon liquidation,
dissolution, bankruptcy, reorganization, or other insolvency proceeding, and upon the winding up of the corporation.
Subject to the above limitations and to the provisions of Section 5(g), dividends may be paid on the Common Stock or any
other junior shares out of any funds legally available for such
purpose when and as declared by the Board of Directors.

2.   *Liquidation Preference.*

(a)   In the event of any liquidation, dissolution, or winding up of the corporation, either voluntary or involuntary, the
Holders of Series A Preferred Stock shall be entitled to receive,

prior and in preference to any distribution of any of the assets of
this corporation to the Holders of Common Stock by reason of
their ownership thereof, an amount per share equal to the sum
of (i) $20.00 for each outstanding share of Series A Preferred
Stock and (ii) all accumulations of unpaid dividends on each share
of Series A Preferred Stock. If upon the occurrence of such event,
the assets and funds thus distributed among the Holders of the
Series A Preferred Stock shall be insufficient to permit the payment to such Holders of the full aforesaid preferential amounts,
then the entire assets and funds of the corporation legally available for distribution shall be distributed ratably among the
Holders of the Series A Preferred Stock in proportion to the
amount of such Stock owned by each such Holder.

    (b)   After the distribution described in Subsection (a) has
been paid, the remaining assets of the corporation available
for distribution to shareholders shall be distributed among the
Holders of Common Stock pro rata based on the number of
shares of Common Stock held by each such Holder.

    (c)   A consolidation or merger of this corporation with or
into any other corporation or corporations, or a sale, convey-
ance, or disposition of all or substantially all of the assets of
this corporation or the effectuation by the corporation of a transaction or series of related transactions in which more than 50
percent of the voting power of the corporation is disposed of,
shall be deemed to be a liquidation, dissolution, or winding up
within the meaning of this Section 2, if the Holders of at least
60 percent of the outstanding Series A Preferred Stock elect to
have such transaction treated as a liquidation.

    3.   *Conversion.* The Holders of the Series A Preferred Stock
shall have conversion rights as follows (the "Conversion Rights"):

    (a)   *Conversion Rights and Automatic Conversion.*

    (i)   Each share of Series A Preferred Stock shall be con-
vertible, at the option of the Holder thereof, at any time after
the date of issuance of such share, at the office of this corporation or any transfer agent for the Series A Preferred Stock, into

such number of fully paid and nonassessable shares of Common Stock as is determined by dividing $20.00 (the "Original Conversion Price") by the Conversion Price at the time in effect for such share. The initial Conversion Price per share for shares of Series A Preferred Stock shall be the Original Conversion Price; provided, however, that the Conversion Price for the Series A Preferred Stock (the "Conversion Price") shall be subject to adjustment as set forth in Subsection 3(c).

(ii)   Each share of Series A Preferred Stock shall automatically be converted into shares of Common Stock at the Conversion Price at the time in effect for such Series A Preferred Stock: (a) immediately upon the consummation of the corporation's sale of its Common Stock in a bona fide, firm commitment underwriting pursuant to a registration statement on Form S-1 under the Securities Act of 1933, as amended (or any equivalent successor form), the public offering price of which was not less than $120.00 per share (adjusted to reflect subsequent changes after June __, ____ in the number of shares of Common Stock outstanding by reason of stock dividends, stock splits, or recapitalizations, or the like) and the net proceeds to the corporation of which were not less than $5,000,000 or (b) upon the approval of the Holders of not less than a majority of the then outstanding Series A Preferred Stock.

(iii)   Upon conversion of any Series A Preferred Stock, no payment or adjustment shall be made on account of dividends accrued but unpaid on the Series A Preferred Stock.

(b) *Mechanics of Conversion.* Before any Holder of Series A Preferred Stock shall be entitled to convert the same into shares of Common Stock, he shall surrender the certificate or certificates therefor, duly endorsed, at the office of the corporation or of any transfer agent for the Series A Preferred Stock, and shall give written notice by mail, postage prepaid, to the corporation at its principal corporate office, of the election to convert the same and shall state therein the name or names in which the certificate or certificates for shares of Common Stock are to be issued. The corporation shall, as soon as practicable thereafter, issue and deliver at such office to such

Holder of Series A Preferred Stock, or to the nominee or nomi- 1
nees or such Holder, a certificate or certificates for the number 2
of whole shares of Common Stock to which such Holder shall 3
be entitled as aforesaid. Such conversion shall be deemed to 4
have been made immediately prior to the close of business on 5
the date of such surrender of the shares of Series A Preferred 6
Stock to be converted, and the person or persons entitled to 7
receive the shares of Common Stock issuable upon such con- 8
version shall be treated for all purposes as the record Holder or 9
Holders of such shares of Common Stock as of such date. If the 10
conversion is in connection with an underwritten offer of secu- 11
rities registered pursuant to the Securities Act of 1933, the 12
conversion may, at the option of any Holder tendering Series A 13
Preferred Stock for conversion, be conditioned upon the closing 14
with the underwriter of the sale of securities pursuant to such 15
offering, in which event the person(s) entitled to receive the 16
Common Stock issuable upon such conversion of the Series A 17
Preferred Stock shall not be deemed to have converted such 18
Series A Preferred Stock until immediately prior to the closing 19
of such sale of securities. 20
  21

(c) *Conversion Price Adjustments of Preferred Stock.* The 22
Conversion Price shall be subject to adjustment from time to 23
time as follows: 24
  25

(i) (A) If the corporation shall issue any Additional Stock 26
(as defined below) for a consideration per share less than the 27
Conversion Price in effect immediately prior to the issuance of 28
such Additional Stock, the Conversion Price in effect immedi- 29
ately prior to each such issuance shall forthwith (except as 30
otherwise provided in this clause (i)) be decreased to a price 31
equal to the least consideration per share received by the cor- 32
poration for such Additional Stock. 33
  34

(B)   No adjustment of the Conversion price for the Se- 35
ries A Preferred Stock shall be made in an amount less than 36
one cent per share, provided that any adjustments which are 37
not required to be made by reason of this sentence shall be 38
carried forward and shall be either taken into account in any 39
subsequent adjustment made prior to three (3) years from the 40

date of the event giving rise to the adjustment being carried forward, or, if no such adjustment is made, shall be made at the end of three (3) years from the date of the event giving rise to the adjustment being carried forward. Except to the limited extent provided for in Subsections (E)(3) and (E)(4), no adjustment of such Conversion Price pursuant to this Subsection 3(c)(i) shall have the effect of increasing the Conversion Price above the Conversion Price in effect immediately prior to such adjustment.

(C)   In the case of the issuance of Common Stock for cash, the consideration shall be deemed to be the amount of cash paid therefor before deducting any discounts, commissions, or other expenses allowed, paid, or incurred by the corporation for any underwriting or otherwise in connection with the issuance and sale thereof.

(D)   In the case of the issuance of the Common Stock for a consideration in whole or in part other than cash, the consideration other than cash shall be deemed to be the fair value thereof as reasonably determined by the Board of Directors, irrespective of any accounting treatment.

(E)   In the case of the issuance of options to purchase or rights to subscribe for Common Stock, securities by their terms convertible into or exchangeable for Common Stock or options to purchase or rights to subscribe for such convertible or exchangeable securities (which are not excluded from the definition of Additional Stock), the following provisions shall apply:

1.   The aggregate maximum number of shares of Common Stock deliverable upon exercise of such options to purchase or rights to subscribe for Common Stock shall be deemed to have been issued at the time such options or rights were issued and for a consideration equal to the consideration (determined in the manner provided in Subsections 3(c)(i)(C) and 3(c)(i)(D)), if any, received by the corporation upon the issuance of such options or rights plus the minimum purchase price provided in such options or rights for the Common Stock covered thereby.

2. The aggregate maximum number of shares of Common Stock deliverable upon conversion of or in exchange for any such convertible or exchangeable securities or upon the exercise of options to purchase or rights to subscribe for such convertible or exchangeable securities and subsequent conversion or exchange thereof shall be deemed to have been issued at the time such securities were issued or such options or rights were issued and for a consideration equal to the consideration, if any, received by the corporation for any such securities and related options or rights (excluding any cash received on account of accrued interest or accrued dividends), plus the additional consideration, if any, to be received by the corporation upon the conversion or exchange of such securities or the exercise of any related options or rights (the consideration in each case to be determined in the manner provided in Subsections 3(c)(i)(C) and 3(c)(i)(D)).

3. In the event of any change in the number of shares of Common Stock deliverable or any increase in the consideration payable to the corporation upon exercise of such options or rights or upon conversion of or in exchange for such convertible or exchangeable securities, including, but not limited to, a change resulting from the anti-dilution provisions thereof, the Conversion Price of the Series A Preferred Stock obtained with respect to the adjustment which was made upon the issuance of such options, rights, or securities, and any subsequent adjustments based thereon, shall be recomputed to reflect such change, but no further adjustment shall be made for the actual issuance of Common Stock or any payment of such consideration upon the exercise of any such options or rights or the conversion or exchange of such securities.

4. Upon the expiration of any such options or rights, the termination of any such rights to convert or exchange or the expiration of any options or rights related to such convertible or exchangeable securities, the Conversion Price of the Series A Preferred Stock obtained with respect to the adjustment that was made upon the issuance of such options, rights, or securities or options or rights related to such securities, and any subsequent adjustments based thereon, shall be recomputed to

1 reflect the issuance of only the number of shares of Common
2 Stock actually issued upon the exercise of such options or rights,
3 upon the conversion or exchange of such securities or upon the
4 exercise of the options or rights related to such securities.
5
6   (ii)   "Additional Stock" shall mean any shares of Com-
7 mon Stock issued (or deemed to have been issued pursuant to
8 Subsection 3(c)(i)(E)) by this corporation after June __, _____
9 (the "Purchase Date") other than:
10
11   (A)   Common Stock issued pursuant to a transaction
12 described in Subsection 3(c)(iii) hereof;
13
14   (B)   shares of Common Stock issuable or issued after
15 the Purchase Date to employees, officers, directors, or consult-
16 ants of this corporation directly or pursuant to a Stock option
17 plan or restricted Stock plan approved by the shareholders and
18 directors of this corporation at any time when the total num-
19 ber of shares of Common Stock so issuable or issued (and not
20 repurchased at cost by the corporation in connection with the
21 termination of employment) does not exceed 15,813; or
22
23   (C)   Common Stock issued or issuable upon conversion
24 of the Series A Preferred Stock.
25
26   (iii)   In the event the corporation should at any time or
27 from time to time after the Purchase Date fix a record date for
28 the effectuation of a split or subdivision of the outstanding
29 shares of Common Stock or the determination of Holders of
30 Common Stock entitled to receive a dividend or other distribu-
31 tion payable in additional shares of Common Stock or other
32 securities or rights convertible into, or entitling the Holder
33 thereof to receive directly or indirectly, additional shares of
34 Common Stock (hereinafter referred to as "Common Stock
35 Equivalents") without payment of any consideration by such
36 Holder for the additional shares of Common Stock or the Com-
37 mon Stock Equivalents (including the additional shares of
38 Common Stock issuable upon conversion or exercise thereof),
39 then, as of such record date (or the date of such dividend distri-
40 bution, split, or subdivision if no record date is fixed), the

Conversion Price of the Series A Preferred Stock shall be ap- 1
propriately decreased so that the number of shares of Common 2
Stock issuable on conversion of each share of such series shall 3
be increased in proportion to such increase of outstanding 4
shares determined in accordance with Subsection 3(c)(i)(E). 5

(iv)   If the number of shares of Common Stock outstand- 7
ing at any time after the Purchase Date is decreased by a 8
combination of the outstanding shares of Common Stock, then 9
following the record date of such combination, the Conversion 10
Price for the Series A Preferred Stock shall be appropriately 11
increased so that the number of shares of Common Stock issu- 12
able on conversion of each share of such series shall be decreased 13
in proportion to such decrease in outstanding shares. 14

(d)   *Other Distributions.* In the event the corporation 16
shall declare a distribution payable in securities of other per- 17
sons, evidences of indebtedness issued by the corporation or 18
other persons, assets (excluding cash dividends), or options or 19
rights not referred to in Subsection 3(c)(iii), then, in each such 20
case for the purpose of this Subsection 3(d), the Holders of the 21
Series A Preferred Stock shall be entitled to a proportionate 22
share of any such distribution as though they were the Holders 23
of the number of shares of Common Stock of the corporation 24
into which their shares of Series A Preferred Stock are convert- 25
ible as of the record date fixed for the determination of the 26
Holders of Common Stock of the corporation entitled to receive 27
such distribution. 28

(e)   *Recapitalizations.* If at any time or from time to time 30
there shall be a recapitalization of the Common Stock (other 31
than a subdivision, combination or merger, or sale of assets 32
transaction provided for elsewhere in this Section 3), provision 33
shall be made so that the Holders of the Series A Preferred 34
Stock shall thereafter be entitled to receive upon conversion of 35
the Series A Preferred Stock the number of shares of stock of 36
other securities or property of the corporation or otherwise, to 37
which a Holder of Common Stock deliverable upon conversion 38
would have been entitled on such recapitalization. In any such 39
case, appropriate adjustment shall be made in the application 40

1 of the provisions of this Section 3 with respect to the rights of
2 the Holders of the Series A Preferred Stock after the recapital-
3 ization to the end that the provisions of this Section 3 (including
4 adjustment of the Conversion Price then in effect and the num-
5 ber of shares purchasable upon conversion of the Series A
6 Preferred Stock) shall be applicable after that event as nearly
7 equivalent as may be practicable.
8
9   (f) *No Impairment.* The corporation will not, by amend-
10 ment of its Articles or through any reorganization,
11 recapitalization, transfer of assets, consolidation, merger, dis-
12 solution, issue, or sale of securities or any other voluntary
13 action, avoid or seek to avoid the observance or performance of
14 any of the terms to be observed or performed hereunder by the
15 corporation, but will at all times in good faith assist in the car-
16 rying out of all the provisions of this Section 3 and in the taking
17 of all such action as may be necessary or appropriate in order
18 to protect the conversion rights of the Holders of the Series A
19 Preferred Stock against impairment.
20
21   (g) *No Fractional Shares; Certificate As to Adjustments.*
22
23   (i) No fractional shares shall be issued upon conversion
24 of the Series A Preferred Stock, and the number of shares of
25 Common Stock to be issued shall be rounded to the nearest whole
26 share. Whether or not fractional shares are issuable upon such
27 conversion shall be determined on the basis of the total number
28 of shares of Series A Preferred Stock the Holder is at the time
29 converting into Common Stock and the number of shares of Com-
30 mon Stock issuable upon such aggregate conversion.
31
32   (ii) Upon the occurrence of each adjustment or read-
33 justment of the Conversion Price of Series A Preferred Stock
34 pursuant to this Section 3, the corporation, at its expense, shall
35 promptly compute such adjustment or readjustment in accor-
36 dance with the terms hereof and prepare and furnish to each
37 Holder of Series A Preferred Stock a certificate setting forth
38 such adjustment or readjustment and showing in detail the
39 facts upon which such adjustment or readjustment is based.
40 The corporation shall, upon the written request at any time of

any Holder of Series A Preferred Stock, furnish or cause to be   1
furnished to such Holder a like certificate setting forth (A) such   2
adjustment and readjustment, (B) the Conversion Price at the   3
time in effect, and (C) the number of shares of Common Stock   4
and the amount, if any, of other property which at the time   5
would be received upon the conversion of a share of Series A   6
Preferred Stock.   7
8
(h)   *Notices of Record Date.* In the event of any taking by   9
the corporation of a record of the Holders of any class of securi-   10
ties for the purpose of determining the Holders thereof who are   11
entitled to receive any dividend (other than a cash dividend) or   12
other distribution, any right to subscribe for, purchase, or other-   13
wise acquire any shares of stock or any class of any other   14
securities or property, or to receive any other right, this corpora-   15
tion shall mail to each Holder of Series A Preferred Stock, at   16
least twenty (20) days prior to the date specified therein, a no-   17
tice specifying the date on which any such record is to be taken   18
for the purpose of such dividend, distribution, or right, and the   19
amount and character of such dividend, distribution, or right.   20
21
(i)   *Reservation of Stock Issuable upon Conversion.* This   22
corporation shall at all times reserve and keep available out of   23
its authorized but unissued shares of Common Stock solely for   24
the purpose of effecting the conversion of the shares of the Se-   25
ries A Preferred Stock such number of its shares of Common   26
Stock as shall from time to time be sufficient to effect the con-   27
version of all outstanding shares of the Series A Preferred Stock;   28
and if at any time the number of authorized but unissued shares   29
of Common Stock shall not be sufficient to effect the conversion   30
of all then outstanding shares of the Series A Preferred Stock, in   31
addition to such other remedies as shall be available to the Holder   32
of such Preferred Stock, this corporation will take such corpo-   33
rate action as may, in the opinion of its counsel, be necessary to   34
increase its authorized but unissued shares of Common Stock to   35
such number of shares as shall be sufficient for such purposes.   36
37
(j)   *Notices.* Any notice required by the provisions of this   38
Section 3 to be given to the Holders of shares of Series A Pre-   39
ferred Stock shall be deemed given if deposited in the United   40

States mail, postage prepaid, and addressed to each Holder of
record at his address appearing on the books of this corporation.

4.   *Voting Rights.*

   (a)   *Election of Directors.*

      (i)   The Board of Directors shall consist of six mem-
bers. The Holders of the Series A Preferred Stock shall have
the right to elect two directors. The Holders of the Common
Stock shall have the right to elect two directors. The Holders of
Preferred Stock and the Holders of the Common Stock voting
as a single class shall have the right to elect two officers of the
corporation to serve as directors.

      (ii)   Each director shall be elected at the annual meeting
of shareholders and shall serve until his successor is elected and
qualified or until his earlier resignation or removal. Any director who shall have been elected by the Holders of Series A
Preferred Stock may be removed during his term of office, either
for or without cause, by and only by, the affirmative vote of the
Holders of a majority of the shares of the Series A Preferred Stock
who elected such director, given at a special meeting of such
shareholders duly called for that purpose, and any vacancy
thereby created may be filled by the Holders of the Series A Preferred Stock represented at that meeting. The two directors
elected by the Holders of the Series A Preferred Stock shall have
the sole and exclusive right to appoint, remove, and re-appoint
from time to time the Chief Executive Officer of the corporation.

   (b)   *Other Voting Rights.* Subject to (a) above, the Holder
of each share of Series A Preferred Stock shall have the right to
one vote for each share of Common Stock into which such Series A Preferred Stock could then be converted (with any
fractional share determined on an aggregate conversion basis
being rounded to the nearest whole share), and with respect to
such vote, such Holder shall have full voting rights and powers
equal to the voting rights and powers of the Holders of Common Stock, and shall be entitled, notwithstanding any provision
hereof, to notice of any shareholders' meeting in accordance

with the bylaws of this corporation, and shall be entitled to
vote, together with Holders of Common Stock, with respect to
any question upon which Holders of Common Stock have the
right to vote; provided however that, notwithstanding the foregoing, the Series A Preferred Stock shall not be entitled to vote
in the election of the two directors to be elected by the Holders
of Common Stock referred to in Section 4(a)(i) hereof.

5. *Protective Provisions.* So long as shares of Series A
Preferred Stock are outstanding, this corporation shall not without first obtaining the approval (by vote or written consent) of
the Holders of at least a majority of the then outstanding shares
of Series A Preferred Stock (voting in accordance with Section
4 above):

(a) sell, lease, convey, or otherwise dispose of any substantial part of its technology, property, or business, or merge
with or into or consolidate with any other corporation (other
than a wholly owned subsidiary corporation), or effect any transaction or series of related transactions in which more than 50
percent of the voting power of the corporation is disposed of;

(b) alter or change the rights, preferences, or privileges
of the shares of Series A Preferred Stock so as to affect adversely the shares;

(c) amend its Articles, except for the filing of Statements
of Reduction of Authorized Shares, or bylaws;

(d) create any new series of stock or any other securities convertible into equity securities of the corporation having
a preference over, or being on a parity with, the Series A Preferred Stock with respect to voting, dividends, liquidation rights,
or otherwise;

(e) do any act or thing which would result in taxation of
the Holders of shares of the Series A Preferred Stock under
Section 305 of the Internal Revenue Code of 1986, as amended
(or any comparable provision of the Internal Revenue Code as
hereafter from time to time amended);

(f)   issue any Additional Stock except for the issuance of up to 15,813 shares of Common Stock to employees of the Company pursuant to an employee benefit plan approved by the directors of the corporation;

(g)   adopt or amend any employee benefit plan or arrangement providing for compensation or benefits to any of the ten most highly compensated employees of, or consultants to, the Company; or

(h)   declare any dividend on any class or series of stock other than the Series A Preferred Stock, or repurchase shares of any class or series.

6.   *Status of Converted Stock.* In the event any shares of Series A Preferred Stock shall be converted pursuant to Section 3 hereof, the shares so converted shall be cancelled and shall not be reissuable by the corporation, and the Articles of this corporation shall be appropriately amended to affect the corresponding reduction in the corporation's authorized capital stock.

7.   *Redemption at Holder's Option.*

(a)   Upon the written request of a Holder of shares of Series A Preferred Stock given not earlier than the Redemption Date (hereinafter defined), for redemption of all or a part of the outstanding shares of Series A Preferred Stock, the corporation shall, within ten (10) days thereafter, send a notice (the "Redemption Notice") to all other Holders of Series A Preferred Stock of such request and of the total number of shares of Series A Preferred Stock which may then be redeemed by the corporation pursuant to this Section 7. Any Holder of shares of Series A Preferred Stock, within thirty (30) days after the Redemption Notice by the Company may elect to tender all or a part of his shares of Series A Preferred Stock for redemption pursuant to this Section 7 (such shares, so tendered, the "Redemption Shares"). Not earlier than thirty (30) days nor later than ninety (90) days after such notice by the Company, the Company shall redeem such Redemption Shares,

out of funds legally available therefor, by paying the Holder 1
of such shares an amount equal to $20.00 per each Redemp- 2
tion Share plus all accumulated but unpaid dividends on each 3
Redemption Share. 4

    (b) The Redemption Date shall be the earliest of the fol- 6
lowing dates or events: (i) five (5) years after closing; (ii) the 7
death of either Entrepreneur 1 or Entrepreneur 2; (iii) the fail- 8
ure to appoint on or before December 31, [of year of closing] a 9
Chief Executive Officer acceptable to the Holders of a majority 10
of the Series A Preferred Stock; (iv) the rejection by the Board 11
of Directors of three candidates for Chief Executive Officer pro- 12
posed by the Holders of a majority of the Series A Preferred 13
Stock; or (v) the failure of the Company to meet any of the fol- 14
lowing financial ratios or results, computed in accordance with 15
generally accepted accounting principles consistently applied, 16
at any time: (1) maintain a ratio of operating expenses to sales 17
of not more than 75 percent, 70 percent, and 67 percent during 18
the years ended December 31 [of year of closing and first and 19
second year after closing], respectively; (2) maintain a ratio of 20
current assets to current liabilities of at least 110 percent at all 21
times; (3) maintain a ratio of total debt to equity of not more 22
than 50 percent at all times; (4) achieve positive net income for 23
the three-month period ending December 31 [of the year of clos- 24
ing]; and (5) achieve net revenues of at least $2,500,000, 25
$4,900,000, and $6,800,000 in the years ended December 31 26
[first, second, and third year after closing], respectively. 27

    (c)   Except as described in this Section 7 the Series A 29
Preferred Stock shall not be redeemable by the corporation. 30

    (d)   *Common Stock.* 32

    1.   *Dividend Rights.* Subject to the prior rights of Hold- 34
ers of all classes of stock at the time outstanding having prior 35
rights as to dividends, the Holders of the Common Stock shall 36
be entitled to receive, when and as declared by the Board of 37
Directors, out of any assets of the corporation legally available 38
therefor, such dividends as may be declared from time to time 39
by the Board of Directors. 40

2. *Liquidation Rights.* Subject to the prior rights of Holders of all classes of stock at the time outstanding having prior rights as to liquidation, upon the liquidation, dissolution, or winding up of the corporation, the assets of the corporation shall be distributed to the Holders of Common Stock.

3. *Redemption.* The Common Stock is not redeemable.

4. *Voting Rights.* The Holder of each share of Common Stock shall have the right to one vote, and shall be entitled to notice of any shareholders' meeting in accordance with the by-laws of this corporation, and shall be entitled to vote upon such other matters and in such manner as may be provided by law.

SIXTH: *Bylaws.* The Board of Directors shall have the power, in addition to the shareholders, to make, alter, or repeal the bylaws of the corporation.

SEVENTH: *No Cumulative Voting.* The shareholders of the corporation shall not have the right to cumulate their votes for the election of directors of the corporation.

EIGHTH: *Action by Written Consent.* Any action which may be taken at a meeting of shareholders or of a class of share-holders may be taken without a meeting if a consent or consents in writing to such action, setting forth the action so taken, shall be signed by shareholders entitled to cast a majority (or such larger percentage as may at the time of such action be required by statute for the taking of action by shareholders without a meeting) of the votes which all such shareholders are entitled to cast thereon.

NINTH: *Reservation of Right to Amend.* The corporation reserves the right to amend, alter, change, or repeal any provi-sion contained in these Articles, in the manner now or hereafter prescribed by statute, and all rights conferred upon stockhold-ers are granted subject to this reservation.

EXHIBIT B OF APPENDIX 3

Notice: This agreement is a legally binding contract which governs, among other things, the terms of your employment and provides for the transfer to ABC, Inc. of rights in certain inventions you might make during the period of your employment. You should consult legal counsel to advise you of your obligations under this agreement.

ABC, INC.

EMPLOYEE AGREEMENT

In consideration of my employment or continued employment with ABC, INC. and the compensation received by me from time to time and the consummation by certain investors of the purchase of capital stock of the Company under a Preferred Stock Purchase Agreement, dated _____, between the Company and such investors, and intending to be legally bound, I hereby agree as follows:

1.   *Definitions.*

For the purposes of this Agreement, I hereby agree that:

(a)   "Company" means ABC, INC., a Pennsylvania corporation, and any of its subsidiaries and affiliates for or with which I may work or perform services;

(b)   "Proprietary Information" means any information created, discovered, or developed by, or otherwise become known to, the Company (including, without limitation, information created, discovered, developed by, or otherwise made known to me during the period of my employment with the Company) or in which property rights have been or may be assigned or otherwise conveyed to the Company, which information has commercial value in the business or planned future business of the Company from time to time; Proprietary Information includes, but is not limited to, formulae, functional specifications, data, processes, techniques, systems, computer programs, discoveries, designs, inventions, developments, im-

1 provements, marketing plans, strategies, forecasts, competi-
2 tive analyses, new products, unpublished financial statements,
3 budgets, projections, licenses, prices, costs, and customer and
4 supplier lists; and
5
6   (c)   "Invention" means any discovery, design, invention,
7 development, improvement, formula, process, technique, sys-
8 tem, computer program, know-how, or data, whether or not
9 patentable or registerable under copyright or similar statutes,
10 made, conceived, learned, or reduced to practice by me, either
11 alone or jointly with others, during the period of my employ-
12 ment that are related to or useful in the business of the
13 Company, result from tasks assigned to me by the Company,
14 or result from the use of premises or property (including com-
15 puter systems and laboratory facilities) owned, leased or
16 contracted for by the Company.
17
18 2.   *Proprietary Information.*
19
20   (a)   The Company shall be the sole owner of all Proprietary
21 Information and all patents, copyrights, trademarks, and other
22 rights related thereto. I agree that I will promptly disclose to
23 the Company all Proprietary Information developed by, or oth-
24 erwise made known to, me. I hereby assign to the Company all
25 rights I may have or acquire, during the period of my employ-
26 ment, in any Proprietary Information.
27
28   (b)   At all times, both during my employment with the Com-
29 pany and after its termination, I will keep in strictest confidence
30 and trust all Proprietary Information and will not use or dis-
31 close any Proprietary Information without the written consent
32 of the Company, except as may be necessary in the ordinary
33 course of performing my duties as an employee of the Com-
34 pany. I will not use Proprietary Information for my own or
35 another's benefit, either during my employment with the Com-
36 pany or after its termination.
37
38   (c)   To the extent that any such Proprietary Information
39 belongs to me, as a condition of my employment by the Com-
40 pany, I hereby transfer and assign forever to the Company and

its successors and assigns all of my right, title, and interest in
and to such Proprietary Information or inventions which relate in any manner to the business of the Company.

3.   *Inventions.*

(a)   I will promptly disclose all Inventions to the Company (or any persons designated by it). I will also promptly
disclose to the Company, and the Company hereby agrees to
receive all such disclosures in strict confidence and trust, all
other discoveries, designs, inventions, developments, improvements, formulae, processes, techniques, systems,
computer programs, know-how, or data, whether or not patentable or registrable under copyright or similar statutes,
made, conceived, learned, or reduced to practice by me, either alone or jointly with others, during the period of my
employment, for the purpose of permitting the Company to
determine in good faith whether they constitute "Inventions"
as defined in this Agreement.

(b)   The Company shall be the sole owner of all Inventions
and all patents, copyrights, trademarks, and other rights related thereto. I hereby assign to the Company all rights I may
have or acquire in such Inventions.

(c)   I will assist the Company in every reasonable way (but
at the Company's expense) to obtain, maintain, and enforce all
patents, copyrights, trademarks, and other rights and protections relating to Inventions in any and all countries. To that
end, I will sign all documents, supply all information, and do
all things (including the giving of evidence and testimony) that
the Company may consider necessary or desirable.

(d)   My obligation to assist the Company in obtaining, main-
taining, and enforcing patents, copyrights, trademarks, and
other rights and protections related to Inventions shall continue beyond the termination of my employment with the
Company, but the Company shall compensate me at a reasonable rate after my termination for time actually spent by me at
the Company's request on such assistance.

1   (e)   If the Company is unable, after reasonable effort, to
2 secure my signature on any document needed to apply for or
3 prosecute any patent, copyright, trademark, or other right or
4 protection relating to an Invention, whether by reason of my
5 physical or mental incapacity or for any other reason whatso-
6 ever other than a bona fide objection to such application or
7 prosecution (which shall mean a good faith belief that such
8 application or prosecution is illegal, wrongful, based on mis-
9 representations or fraud, or other similar reason), I hereby
10 irrevocably designate and appoint the Company and its duly
11 authorized officers and agents as my agents and attorneys-in-
12 fact, to act for and on my behalf to execute and file any such
13 application and to do all other lawful acts to further the pros-
14 ecution and issuance of patents, copyrights, trademarks, or
15 similar rights or protections thereon with the same legal force
16 and effect as if executed by me.
17
18   (f)   I represent that I have identified on Item 1 of Annex A
19 attached hereto all Inventions or improvements relevant to the
20 subject matter of my employment with the Company that have
21 been made, conceived, learned, or first reduced to practice by
22 me, alone or jointly with others, prior to my employment with
23 the Company and that I desire to remove from the operation of
24 this Agreement. I represent and warrant that such list is com-
25 plete. I agree that the Company is under no obligation at any
26 time based on any claim of right on my part because of any
27 listing on Annex A. If there is no such list on Annex A, I repre-
28 sent that I have made no such Inventions or improvements at
29 the time of signing this Agreement.
30
31   (g)   IF I AM A CALIFORNIA RESIDENT OR EMPLOYED
32 BY THE COMPANY IN CALIFORNIA, any provision in this
33 Agreement requiring me to assign my rights in any Invention
34 does not apply to an Invention that qualifies fully under the
35 provisions of Section 2870 of the California Labor Code. That
36 section provides that the requirement to assign "shall not ap-
37 ply to an Invention for which no equipment, supplies, facility,
38 or trade secret information of the employer was used and which
39 was developed entirely on the employee's own time, and (a)
40 which does not relate (1) to the business of the employer or (2)

to the employer's actual or demonstrably anticipated research
and development, or (b) which does not result from any work
performed by the employee for the employer." I understand that
I have the full burden of proving to the Company that an In-
vention qualifies fully under Section 2870. By signing this
Agreement, I acknowledge receipt of a copy of this Agreement
and of written notification of the provisions of Section 2870.
Notwithstanding the foregoing, I also assign to the Company
(or as directed by it) any rights I may have or acquire in any
Invention, full title to which is required to be in the United
States by a contract between the Company and the United
States or any of its agencies.

4.   *Documents, Materials, and Tangible Property.*

All documents, notes, drawings, specifications, computer programs, data, and other materials of any nature relating in any
way to any Proprietary Information or the business of the Company which are generated by me or come into my possession
from the Company or its consultants or affiliates shall be and
remain the exclusive property of the Company. I will not take
any of the foregoing, or any reproduction of any of the foregoing, and will return the same to the Company in the event of
the termination of my employment for any reason or at such
earlier time as requested by the Company.

5.   *Other Employment and Competitive Activities.*

During my employment, I will not engage in any other employment or plan, organize or engage in any other business (on either
a full-time or a part-time basis) without the Company's prior
written consent, which consent shall not be unreasonably withheld by the Company.

6.   *Publishing.*

I agree that, during the period of my employment with the Company, I will not publish anything relating to areas in which the
Company has an interest without the Company's prior written
consent.

7. *Prior Employment-Related Obligations.*

(a) I represent and warrant that my performance of all the terms of this Agreement and as an employee of the Company does not and will not breach any agreement to keep in confidence proprietary information acquired by me in confidence or in trust prior to my employment by the Company. I have not entered into and shall not enter into any agreement, either written or oral, in conflict herewith.

(b) I represent that I have identified on Item 2 of Annex A attached hereto all agreements (whether written or oral, express or implied) which I have executed or by which I am bound and which presently or in the future may affect my compliance with the terms of this Agreement or the scope and nature of the duties and responsibilities which may now or in the future be assigned to me by the Company. If there is no such list on Annex A, I represent that I have not executed and that I am not bound by any such agreement at the time of signing this Agreement.

8. *Proprietary Information of Others.*

I represent, as part of the consideration for the offer of employment extended to me by the Company and of my employment or continued employment by the Company, that I have not brought and will not bring with me to the Company or use in the performance of my responsibilities at the Company any materials or documents of a former employer that are not generally available to the public, unless express written authorization from the former employer for their possession and use has been obtained. I also understand that, in my employment with the Company, I am not to breach any obligation of confidentiality that I have to any former employer and agree to fulfill all such obligations during by employment with the Company.

9. *No Contract of Employment.*

I acknowledge that nothing contained in this agreement shall be deemed to require the Company to continue my employment.

I further acknowledge that, except as may be provided in a   1
written employment contract executed by a duly authorized   2
officer of the Company and approved by the Board of Directors   3
of the Company, I shall at all times be an employee-at-will of   4
the Company and the Company may discharge me at any time   5
for any reason, with or without cause, and with or without sev-   6
erance compensation.   7
 8
10.   *Employee Manuals, Etc.*   9
 10
From time to time, the Company may distribute employee   11
manuals or handbooks, and officers or other representatives of   12
the Company may make written or oral statements relating to   13
the Company's policies and procedures. Such manuals, hand-   14
books, and statements are intended only for the general   15
guidance of employees. No policies, procedures, or statements   16
of any nature by or on behalf of the Company (whether written   17
or oral, and whether or not contained in any formal employee   18
manual or handbook) shall be construed to modify this Agree-   19
ment or to create express or implied obligations to me of any   20
nature.   21
 22
11.   *Non-Competition.*   23
 24
I acknowledge that I have specialized knowledge and experi-   25
ence in the Company's business, that my reputation and   26
contacts within the industry are considered of great value to   27
the Company and that if my knowledge, experience, reputa-   28
tion, or contacts are used to compete with the Company, serious   29
harm to the Company may result. Thus, I agree that during   30
my employment by the Company and for a period of two (2)   31
years thereafter, I shall not, unless acting pursuant hereto or   32
with the prior written consent of the Board of Directors of the   33
Company, directly or indirectly: 34
 35
    (a)   solicit business from or perform services for, any per-   36
sons, company, or other entity, which at any time during my   37
employment by the Company is a client of the Company, if such   38
business or services are of the same general character as those   39
engaged in or performed by the Company;   40

1   (b)   solicit for employment or in any other fashion hire any
2 of the employees of the Company;
3
4   (c)   own, manage, operate, finance, join, control, or partici-
5 pate in the ownership, management, operation, financing or
6 control of, or be connected as an officer, director, employee, part-
7 ner, principal, agent, representative, consultant, or otherwise
8 with any business or enterprise engaged in any business or
9 activities which compete with or adversely affect any business
10 engaged in by the Company, in any state or jurisdiction of the
11 United States in which the Company or any of its affiliates is
12 doing business at the time of termination of employment; or
13
14   (d)   use, or permit my name to be used in connection with,
15 any business or enterprise engaged in any business or activi-
16 ties which compete with or adversely affect any business
17 engaged in by the Company; provided, however, that this pro-
18 vision shall not be construed to prohibit the ownership by me
19 of not more than one of any class of securities of any corpora-
20 tion which is engaged in any of the foregoing businesses having
21 a class of securities registered pursuant to the Securities Ex-
22 change Act of 1934. In the event that the provisions of this
23 Section should ever be adjudicated to exceed the time, geo-
24 graphic, service, or product limitations permitted by applicable
25 law in any jurisdiction, then such provisions shall be deemed
26 reformed in such jurisdiction to the maximum time, geographic,
27 service, or product limitations permitted by applicable law.
28
29 12.   *Equitable Relief.*
30
31 I acknowledge that the provisions of this Agreement are, in
32 view of the nature of the business of the Company, reasonable
33 and necessary to protect the legitimate interests of the Com-
34 pany, and that any violation of any provisions of those Sections
35 will result in irreparable injury to the Company. I also ac-
36 knowledge that the Company shall be entitled to temporary
37 and permanent injunctive relief, without the necessity of prov-
38 ing actual damages, and to an equitable accounting of all
39 earnings, profits, and other benefits arising from any such
40 violation, which rights shall be cumulative and in addition to

any other rights or remedies to which the Company may be
entitled. In the event of any such violation, the Company shall
be entitled to commence an action for temporary and permanent injunctive relief and other equitable relief in any court
of competent jurisdiction.

13.   *Miscellaneous.*

(a)   In the event that any provision of this Agreement is
held invalid or unenforceable by a court of competent jurisdiction, such provision shall be considered separate and apart from
the remainder of this Agreement, which shall remain in full
force and effect. In the event that any provision is held to be
over-broad as written, such provision shall be deemed amended
to narrow its application to the extent necessary to make the
provision enforceable according to applicable law and shall be
enforced as amended.

(b)   The waiver or failure of the Company to enforce any
violation or provision of this Agreement shall not constitute a
waiver of its rights hereunder with respect to any other violation or provision of this Agreement.

(c)   This Agreement and any disputes arising under or in
connection therewith shall be governed by the laws of the Commonwealth of Pennsylvania.

(d)   This Agreement shall inure to the benefit of and be binding upon and enforceable by the heirs, personal representatives,
successors, and assigns of the parties hereto and may be transferred by the Company to any successor or assign by merger,
consolidation, sale of assets, or otherwise. This Agreement shall
also inure to the benefit of and be binding upon and enforceable by any subsidiary or affiliate included within the meaning
of the term "Company."

(e)   I acknowledge that a violation of this Agreement will
result in harm to the Company, which will be difficult to assess
in terms of monetary damages, and agree that the remedy at
law for any breach of this Agreement shall be inadequate and

1 that the Company, in addition to any other relief available to
2 it, shall be entitled to temporary and permanent injunctive relief
3 and other equitable remedies without the necessity of proving
4 actual damages.

6   (f)   This Agreement sets forth the entire understanding of
7 the parties with respect to the subject matter of this Agree-
8 ment and shall not be amended or modified except by written
9 instrument duly executed by each of the parties hereto and
10 approved by the Board of Directors of the Company. Section
11 headings are for convenience of reference only and are not a
12 part of this Agreement.

14   (g)   I will provide (and the Company may similarly provide)
15 a copy of this Agreement to subsequent employers for whom I
16 may work.

18 I HAVE READ AND UNDERSTOOD THE FOREGOING
19 AGREEMENT, AND I UNDERSTAND THAT BY SIGNING I
20 AM AGREEING TO BE LEGALLY BOUND BY ALL OF THE
21 PROVISIONS OF THIS AGREEMENT.

23 WITNESS my hand and seal this _____ day of _____, _____.

27   Employee Signature

30   Address

33 Accepted for ABC, INC.:

35 By: _____

37 Title: _____

39 Date: _____

ANNEX A

ABC, INC.
3624 Market Street
Philadelphia, PA 19104

Dear Sir or Madam:

1. The following is a complete list of all inventions or improvements relevant to the subject matter of my employment by _____ (the "Company") that have been made, conceived, learned, or first reduced to practice by me alone or jointly with others prior to my engagement by the Company:

[ ] No inventions or improvements.

[ ] See below:

_____

_____

_____

_____

[ ] Additional sheets attached.

2. The following is a complete list of all agreements, which I have executed or by which I am bound, that presently or in the future may affect my compliance with the terms of the Employee Agreement between the Company and me or the scope and nature of the duties and responsibilities, which may now or in the future be assigned to me by the Company.

[ ] No agreements.

[ ] See below:

_____

_____

_____

_____

1   [ ]   Additional sheets attached.

2

3   3.   I propose to bring to my employment the following ma-
4 terials and documents of a former employer that are not
5 generally available to the public, which materials and docu-
6 ments may be used in my employment pursuant to the express
7 written authorization of my former employer (a copy of which
8 is attached hereto):

9

10   [ ]   No materials.

11

12   [ ]   See below:

13 _____

14 _____

15 _____

16 _____

17

18   [ ]   Additional sheets attached.

19

20   Very truly yours,

21

22   _____

23   Employee Signature

24

25

26

27

28

29

30

31

32

33

34

35

36

37

38

39

40

Exhibit C of Appendix 3   301

EXHIBIT C OF APPENDIX 3

ABC, INC.

STOCK RESTRICTION AGREEMENT

This Agreement is made as of _____, by and between ABC, INC., a Pennsylvania corporation (the "Company"), and _____ ("Stockholder"), with reference to the following Preamble:

> On the date hereof, the Stockholder owns of record and beneficially the number of shares (the "Shares") of the Company's Common Stock set forth after his name on the signature page hereof. In order to induce a group of investors to consummate the transactions contemplated by that certain Stock Purchase Agreement, of even date herewith, between the Company and such investors, and in view of the benefits which will redound to the Stockholder because of the consummation of such agreement, the Stockholder is willing to enter into and comply with the terms and provisions hereof.

In consideration of the Preamble and the mutual covenants and representations herein set forth and intending to be legally bound, the Company and the Stockholder agree as follows:

1.   *Purchase Option.*

(a)   The Stockholder hereby grants to the Company the right and option ("Purchase Option"), at the election of the Company in its sole discretion, to repurchase up to 60 percent of the Shares (the "Option Shares") as set forth in this Section 1. Upon the occurrence of a Termination (as hereinafter defined), the Company shall thereafter have the right, as provided in (b) below, to purchase from the Stockholder or the Stockholder's executors, administrators, or personal representative, as the case may be, at the purchase price per share of [$.01], being the purchase price originally paid therefor by the Stockholder

("Option Purchase Price"), a portion of the Option Shares computed as follows:

(i)   If the Termination giving rise to the right to exercise the Purchase Option occurs on or prior to the first anniversary of the date hereof, the Purchase Option shall apply to 100 percent of the Option Shares.

(ii)   If the Termination giving rise to the right to exercise the Purchase Option occurs after the first anniversary of the date hereof but on or prior to the second anniversary of the date hereof, the Purchase Option shall apply to 75 percent of the Option Shares.

(iii)   If the Termination giving rise to the right to exercise the Purchase Option occurs after the second anniversary of the date hereof but on or prior to the third anniversary of the date hereof, the Purchase Option shall apply to 50 percent of the Option Shares.

(iv)   If the Termination giving rise to the right to exercise the Purchase Option occurs after the third anniversary of the date hereof but on or prior to the fourth anniversary of the date hereof, the Purchase Option shall apply to 25 percent of the Option Shares.

(v)   After the fourth anniversary of the date hereof the Purchase Option shall be terminated.

(b)   Within 45 days following a Termination, the Company shall notify the Stockholder in writing as to whether it wishes to purchase the Option Shares pursuant to exercise of the Purchase Option. If the Company (or its assignee) elects to purchase the Option Shares, it shall set a date for the closing of the transaction at a place specified by the Company not later than 15 days from the date of such notice. At such closing, the Company (or its assignee) shall tender payment for the Option Shares and the certificates representing the Option Shares so purchased shall be cancelled and new certificates issued in the name of the Company or its assignee. The Stockholder hereby

Exhibit C of Appendix 3 303

authorizes and directs the Secretary or Transfer Agent of the 1
Company to transfer the Option Shares as to which the Pur- 2
chase Option has been exercised from the Stockholder to the 3
Company or its assignee. The Option Purchase Price may be 4
payable, at the option of the Company, in cancellation of all or 5
a portion of any outstanding indebtedness of Stockholder to 6
the Company or in cash (by check), or by a combination of both. 7

8

(c) The date of Termination shall be understood to be the 9
last day of the Stockholder's relationship with the Company as 10
director, officer, employee, or consultant and not the day upon 11
which the Stockholder or the Company may have given prior 12
notice of such event. 13

14

(d) The term "Termination" shall mean the occurrence of 15
one or more of the following events: 16

17

(i) the cessation of the Stockholder to be a director, of- 18
ficer, or employee of (or, pursuant to the terms of a written 19
consulting agreement, consultant to) the Company or any of 20
its subsidiaries due to the termination of such relationship by 21
the Stockholder for any reason other than the death or disabil- 22
ity of the Stockholder (as used herein the term "disability" shall 23
mean the inability of the Employed to perform his duties and 24
responsibilities to the Company to the full extent required by 25
the Board of Directors of the Company by reason of illness, 26
injury, or incapacity for 26 consecutive weeks, and in connec- 27
tion therewith the Stockholder agrees, in the event of any 28
dispute under this Section 1(d), to submit to a physical exami- 29
nation by a licensed physician selected by the Board of Directors 30
of the Company); 31

32

(ii) the cessation of the Stockholder to be a director, of- 33
ficer, or employee of (or, pursuant to the terms of a written 34
consulting agreement consultant to) the Company or any of its 35
subsidiaries due to the involuntary termination by the Com- 36
pany of the Stockholder on the grounds of cause (as used herein 37
the term "cause" shall mean (a) any failure of the Stockholder 38
to follow in any material respect the directions of the Board of 39
Directors of the Company which such Board in its reasonable 40

business judgment considers to be appropriate or to perform or
observe the terms of any agreements which the Stockholder
may have from time to time with the Company; (b) any dishon-
esty misconduct, habitual insobriety, substance abuse,
misappropriation of funds, or public disparagement of the Company or its management, shareholders, or key employees by
the Stockholder (c) the conviction of the employee for any crime
involving moral turpitude; or (d) any other proper cause as determined by the Board of Directors of the Company); or

(iii)   any sale, assignment, transfer, pledge, or disposition
or any attempted sale, assignment, transfer, pledge, or disposition of any nature of Shares subject to the Purchase Option.

2.   *Stock Splits, etc.* If, from time to time during the term
of this agreement:

(a)   there is any stock dividend or liquidating dividend of
cash and/or property, stock split, or other change in the character or amount of any of the outstanding securities of the
Company; or

(b)   there is any consolidation merger or sale of all, or substantially all, of the assets of the Company; then, in such event,
any and all new, substituted or additional securities or other
property to which Stockholder is entitled by reason of
Stockholder's ownership of Shares shall be immediately subject to this agreement and be included in the word "Shares" for
all purposes with the same force and effect as the Shares presently subject to this agreement. While the total Option Price
shall remain the same after each such event, the Option Price
per Share upon execution of the Purchase Option shall be appropriately adjusted.

3.   *Representations and Warranties.* The Stockholder
hereby represents and warrants that:

(a)   he has all requisite legal capacity to execute and deliver this Agreement; this Agreement has been duly and validly
executed and delivered by him; this Agreement is enforceable

EXHIBIT C OF APPENDIX 3   305

against him in accordance with its terms; the execution, deliv- 1
ery, and performance by him of his obligations under this 2
agreement do not conflict with, or result in a breach of, any 3
agreement, document, or instrument to which he is a party or 4
by which any of his assets are otherwise bound or affected; and 5

6

(b)   he owns the Shares of record and beneficially, free and 7
clear of any liens, claims, encumbrances, or other charges 8
thereon; and no person or entity has any right with respect to 9
the Shares, including without limitation any option thereon, 10
or right of first refusal or voting rights with respect thereto. 11

12

4.   *Share Legend.* The certificate or certificates represent- 13
ing the Shares shall bear the following legend, in addition to 14
any other legend required or advisable pursuant to applicable 15
Blue Sky laws: 16

17

> The shares represented by this certificate have not been 18
> registered under the Securities Act of 1933. Such shares 19
> have been acquired for investment and may not be sold, 20
> transferred, pledged, or hypothecated in the absence of 21
> an effective registration statement for such shares un- 22
> der the Securities Act of 1933, unless, in the opinion 23
> (which shall be in form and substance satisfactory to the 24
> company) of counsel satisfactory to the company, such 25
> registration is not required. 26

27

The shares represented by this certificate are also further sub- 28
ject to the provisions of a Stock Restriction Agreement dated 29
_____, as the same may be amended from time to time, a 30
copy of which is available for inspection at the principal offices 31
of the company, and, without limiting the generality of the fore- 32
going, no sale, assignment, transfer, or other disposition of these 33
shares shall be valid or effective unless made in compliance 34
with all of the terms and conditions of such agreement. 35

36

5.   *No Contract of Employment.* 37

38

(a)   Nothing contained in this Agreement shall be deemed to 39
require the Company to continue the Stockholder's employment. 40

1 Except as may be provided in a written employment contract
2 executed by a duly authorized officer of the Company and
3 approved by the Board of Directors of the Company, the
4 Stockholder shall at all times be an employee-at-will of the
5 Company and the Company may discharge the Stockholder
6 at any time for any reason, with or without cause, and with
7 or without severance compensation.
8
9   (b)   From time to time, the Company may distribute em-
10 ployee manuals or handbooks, and officers or other
11 representatives of the Company may make written or oral
12 statements relating to the Company's policies and procedures.
13 Such manuals, handbooks, and statements are intended only
14 for the general guidance of employees. No policies, procedures,
15 or statements of any nature by or on behalf of the Company
16 (whether written or oral, and whether or not contained in
17 any formal employee manual or handbook) shall be construed
18 to modify this Agreement (including without limitation Sec-
19 tion 5(a)) or to create express or implied obligations to the
20 Stockholder of any nature.
21
22 6.   *Escrow.* As security for the faithful performance of
23 the terms of this Agreement and to insure the availability
24 for delivery of the Stockholder's Shares upon exercise of the
25 Purchase Option provided for herein, the Stockholder agrees
26 to deliver to and deposit with the Secretary of the Company,
27 or such other person designated by the Company as Escrow
28 Agent ("Escrow Agent"), in this transaction, a Stock Assign-
29 ment duly endorsed (with date and number of shares blank)
30 in the form attached hereto as Annex A, together with the
31 certificate or certificates evidencing the Shares; said docu-
32 ments are to be held by the Escrow Agent and delivered by
33 said Escrow Agent pursuant to the Joint Escrow Instruc-
34 tions of the Company and the Stockholder set forth in Annex
35 C attached hereto, which instructions shall also be deliv-
36 ered to the Escrow Agent. Subject to the provisions of this
37 Agreement and the Joint Escrow Instructions, the Stock-
38 holder shall exercise all rights and privileges of a shareholder
39 of the Company with respect to the Shares deposited in said
40 escrow.

EXHIBIT C OF APPENDIX 3   307

7.   *Specific Performance.*   1

2

(a)   Because of the unique character of the Shares, the par- 3
ties hereto agree that they will be irreparably damaged in the 4
event that this Agreement is not specifically enforced. Should 5
any dispute arise concerning the sale or transfer of the Shares, 6
an injunction may be issued restraining any sale or transfer 7
pending the determination of such controversy. In the event of 8
any controversy concerning the right or obligation to purchase 9
or sell any of the Shares, such right or obligation shall be en- 10
forceable in a court of equity by a decree of specific performance. 11
Such remedy shall, however, be in addition to any other rem- 12
edies which the parties may have.   13

14

(b)   The Stockholder agrees that in the event of any viola- 15
tion of this Agreement, an action may be commenced by the 16
Company for any such preliminary and permanent injunctive 17
relief and other equitable relief in any court of competent ju- 18
risdiction in the Commonwealth of Pennsylvania or in any other 19
court of competent jurisdiction. The Stockholder hereby waives 20
any objections on the grounds of improper jurisdiction or venue 21
to the commencement of an action in the Commonwealth of 22
Pennsylvania and agrees that effective service of process may 23
be made upon him by mail under the Notice provisions con- 24
tained in Section 9 hereof.   25

26

8.   *Indemnification.* The Stockholder agrees to hold harm- 27
less and indemnify the Company for any and all liabilities 28
resulting to it through violation by the Stockholder of the war- 29
ranties and representations made by the Stockholder in, and 30
other provisions of, this Agreement.   31

32

9.   *Miscellaneous.*   33

34

(a)   This Agreement sets forth the entire understanding 35
between the parties hereto with respect to the subject matter 36
hereof and may only be changed by agreement in writing ex- 37
ecuted by the parties hereto.   38

39

(b)   The parties agree to execute such further instruments 40

1 and to take such further action as may reasonably be necessary to
2 carry out the intent of this Agreement.
3
4 (c) Any notice required or permitted hereunder shall be
5 given in writing and shall be deemed effectively given upon
6 personal delivery or upon deposit in the United States Post
7 Office, by registered or certified mail with postage and fees pre-
8 paid, addressed to the Stockholder at his address shown on the
9 Company's employment records and to the Company at the ad-
10 dress of its principal corporate offices (attention: President) or
11 at such other address as such party may designate by ten days'
12 advance written notice to the other party hereto.
13
14 (d) The Company may assign its rights and delegate its
15 duties under Section 1 hereof. This Agreement shall inure to
16 the benefit of the successors and in set forth, be binding upon
17 the Stockholder, his heirs, executors, administrators, succes-
18 sors, and assigns. Without limiting the generality of the
19 foregoing, the Stockholder agrees that any such assignees of
20 the Company's rights shall be intended third-party beneficia-
21 ries of this Agreement with all rights the Company would have
22 otherwise had hereunder.
23
24 (e) Captions in this Agreement are for convenience of ref-
25 erence only and shall not be considered in the construction
26 hereof. Words used herein, regardless of the number and gen-
27 der specifically used, shall be deemed and construed to include
28 any other number, singular or plural, and any other gender,
29 masculine, feminine, or neuter, as the context requires. Any
30 requirement of time made hereinabove shall be of the essence
31 of this Agreement.
32
33 10. *Governing Law.* This Agreement shall be construed in
34 accordance with and governed in all respects by the laws of the
35 Commonwealth of Pennsylvania.
36
37
38
39
40

Exhibit C of Appendix 3   309

IN WITNESS WHEREOF, the parties hereto have executed this   1
Agreement as of the day and year first above written.   2
                                                               3
                        ABC, INC.   4
                                                               5
                        By: _____   6
                                                               7
                        Title: _____   8
                                                               9
                        Stockholder:_____   10
                                                               11
                        _____   12
                        (Signature)   13
                                                               14
                        _____   15
                        (Please Print Name)   16
                                                               17
                                                               18
                        Address: 19
                                                               20
                        _____   21
                                                               22
                        _____   23
                                                               24
                        Number of Shares Owned: _____   25
                                                               26
                   CONSENT OF SPOUSE   27
                                                               28
The undersigned spouse of the Stockholder executing this Stock   29
Restriction Agreement irrevocably agrees that such spouse (and   30
such spouse's equitable or community property interests, if any, 31
in the Shares subject to this Agreement) shall be bound in all   32
respects by this Agreement, including without limitation any   33
exhibits or annexes hereto.   34
                                                               35
                        _____   36
                        Spouse of the Stockholder   37
                                                               38
                                                               39
                                                               40

ANNEX A

ASSIGNMENT SEPARATE FROM CERTIFICATE

FOR VALUE RECEIVED and pursuant to that certain Stock Restriction Agreement dated as of _____, hereby sells, assigns, and transfers unto _____ (____) shares of the Common Stock of ABC, INC., a Pennsylvania corporation, standing in the undersigned's name on the books of said corporation represented by certificate No. ___ herewith, and do hereby irrevocably constitute and appoint _____ attorney to transfer, solely for purposes of facilitating the exercise by the Company of its rights set forth in the Stock Purchase Agreement to which this Assignment is attached as Annex A, said stock on the books of the corporation, with full power of substitution in the premises.

Dated: _____

_____
(Signature)

_____
(Please Print Name)

Exhibit C of Appendix 3   311

ANNEX B

JOINT ESCROW INSTRUCTIONS

Secretary
ABC, INC.

Dear Sir or Madam:

As Escrow Agent for both ABC, INC., a Pennsylvania corporation (the "Company") and the undersigned owner of stock of the Company (the "Stockholder"), you are hereby authorized and directed to hold the documents delivered to you pursuant to the terms of that certain Stock Restriction Agreement ("Agreement"), dated as of _____, to which a copy of these Joint Escrow Instructions is attached as Annex B, in accordance with the following instructions:

1.   In the event the Company or any assignee of the Company (referred to collectively for convenience herein as the "Company") exercises the Purchase Option set forth in the Agreement, the Company shall give to the Stockholder and you a written notice specifying the number of shares of stock to be purchased, the purchase price, and the time for a closing hereunder at the principal office of the Company. The Stockholder and the Company hereby irrevocably authorize and direct you to close the transaction contemplated by such notice in accordance with the terms of said notice.

2.   At the closing, you are directed (a) to complete and date the stock assignments necessary for the transfer in question, and (b) to deliver such stock assignment, together with the certificate evidencing the shares of stock to be transferred, to the Company against the simultaneous delivery to you of the purchase price as contemplated in the Agreement for the number of shares of stock being purchased pursuant to the exercise of the Purchase Option.

3. The Stockholder irrevocably authorizes the Company to deposit with you any certificates evidencing shares of stock to be held by you hereunder and any additions and substitutions to said shares as defined in the Agreement. The Stockholder does hereby irrevocably constitute and appoint you as his attorney-in-fact and agent for the term of this escrow to execute with respect to such securities all documents necessary or appropriate to make such securities negotiable and to complete any transaction herein contemplated. Subject to the provisions of this Section 3, the Stockholder shall exercise all rights and privileges of a stockholder of the Company while the stock is held by you.

4. Upon written request of the Stockholder after each successive one-year period from the Commencement Date set forth in Section 1 of the Agreement, unless the Purchase Option has been exercised, you will deliver to the Stockholder a certificate or certificates representing so many shares of stock as are not then subject to the Purchase Option. Ninety days after the occurrence of a Termination as defined in the Agreement, you will deliver to the Stockholder a certificate or certificates representing the aggregate number of shares sold and issued pursuant to the agreement and not purchased by the Company or its assignees pursuant to exercise of the Purchase Option.

5. If at the time of termination of this escrow you should have in your possession any documents, securities, or other property belonging to the Stockholder, you shall deliver all of the same to the Stockholder and shall be charged of all further obligations hereunder.

6. Your duties hereunder may be altered, amended, modified, or revoked only by a writing signed by all of the parties hereto.

7. You shall be obligated only for the performance of such duties as are specifically set forth herein and may rely and shall be protected in relying or refraining from acting on any instrument reasonably believed by you to be genuine and to have been signed or presented by the proper party or parties. You shall not be personally liable for any act you may do or omit to do hereunder as Escrow Agent or as attorney-in-fact for

EXHIBIT C OF APPENDIX 3 313

the Stockholder while acting in good faith and in the exercise 1
of your own good judgment, and any act done or omitted by you 2
pursuant to the advice of an attorney shall be conclusive evi- 3
dence of such good faith. 4

5

8. You are hereby expressly authorized to disregard any 6
and all earnings given by any of the parties hereto or by any 7
other person or corporation excepting only orders or process of 8
courts of law, and are hereby expressly authorized to comply 9
with and obey orders, judgments, or decrees of any court. In 10
case you obey or comply with any such order, judgment, or de- 11
cree, you shall not be liable to any of the parties hereto or to 12
any other person, firm, or corporation by reason of such com- 13
pliance, not withstanding any such order, judgment, or decree 14
being subsequently reversed, modified, annulled, set aside, 15
vacated, or found to have been entered without jurisdiction. 16

17

9. You shall not be liable in any respect on account of the 18
identity, authorities, or rights of the parties executing or deliv- 19
ering or purporting to execute or deliver the Agreement or any 20
documents or papers deposited or called for hereunder. 21

22

10. You shall not be liable for the outlawing of any rights 23
under the Statute of Limitations with respect to these Joint 24
Escrow Instructions or any documents deposited with you. 25

26

11. You shall be entitled to employ such legal counsel and 27
other experts as you may deem necessary properly to advise 28
you in connection with your obligations hereunder, may rely 29
upon the advice of such counsel, and may pay such counsel 30
reasonable compensation therefor. 31

32

12. Your responsibilities as Escrow Agent hereunder shall 33
terminate if you shall cease to be Secretary of the Company or 34
if you shall resign by written notice to each party. In the event 35
of any such termination, the Company shall appoint a succes- 36
sor Escrow Agent. 37

38

13. If you reasonably require other or further instru- 39
ments in connection with these Joint Escrow Instructions or 40

1 obligations in respect hereto, the necessary parties hereto shall
2 join in furnishing such instruments.
3
4   14. It is understood and agreed that should any dispute arise
5 with respect to the delivery and/or ownership or right of posses-
6 sion of the securities held by you hereunder, you are authorized
7 and directed to retain in your possession without liability to any-
8 one all or any part of said securities until such disputes shall
9 have been settled either by mutual written agreement of the
10 parties concerned or by a final order, decree, or judgment of a
11 court of competent jurisdiction after the time for appeal has ex-
12 pired and no appeal has been perfected, but you shall be under
13 no duty whatsoever to institute or defend any such proceedings.
14
15   15. Any notice required or permitted hereunder shall be
16 given in writing and shall be deemed effectively given upon
17 personal delivery or upon deposit in the United States Post
18 Office, by registered or certified mail with postage and fees
19 prepaid, addressed to each of the other parties thereunto en-
20 titled at the following addresses, or at such other addresses as
21 a party may designate by ten days' advance written notice to
22 each of the other parties hereto.
23
24
25   Company: ABC, INC.
26   Philadelphia, PA 19104
27   Stockholder: _____
28   _____
29   _____
30
31   ESCROW AGENT: Secretary
32   c/o ABC, INC.
33   Philadelphia, PA 19104
34
35   16. By signing these Joint Escrow Instructions, you become
36 a party hereto only for the purpose of said Joint Escrow In-
37 structions; you do not thereby become a party to the Agreement.
38
39   17. This Agreement sets forth the entire Understanding be-
40 tween the parties hereto with respect to the subject matter

Exhibit C of Appendix 3   315

hereof and may only be changed by agreement in writing executed by the parties hereto.

18.   This Agreement shall inure to the benefit of the successors and assigns of the Company and, subject to the restrictions
on transfer herein set forth, be binding upon the Stockholder,
his heirs, executors, administrators, successors, and assigns.

19.   Words used herein, regardless of the number and gender specifically used, shall be deemed and construed to include
any other number, singular or plural, and any other gender,
masculine, feminine, or neuter, as the context requires.

20.   This Instrument shall be construed in accordance with
and governed in all respects by the laws of the Commonwealth
of Pennsylvania.

IN WITNESS WHEREOF, the parties hereto, intending to be
legally bound have executed these Joint Escrow Instructions
as of the day and year first above written.

ABC, INC.

By: _____

Title: _____

Stockholder: _____

_____
(Signature)

_____
(Please Print Name)

ACCEPTED AND AGREED TO:
ESCROW AGENT:

_____

1   **EXHIBIT D OF APPENDIX 3**
2
3   ABC, INC.
4
5   STOCKHOLDERS' AGREEMENT
6
7   AGREEMENT, dated _____, by and among ABC,
8   INC., a Pennsylvania corporation (the "Company"), those per-
9   sons who are current holders of Common Stock of the Company
10   who are identified on the signature pages hereof as being the
11   Current Holders (the "Current Holders"), and those persons who
12   are purchasing shares of Series A Convertible Preferred Stock of
13   the Company contemporaneously with the execution hereof who
14   are identified on the signature pages hereof as being the Inves-
15   tors (the "Investors"), with reference to the following Preamble:
16
17   Each Current Holder presently owns the number of shares
18   of the Common Stock of the Company set forth opposite
19   their name on Annex A hereto and may in the future ac-
20   quire, or obtain the right to acquire, additional equity
21   securities of the Company (all such shares and equity se-
22   curities, the "Current Holder Shares"). The Investors are
23   acquiring simultaneously herewith an aggregate of 50,000
24   shares of Series A Convertible Preferred Stock pursuant to
25   a Stock Purchase Agreement, of even date herewith (the
26   "Purchase Agreement"), by and among the Investors and
27   the Company (all such shares and the Common Stock into
28   which they are convertible, the "Investor Shares"). The
29   Current Holders and the Investors (together, the "Stock-
30   holders") wish to place certain restrictions on the Current
31   Holder Shares and the Investor Shares to the extent pro-
32   vided for herein as required by the Purchase Agreement.
33
34   NOW, THEREFORE, in consideration of the mutual cov-
35   enants herein contained and other valuable consideration, the
36   receipt and sufficiency of which is hereby acknowledged, the
37   Stockholders, intending to be legally bound, agree as follows:
38
39   1.   *Prohibited Transfers.* None of the Current Holders shall
40   sell, assign, transfer, pledge, hypothecate, mortgage, or dispose

of, by gift or otherwise, or in any way encumber, all or any part 1
of the Shares owned by him except in compliance with the terms 2
of this Agreement. With respect to Current Holder Shares, if 3
any, owned by the Current Holders which are subject to repur- 4
chase rights of the Company, the provisions of Sections 2 and 3 5
shall only apply to such Shares as the Company does not elect 6
to repurchase. 7

8
2.   *Right of First Refusal on Dispositions.* 9

10
(a)   If at any time any of the Current Holders wishes to sell 11
all or any part of the Current Holder Shares owned by him, 12
such Stockholder (the "Offeror") shall submit a written offer to 13
sell such Current Holder Shares to the Company on terms and 14
conditions, including price, not less favorable to the Company 15
than those on which the Offeror proposes to sell such Shares to 16
any other purchaser (the "Offer"). The Offer shall disclose the 17
identity of the proposed purchaser or transferee, the Shares 18
proposed to be sold, the terms of the sale, any amounts owed to 19
the Company with respect to such Shares, and any other mate- 20
rial facts relating to the sale; and copies of the Offer shall be 21
sent to each Investor who holds at least ten percent of the ag- 22
gregate number of shares of Series A Preferred Stock and 23
Common Stock issued upon conversion thereof (adjusted to re- 24
flect subsequent changes after the date hereof in the number 25
of shares of Common Stock outstanding by reason of stock divi- 26
dends, stock splits, or recapitalizations, or the like) purchased 27
by all of the Investors under the Purchase Agreement (collec- 28
tively the "Offerees" and individually an "Offeree"). The 29
Company shall have the right to accept the Offer as to all or 30
any part of the Shares covered thereby. The Company shall act 31
upon the Offer as soon as practicable after receipt thereof, and 32
in all events within thirty (30) days after receipt thereof. In the 33
event that the Company shall elect on a timely basis to pur- 34
chase all or part of the Shares covered by the Offer, the Company 35
shall communicate in writing such election to purchase to the 36
Offeror, which communication shall be delivered by hand or 37
mailed to the Offeror at the address set forth in Section 10 38
below and shall, when taken in conjunction with the Offer, be 39
deemed to constitute a valid, legally binding, and enforceable 40

1 agreement for the sale and purchase of the Shares covered
2 thereby.
3
4   (b)   If the Company rejects the Offer or does not respond
5 thereto within such 30-day period, the Offeror shall notify all
6 Offerees, each of whom shall have the right to purchase that
7 number of Shares covered by the Offer as shall be equal to the
8 aggregate number of Shares covered by the Offer multiplied by
9 a fraction, the numerator of which shall be the number of Shares
10 then owned by such Offeree and the denominator of which shall
11 be the aggregate number of Shares then owned by all of the
12 Offerees. (The amount of Shares that each Offeree is entitled
13 to purchase under this Section 2 shall be referred to as its "Pro
14 Rata Fraction.") In the event an Offeree does not elect to pur-
15 chase its Pro Rata Fraction, then any Offeree who elects to
16 purchase its Pro Rata Fraction shall have the right to purchase,
17 on a pro rata basis with any other Offerees who so elect, any
18 Pro Rata Fraction or portion thereof not purchased by an Of-
19 feree. Each Offeree shall act upon the Offer as soon as
20 practicable after receipt of notice of the rejection thereof by the
21 Company, and in all events within thirty (30) days after receipt
22 of such notice. Each Offeree shall have the right to accept the
23 Offer as to all or any part of the Shares offered thereby. In the
24 event that an Offeree shall elect on a timely basis to purchase
25 all or part of the Shares covered by the Offer, said Offeree shall
26 individually communicate in writing such election to purchase
27 to the Offeror, which communication shall be delivered by hand
28 or mailed to the Offeror at the address set forth in Section 10
29 below and shall, when taken in conjunction with the Offer, be
30 deemed to constitute a valid, legally binding, and enforceable
31 agreement for the sale and purchase of the Shares covered
32 thereby (subject to the aforesaid limitations as to an Offeree's
33 right to purchase more than its Pro Rata Fraction).
34
35   (c)   In the event that the Company and the Offerees do not
36 purchase all of the Shares offered by the Offeror pursuant to
37 the Offer, the Shares not so purchased may be sold by the Off-
38 eror at any time within ninety (90) days after the expiration of
39 the Offer, subject to the provisions of Section 3 below. Any such
40 sale shall be to the same proposed purchaser or transferee, at

not less than the price and upon other terms and conditions, if   1
any, not more favorable to the purchaser than those specified   2
in the Offer. Any Shares not sold within such 90-day period   3
shall continue to be subject to the requirements of a prior offer   4
pursuant to this Section. In the event that Shares are sold pur-   5
suant to this Section to any purchaser other than a Stockholder,   6
said Shares shall no longer be entitled to the benefits conferred   7
by, or subject to the restrictions imposed by, this Agreement.   8
   9
3.   *Right of Participation in Sales.* If at any time any of the   10
Current Holders wishes to sell any Shares owned by him ("Sell-   11
ing Party") to any person or entity other than one or more of the   12
Investors (the "Purchaser"), each of the Investors shall have the   13
right to offer for sale to the Purchaser, as a condition of such sale   14
by the Selling Party, at the same price per Share and on the   15
same terms and conditions as involved in such sale by the Sell-   16
ing Party, the same proportion of the Shares owned by the   17
Investor as the proposed sale represents with respect to said   18
Shares then owned by such Selling Party. Each Investor desir-   19
ing so to participate in any such sale shall notify the Selling   20
Party of such intention as soon as practicable after receipt of the   21
Offer made pursuant to Section 2, and in all events within thirty   22
(30) days after receipt thereof. In the event that an Investor shall   23
elect to participate in such sale by the Selling Party, said Party   24
shall individually communicate such election to the Selling Party,   25
which communication shall be delivered by hand or mailed to   26
such Selling Party at the address set forth in Section 10 below.   27
The Selling Party and each participating Party shall sell to the   28
Purchaser all or, at the option of the Purchaser, any part of the   29
Shares proposed to be sold by them at not less than the price per   30
Share and upon other terms and conditions, if any, not more   31
favorable to the Purchaser than those in the Offer provided by   32
the Selling Party under Section 2 above; provided, however, that   33
any purchase of less than all of such Shares by the Purchaser   34
shall be made from the Selling Party and each participating   35
Stockholder pro rata based upon the number of Shares proposed   36
to be sold by each. Any Shares sold by a Stockholder (including   37
Shares sold by the Selling Party) pursuant to this Section 3 shall   38
no longer be entitled to the benefits conferred by, or subject to   39
the restrictions imposed by, this Agreement. As a condition to   40

1 selling Shares to the Purchaser pursuant to this Section 3, all
2 Shares to be sold by the Current Holders shall be fully paid and
3 vested Shares.
4
5 4.   *Permitted Transfers.* Anything herein to the contrary
6 notwithstanding, the provisions of Sections 1, 2, and 3 shall
7 not apply to: (a) any transfer of Shares by a Current Holder by
8 gift or bequest or through inheritance to, or for the benefit of,
9 any member or members of such Current Holder's immediate
10 family; or (b) any transfer of Shares by a Current Holder to a
11 trust in respect of which such Stockholder serves as trustee,
12 provided that the trust instrument governing said trust shall
13 provide that such Stockholder, as trustee, shall retain sole and
14 exclusive control over the voting and disposition of said Shares
15 until the termination of this Agreement. In the event of any
16 such transfer, the transferee of the Shares shall hold the Shares
17 so acquired with all the rights conferred by, and subject to all
18 the restrictions imposed by, this Agreement and shall be deemed
19 a Current Holder for all purposes hereof.
20
21 5.   *Market Standoff.* Each Stockholder hereby agrees that
22 if so requested by the Company or any representative of the
23 underwriters in connection with any registration of any securi-
24 ties of the Company under the Securities Act of 1933, as
25 amended (the "Act"), the Stockholder shall not sell or other-
26 wise transfer any Shares or other securities of the Company
27 during the 90-day period following the effective date of a regis-
28 tration statement of the Company filed under the Act; provided,
29 however, that such restriction shall only apply to the first reg-
30 istration statements of the Company to become effective under
31 the Act which include securities to be sold on behalf of the Com-
32 pany to the public in an underwritten public offering under the
33 Act. The Company may impose stop-transfer instructions with
34 respect to securities subject to the foregoing restrictions until
35 the end of such 90-day period.
36
37 6.   *Board of Directors.* The Stockholders agree to vote
38 their shares of the Company's Common Stock and Series A
39 Preferred Stock and any other shares of voting securities of
40 the Company now owned or hereafter acquired or controlled

by them (collectively, the "Voting Stock"), and otherwise to use 1
their best efforts as shareholders or directors of the Company, 2
to set and maintain the number of directors of the Company at 3
no more than six and to elect and maintain as members of the 4
Board of Directors: (i) two designees of the holders of a major- 5
ity of the outstanding Series A Preferred Stock; (ii) two designees 6
of the holders of a majority of the outstanding Common Stock; 7
and (iii) two persons who are officers of the Company and who 8
are approved as directors by the holders of a majority of the 9
outstanding Common Stock and the holders of a majority of 10
the outstanding Series A Preferred Stock. In the event of any 11
vacancy on the Board of Directors, each stockholder covenants 12
and agrees that it shall vote a sufficient number of shares of 13
Voting Stock in accordance with the procedure described above 14
in order to fill such vacancy. 15
  16
7.   *Director Indemnification.* In the event that any direc- 17
tor elected pursuant to the terms of this agreement shall be 18
made or threatened to be made a party to any action, suit, or 19
proceeding with respect to which he may be entitled to indem- 20
nification by the Company pursuant to its corporate charter, 21
bylaws, or otherwise, he shall be entitled to be represented in 22
such action, suit, or proceeding by counsel of his choice and the 23
expenses of such presentation shall be reimbursed by the Com- 24
pany and such director shall be entitled to indemnification by 25
the Company to the full extent permitted by law. 26
  27
8.   *Sale Agreement.* The Current Holders agree to join at 28
any time in any agreement to which the holders of a majority 29
of the outstanding Investor Shares are parties at any time pro- 30
viding for the sale of the capital stock of the Company to any 31
third party under which the Current Holders will sell the Cur- 32
rent Holder Shares to such third party on the same terms and 33
conditions (on a per common share basis) as those terms and 34
conditions under which such holders agree to sell their shares 35
of the Company's Series A Preferred Stock. The Current Hold- 36
ers acknowledge that their agreement pursuant to this Section 37
8 is for the benefit of, and may be enforced by, the holders of a 38
majority of the shares of the Company's Series A Convertible 39
Preferred Stock. The Current Holders also acknowledge that 40

1 this Section 8 shall in no way limit, diminish, or modify the
2 rights of the Investor or Company to purchase the Current
3 Holder Shares under any other Section of this Agreement or
4 any other agreement to which such Current Holder is a party,
5 or require the Investor to include any of the Current Holder
6 Shares in any sale by the Investors of the Investor Shares.
7
8 9.   *Termination.* This Agreement, and the respective rights
9 and obligations of the Stockholders hereto, shall terminate upon
10 the earliest to occur of the following: (i) the expiration of ten
11 (10) years from the date of this Agreement or (ii) the consum-
12 mation of the Company's sale of its Common Stock in a bona
13 fide, firm commitment underwriting pursuant to a registra-
14 tion statement on Form 5-1 under the Securities Act of 1933,
15 as amended (or any equivalent successor form), the public of-
16 fering price of which was not less than $120.00 per share
17 (adjusted to reflect subsequent stock dividends, stock splits, or
18 recapitalization) and the net proceeds to the Company of which
19 was not less than $5,000,000.
20
21 10.   *Termination of Existing Agreements.* By their execution
22 hereof, the Current Holders hereby terminate any existing
23 agreements among them with respect to the capital stock of
24 the Company, and all rights and obligations thereunder of any
25 of the parties thereto.
26
27 11.   *Notices.* All notices and other communications hereun-
28 der shall be in writing and shall be deemed to have been given
29 when delivered or mailed by first-class, registered, or certified
30 mail, postage prepaid, to each Stockholder at his respective ad-
31 dress set forth on the signature pages hereof, or to such other
32 address as the addressee shall have furnished to the other Stock-
33 holders hereto in the manner prescribed by this Section 11.
34
35 12.   *Specific Performance.* The rights of the Stockholders
36 under this Agreement are unique and, accordingly, the Stock-
37 holders shall, in addition to such other remedies as may be
38 available to any of them at law or in equity, have the right to
39 enforce their rights hereunder by actions for specific perfor-
40 mance to the extent permitted by law.

13. *Legend.* The certificates representing the Shares sub- 1
ject to this Agreement shall bear on their face a legend indicating 2
the existence of the restrictions imposed hereby. 3

4

14. *Entire Agreement.* This Agreement constitutes the en- 5
tire agreement among the Parties with respect to the subject 6
matter hereof and supersedes all prior agreements and under- 7
standing between them or any of them as to such subject matter. 8

9

15. *Waivers and Further Agreements.* Any waiver by any 10
party of a breach of any provision of this Agreement shall not 11
operate or be construed as a waiver of any subsequent breach 12
of that provision or of any other provision hereof. Each of the 13
parties hereto agrees to execute all such further instruments 14
and documents and to take all such further action as any other 15
Party may reasonably require in order to effectuate the terms 16
and purposes of this Agreement. 17

18

16. *Amendments.* Except as otherwise expressly provided 19
herein, this Agreement may not be amended except by an in- 20
strument in writing executed by (a) all of the Current Holders 21
and (b) Investors owning a majority of the Shares then owned 22
by all Investors. 23

24

17. *Assignment; Successor and Assigns.* This Agreement 25
shall be binding upon and shall inure to the benefit of the Stock- 26
holders and their respective heirs, executors, legal 27
representative, successors, and permitted transferees, except 28
as may be expressly provided otherwise herein. 29

30

18. *Severability.* In case any one or more of the provisions 31
contained in this Agreement shall for any reason be held to be 32
invalid, illegal, or unenforceable in any respect, such invalidity, 33
illegality, or unenforceability shall not affect any other provision 34
of this Agreement and such invalid, illegal, and unenforceable 35
provision shall be reformed and construed so that it will be valid, 36
legal, and enforceable to the maximum extent permitted by law. 37

38

19. *Counterparts.* This Agreement may be executed in two or 39
more counterparts, each of which shall be deemed an original, 40

but all of which together shall constitute one and the same instrument.

20.   *Section Headings.* The headings contained in this Agreement are for reference purposes only and shall not in any way affect the meaning or interpretation of this Agreement

21.   *Governing Law.* This Agreement shall be governed by and construed and enforced in accordance with the laws of the Commonwealth of Pennsylvania.

22.   *Aggregation of Stock.* All shares of Series A Preferred Stock and Common Stock issued upon conversion thereof which is held or acquired by affiliated entities or persons shall be aggregated together for the purpose of determining the availability of any rights under this Agreement.

IN WITNESS WHEREOF, the undersigned have executed this Agreement as a sealed instrument as of the day and year first above written.

The Company: ABC, INC.

By: _____
Title: _____

The Current Holders:

By: _____
As its: _____

The Investors:

By: _____
As its: _____

EXHIBIT E OF APPENDIX 3

EMPLOYMENT AGREEMENT

EMPLOYMENT AGREEMENT (the "Agreement") dated as of _____, by and between ABC, INC., a Pennsylvania corporation (the "Company"), and _____ (the "Employee").

WHEREAS, Employee desires to be employed by the Company upon the terms and conditions hereinafter set forth; and

WHEREAS, the Company desires to employ Employee upon the terms and conditions hereinafter set forth;

WHEREAS, the execution of this Employment Agreement is a condition to the Stock Purchase Agreement, dated _____ (the "Purchase Agreement"), between the Company and the investors described therein;

NOW, THEREFORE, the parties hereto, intending to be legally bound, agree as follows:

1.   *Employment.* The Company hereby employs Employee, and Employee hereby accepts such employment and agrees to perform his duties and responsibilities hereunder, in accordance with the terms and conditions hereinafter set forth.

1.1.   *Employment Term.* The employment term of this Agreement (the "Employment Term") shall commence as of the date hereof and shall continue for a period of two (2) years unless terminated prior thereto in accordance with Section 8 hereof. Notwithstanding anything to the contrary set forth in this Agreement, this Agreement (and the attached Stock Option Agreement) shall be null and void and of no further effect unless and until there shall have been a closing under the Purchase Agreement prior to ninety (90) days from the date thereof.

1.2.   *Duties and Responsibilities.*

(a)   During the Employment Term, the Employee shall serve as_____ of the Company and shall perform all duties and accept all responsibilities incidental to such position or as may be assigned to him by the Company's Board of Directors, and he shall cooperate fully with the Board of Directors and other executive officers of the Company. The scope of the Employee's authority shall at all times be subject to the direction of the Board of Directors of the Company.

(b)   The Employee represents and covenants to the Company that he is not subject or a party to any employment agreement, non-competition covenant, non-disclosure agreement or any similar agreement, covenant, understanding, or restriction that would prohibit the Employee from executing this Agreement and performing his duties and responsibilities hereunder, or that would in any manner, directly or indirectly, limit or affect the duties and responsibilities that may now or in the future be assigned to the Employee by the Company.

(c)   The Employee shall at all times comply with policies and procedures adopted by the Company for its employees, including without limitation the procedures and policies adopted by the Company regarding conflicts of interest, but only to the extent such policies are not in conflict with the express provisions of this Agreement.

1.3.   *Extent of Service.* During the Employment Term, the Employee agrees to use his best efforts to carry out his duties and responsibilities under Section 1.2 hereof and to devote his full professional time, attention, and energy thereto. Except as provided in Section 5 hereof, the foregoing shall not be construed as preventing the Employee from making investments in other businesses or enterprises provided that the Employee agrees not to become engaged in any other business activity that may interfere with his ability to discharge his duties and responsibilities to the Company. The Employee further agrees not to work either on a part-time or independent contracting basis for any other business or enterprise during the Employment Term without the prior

written consent of Board of Directors. The Employee further agrees   1
not to serve as an officer or director of any other business or enter- 2
prise without the prior written consent of the Board of Directors   3
of the Company, and not to work in any other capacity for any   4
other business or enterprise without promptly notifying the Board   5
of Directors of the Company.   6
                                                                        7
1.4.   *Base Compensation.* For all the services rendered by the   8
Employee hereunder, the Company shall pay the Employee an an-   9
nual salary at the rate of $ _____ for each full year of the   10
Employment Term, plus such additional amounts, if any, as may be   11
approved by the Company's Board of Directors, less withholding   12
required by law or agreed to by the Employee, payable in install-   13
ments at such times as the Company customarily pays its other   14
senior officers (but in any event no less often than monthly). The   15
Company agrees that the Employee's salary will be reviewed at least   16
annually by the Company's Board of Directors to determine if an   17
increase (but not a decrease) is appropriate, which increase shall be 18
in the sole discretion of the Company's Board of Directors. During   19
the Employment Term, Employee shall also be entitled to partici-   20
pate in such vacation pay and other fringe benefit plans as may   21
exist from time to time for the senior officers of the Company. The   22
Employee alone, and not the Company, shall be responsible for the   23
payment of all federal, state, and local taxes in respect of the pay- 24
ments to be made and benefits to be provided under this Agreement   25
or otherwise (except to the extent withheld by the Company).   26
                                                                        27
1.5.   *Incentive Compensation.* In addition to the compensa-   28
tion set forth in Section 1.4 hereof, the Employee shall be   29
entitled to participate in an annual bonus plan providing for   30
the payment of annual bonuses equal to 25 percent of the   31
Employee's salary if the Company achieves performance goals   32
set annually by the Compensation Committee of the Company's   33
Board of Directors in the exercise of their sole discretion.   34
                                                                        35
2.   *Expenses.* Employee shall be reimbursed for the rea-   36
sonable business expenses incurred by him in connection with   37
his performance of services hereunder during the Employment   38
Term upon presentation of an itemized account and written   39
proof of such expenses.   40

3.   *Proprietary Information; Non-Disclosure and Non-Competition.* In connection with his employment by the Company hereunder, and ancillary to the commencement of such employment, the Employee has also executed the agreement attached hereto, which agreement is expressly made a part of this Agreement.

4.   *Termination.* This Agreement shall terminate prior to the expiration of its term set forth in Section 1.1 above upon the occurrence of any one of the following events:

4.1.   *Disability.* In the event that the Employee is unable to perform his duties and responsibilities hereunder to the full extent required by the Board of Directors of the Company by reason of illness, injury, or incapacity for twenty-six consecutive weeks, during which time he shall continue to be compensated as provided in Section 1.4 hereof (less any payments due the Employee under disability benefit programs, including Social Security disability, worker's compensation, and disability retirement benefits), this Agreement may be terminated by the Company, and the Company shall have no further liability or obligation to the Employee for compensation hereunder; provided, however, that the Employee will be entitled to receive the payments prescribed under any disability benefit plan that may be in effect for employees of the Company and in which he participated, and a pro rata portion of the incentive compensation, if any, referred to in Section 1.5 hereof in respect of the period prior to the date on which the Employee first became disabled. The Employee agrees, in the event of any dispute under this Section 4.1, to submit to a physical examination by a licensed physician selected by the Board of Directors of the Company.

4.2.   *Death.* In the event that the Employee dies during the Employment Term, the Company shall pay to his executors, legal representatives, or administrators an amount equal to the installment of his salary set forth in Section 1.4 hereof for the month in which he dies, and thereafter the Company shall have no further liability or obligation hereunder to his executors, legal representatives, administrators, heirs or assigns, or any other person claiming under or through him; provided, however, that the Employee's estate or designated beneficiaries shall be entitled to receive the payments prescribed for such recipients under any death benefit plan that may be in effect for employees of the Company and in which the Employee participated, and a pro-rata portion of the incentive compensation, if any, referred to in Section 1.5 hereof in respect of the year during which the Employee died.

4.3.   *Cause.* Nothing in this Agreement shall be construed to prevent its termination by majority vote of the Board of Directors of the Company at any time for "cause." For purposes of this Agreement, "cause" shall mean the failure of the Employee to perform or observe any of the material terms or provisions of this Agreement, conviction of a crime involving moral turpitude, habitual insobriety, substance abuse, misappropriation of funds, disparagement of the Company or its management, or other proper cause determined in good faith by majority vote of the Board of Directors of the Company. Such termination shall be effected by notice thereof delivered by the Company to the Employee and, except as hereinafter provided, shall be effective as of the date of such notice; provided, however, that the termination shall not be effective if (i) such termination is because of the Employee's failure to perform or observe any of the terms or provisions of this Agreement or other proper cause determined in good faith by majority vote of the Board of Directors of the Company, (ii) such notice is the first such notice of termination for any reason delivered by the Company to the Employee hereunder, and (iii) within fifteen (15) days following the date of such notice the Employee shall cease his refusal and shall use his best efforts to perform such obligations. The Company's liability, if any, for payments to the Employee by virtue of any wrongful termination of the Employee's employment pursuant to this Agreement shall be reduced by and to the extent of any earnings received by or accrued for the benefit of the Employee during any unexpired part of the Employment Term.

5.   *Offset.* The Company, in addition to all other rights and remedies, shall have the right to offset against all monies due

1   to the Employee any sums due to the Company from the Em-
2   ployee under this Agreement.

3

4   6.   *Survival*. Notwithstanding the termination of this Agree-
5   ment by reason of the Employee's disability under Section 4.1
6   hereof, or for cause under Section 4.3 hereof, his obligations un-
7   der the Confidentiality Agreement shall survive and remain in
8   full force and effect for the periods therein provided.

9

10   7.   *Governing Law*. This Agreement shall be governed by
11   and interpreted under the laws of the Commonwealth of Penn-
12   sylvania without giving effect to any conflict of law's provisions.

13

14   8.   *Litigation Expenses*. In the event of a lawsuit by either
15   party to enforce the provisions of this Agreement, the prevail-
16   ing party shall be entitled to recover reasonable costs, expenses,
17   and attorney's fees from the other party.

18

19   9.   *Notices*. All notices and other communications required
20   or permitted hereunder or necessary or convenient in connec-
21   tion herewith shall be in writing and shall be deemed to have
22   been given when hand-delivered or mailed by registered or cer-
23   tified mail, as follows (provided that notice of change of address
24   shall be deemed given only when received):

25

26   If to the Company, to:

27

28   ABC, INC.
29   Philadelphia, PA 19104

30

31

32   If to the Employee, to:

33   _____

34   _____

35   _____

36

37   or to such other names or addresses as the Company or the
38   Employee, as the case may be, shall designate by Notice to each
39   other person entitled to receive notices in the manner specified
40   in this Section.

10.   *Contents of Agreement; Amendment and Assignment.*   **1**

   2

(a)   This Agreement supersedes all prior agreements and   **3**
sets forth the entire understanding among the parties hereto   **4**
with respect to the subject matter hereof and cannot be changed,   **5**
modified, extended, or terminated except upon written amend-   **6**
ment approved by the Board of Directors of the Company and   **7**
executed on its behalf by a duly authorized officer. Without limi-   **8**
tation, nothing in this Agreement shall be construed as giving   **9**
the Employee any right to be retained in the employ of the   **10**
Company beyond the expiration of the Employment Term, and   **11**
the Employee specifically acknowledges that he shall be an em-   **12**
ployee-at-will of the Company thereafter, and thus subject to   **13**
discharge by the Company with or without cause and without   **14**
compensation of any nature.   **15**

   16

(b)   All of the terms and provisions of this Agreement shall   **17**
be binding upon and inure to the benefit of and be enforceable   **18**
by the respective heirs, executors, administrators, legal repre-   **19**
sentatives, successors, and assigns of the parties hereto, except   **20**
that the duties and responsibilities of the Employee hereunder   **21**
are of a personal nature and shall not be assignable or del-   **22**
egable in whole or in part by the Employee.   **23**

   24

11.   *Severability.* If any provision of this Agreement or ap-   **25**
plication thereof to anyone or under any circumstances is   **26**
adjudicated to be invalid or unenforceable in any jurisdiction,   **27**
such invalidity or unenforceability shall not affect any other   **28**
provision or application of this Agreement that can be given   **29**
effect without the invalid or unenforceable provision or appli-   **30**
cation and shall not invalidate or render unenforceable such   **31**
provision or application in any other jurisdiction.   **32**

   33

12.   *Remedies Cumulative; No Waiver.* No remedy conferred   **34**
upon the Company by this Agreement is intended to be exclu-   **35**
sive of any other remedy, and each and every such remedy shall   **36**
be cumulative and shall be in addition to any other remedy given   **37**
hereunder or now or hereafter existing at law or in equity. No   **38**
delay or omission by the Company in exercising any right, rem-   **39**
edy, or power hereunder or existing at law or in equity shall be   **40**

1 construed as a waiver thereof, and any such right, remedy, or
2 power may be exercised by the Company from time to time and
3 as often as may be deemed expedient or necessary by the Com-
4 pany in its sole discretion.
5
6 13.   *Miscellaneous.* All section headings are for convenience
7 only and shall not define or limit the provisions of this Agree-
8 ment. This Agreement may be executed in several counterparts,
9 each of which shall be deemed an original, but all of which to-
10 gether shall constitute but one and the same agreement. It shall
11 not be necessary in making proof of this Agreement or any coun-
12 terpart hereof to produce or account for any of the other
13 counterparts.
14
15 IN WITNESS WHEREOF, the undersigned have executed this
16 Agreement as of the date first above written.
17
18 ABC, INC.
19
20 By: _____
21 Name:
22 Title:
23
24 EMPLOYEE
25
26
27 _____
28
29
30
31
32
33
34
35
36
37
38
39
40

EXHIBIT F OF APPENDIX 3

TERM NOTE

$_____

    FOR VALUE RECEIVED,_____,
a _____ corporation ("Payor"), hereby promises to pay
to the order of ABC, INC., a Pennsylvania corporation ("Payee"),
at Payee's offices at Philadelphia, PA 19104, the principal sum
of _____ Dollars ($_____), without interest,
on December 31, _____. All payments of principal hereunder
shall be made in lawful money of the United States of America.

    Prepayment. This Note may be prepaid, without premium
or penalty, in whole or in part at any time.

    Waivers. Presentment for payment, protest, dishonor, and
notice of dishonor and of protest are hereby waived. Any failure by any holder hereof to exercise any right hereunder shall
not be construed as a waiver of the right to exercise the same
or any other right at any other time.

    Related Agreements. This Note is being issued by Payor pur-
suant to a Stock Purchase Agreement, dated _____,
between the Payor and the Payee.

    IN WITNESS WHEREOF, Payor, intending to be legally
bound hereby, has duly executed this Note the day and year
first above written.

[CORPORATE SEAL] _____

ATTEST

By: _____   By: _____
   As its   As its

APPENDIX 4

A PRIMER ON IPO ROLL-UPS

ADAM J. FEIN, PH.D.*

T he following is a discussion of roll-ups in the industrial distribution industry and additional contractor and distribution related IPO roll-ups.

Executive Summary: IPO roll-ups are an increasingly popular strategy for industrial distributors. This article takes a critical look at these transactions along with the management and operational issues for distributors that are considering taking part in a roll-up.

"Should I be a buyer or a seller?" This is how most independent distributors view their strategy for surviving consolidation. The IPO roll-up, a Wall Street–driven financing trend, now offers a distributor the possibility to be both a buyer and a seller. Despite the many potential benefits of these deals, deciding whether this transaction is right for your business is not simple.

---

*© 1998 Pembroke Consulting, Inc. Adam J. Fein, Ph.D., is president of Pembroke Consulting, a Philadelphia-based strategy consulting firm. He can be reached at (215)238-1505/adam@pembroke-consulting.com. This article originally appeared in *Modern Distribution Management,* April 1998.

In an IPO roll-up transaction, a group of private companies from the same line of trade (the founding companies) simultaneously merge into a newly created holding company (the go-forward company). At the same time as the mergers, the holding company goes public and lists its shares on the stock market. The process of going public is called an Initial Public Offering (IPO).

These new companies are sometimes called "poof companies," as in "Poof! We've just created a $300 million company." The simultaneous combination of companies distinguishes these deals from more traditional industry consolidation strategies, which rely on the sequential acquisition of regional and local distributors by a few well-financed buyers.

Some recent distribution IPO roll-ups include Industrial Distribution Group, which brought together nine MROP distributors with combined sales of $251 million, and USA Floral, which combined nine floral products distributors with combined sales of $175 million.

IPO roll-ups are designed for small- to medium-sized companies. Table 1 shows information about nine selected contractor and distribution-related transactions that occurred within the last two years. The 66 companies that took part in these seven transactions had annual sales ranging from $2.0 million to $81.0 million. The average founding company had annual sales of $23 million.

IPO roll-ups reflect the marriage of two hot Wall Street crazes—industry consolidations and initial public offerings. Right now, consolidation is hot. Consolidation Capital Corporation, which is not an IPO roll-up, raised nearly $500 million in November to "become the leading consolidator of distribution companies and service providers in one or more fragmented industries." Sanders Morris Mundy, a Houston-based investment bank, tracks the stock market performance of industry consolidators and roll-up companies. Their SMM Twenty consolidator index is up 18 percent this year, topping the S&P 500's year-to-date gain of 12.9 percent.[1]

These transactions also reflect the belief by outside investors that there is room for substantial consolidation in traditionally fragmented industries such as industrial distribution. Witness an investment report issued by NationsBanc

Montgomery Securities last fall: "Main Street meets Wall Street: Mom & Pop Give Way to the Consolidators."

The rising stock market has created the conditions for a booming IPO market. During the past three years, 2,083 companies went public, raising a combined total of $124.1 billion. In other words, 13 companies per week raised $60 million each. IPO roll-ups are benefitting from this boom.

IPO roll-ups can be an amazing source of wealth creation for distributors in fragmented lines of trade, but the strategy has important risks. It is important for a participating distributor to understand the management and operational issues involved in a roll-up. Why should a distributor take part in this transaction? How does an IPO roll-up affect a distributor's day-to-day operations? How does the new public holding company operate? And who benefits the most from these deals—the participating companies or the financial sponsors that put the deals together?

Why Distributors Are Participating in IPO Roll-ups

For the independent distributor, an IPO roll-up can be an alternative to alliances or marketing groups.[2] Both strategies give participants broader geographic reach. Both strategies enable bidding on national or multi-regional contracts. Both strategies create opportunities for volume purchasing from suppliers. Since the go-forward company in a roll-up is highly decentralized, both strategies also retain operational autonomy for the participating independent companies.

However, there are crucial differences between alliances and roll-ups. Most importantly, distributors that come together through a roll-up formally and legally combine their ownership structure. The newly created public company has the authority to eliminate redundant activities and assets among its member companies. This can be a crucial source of competitive advantage in the face of margin pressure and other challenges.

Following an IPO roll-up, the founding companies are formally bound together. In contrast, an alliance always faces the risk that one or more member companies will be acquired or that disagreements will tear the alliance apart.

Legal combination gives the newly formed company the size needed to tap the public capital markets. Typically, non-technology companies with sales below $100 million are not able to go public. Bundling a group of similar companies together allows the combined entity to go public.

In addition, a corporation's "cost of capital" is lower through the public equity markets than through private sources, such as private investors or venture capital. One reason for this discrepancy is that the public markets will pay more for a dollar of earnings than the private capital markets. For example, the valuation of a privately held distributor usually ranges from four to seven times EBITDA (Earnings Before Interest, Taxes, and Depreciation). In contrast, public distributors are valued at fifteen to twenty-five times earnings.

There are many other benefits to the founding distributors. You can participate in building a leading company in your line of trade. You gain some liquidity for your personal investments in the business. (As I discuss below, IPO roll-ups provide much less liquidity than many owners believe.) And like an alliance strategy, participating in an IPO roll-up allows owners of the founding distributors to retain some degree of day-to-day operational control.

For an entrepreneur, the roll-up model can be an alternative to selling out to a large chain. Selling the company to an external consolidator often entails a substantial loss of independence for a distributor. Even worse, a consolidator may simply acquire a distributor's customer list and then dismantle the rest of the acquired company's organization.

An IPO Roll-up Is Not an Exit Strategy

Despite these many potential benefits, do not think of a roll-up as an exit strategy for you, your family, or other owners of the business. Instead, you should view participation in an IPO roll-up as a way to recommit to the growth of your business. Being a founding company of a roll-up is very different than selling the business and retiring.

The public markets drive this reality. Investors who evaluate a company do not want to see owners fleeing for the exits.

Instead, Wall Street prefers to see the owners with operating responsibilities stay on to maintain their companies. The decentralized nature of a roll-up means that the owners and senior management of the founding companies are expected to remain after the IPO.

The need for management stability influences how payment for a founding company is structured. (The price paid for a company is referred to as the "consideration.") In a roll-up, ownership in a private distributor is exchanged for a mix of cash payments, stock in the new public company, and the assumption of founding company debt. In the IPO roll-ups in Table 1, an average of 55 percent of consideration paid was in the form of stock in the new company. In some transactions, it can be substantially higher. For instance, the consideration paid to the nine founding companies of Industrial Distribution Group was 91 percent of total payments.

Owners also have to sign non-compete agreements for two to five years and agree not to sell their stock for one or two years after the IPO. You also become an "insider" whose stock transactions are closely monitored and subject to legal limitations on the timing and amount of stock sales. These restrictions, along with a high proportion of payment in stock, signal to potential investors that the founding companies are committed to the new company.

If you are the owner of a founding company, these restrictions limit your ability to simply walk away from your company. One investor put it to me this way: "I want the founding company owners to see themselves as swapping ownership with each other rather than cashing out." Thus, a roll-up is definitely not an exit strategy for the owner of a distributor that wants to retire quietly after the IPO.

The Transition from Owner to Employee

After taking part in an IPO roll-up, the former owners of the founding companies become employees of the new public company. This has two effects. One, it reduces the annual compensation for company presidents. Two, it redefines management responsibilities of the former owners.

In the offering documents for IPO roll-ups, there is a section that is euphemistically referred to as the "compensation differential." In reality, the differential translates into a reduction in annual compensation for the owners of the founding companies. For instance, the owners of the USA Floral founding companies collectively agreed to reduce their compensation by $3.6 million, or 8 percent of Selling, General, and Administrative expenses (SG&A).

To some extent, any compensation reduction is offset by cash proceeds from the IPO. The USA Floral companies collectively received $43 million in cash for their companies. In contrast, the participants in IDG reduced their compensation by only $282,000 (0.5 percent of combined SG&A), but received over 90 percent of payment in the form of stock. Keep in mind that the mix of stock versus cash is based on the business fundamentals of the transaction, not on the level of the compensation differential.

The reduction in compensation serves multiple purposes. One, it harmonizes compensation across the participating companies. No one makes more than their counterpart in another company. Two, it allows the go-forward company to report higher operating profits following combination. The amount and impact of the compensation reduction are always presented in the IPO prospectus.

Another big change is the creation of management oversight for executives at the founding companies. The founding company presidents, who may have never had a boss, now report to the CEO of the go-forward company. In other words, rather than being president of your own distribution company, you become president of a business unit at the go-forward public company. Business plans must be approved at the corporate level. Outside commercial banks and private investors are replaced with an internal corporate "bank" that exercises financial controls on each formerly independent company.

The situation is not completely straightforward because most, but not all, business unit presidents/former owners will hold a seat on the board of the newly formed public company. Since the CEO reports to the board of directors, you become the boss of your boss.

Managing the Go-Forward Company

Founding company owners need to face another hard reality about IPO roll-ups: The CEO and CFO of the new public company will probably not come from the ranks of the founding companies. Your boss is likely to be an outsider, possibly even someone with limited experience in your line of trade.

The CEO is likely to be an executive who has had experience working in a large public company and dealing with Wall Street. Ideally, it will be someone that Wall Street investors know by reputation. Usually, the presidents of the founding companies lack the experience, qualifications, and reputations to fulfill that role. For instance, Marty Pinson, the CEO of Industrial Distribution Group, had previously been the executive vice-president and CFO of U.S. Office Products, a leading consolidator in the office products channel. Choosing an outsider also avoids many political problems and disagreements among the founding companies.

Since the owners of the founding companies are represented on the board, the CEO acts as both a facilitator and a leader. The CEO sets the strategic vision of the company, interacts with Wall Street, and oversees the functions that are centralized within the larger company, such as accounting and credit.

As a public company, the CFO's role is even more crucial. Reporting requirements are particularly stringent for public companies. Both the stock exchange and the Securities and Exchange Commission (SEC) mandate a very high level of financial disclosure. The CFO also needs to manage Wall Street expectations about quarterly earnings reports and future financial prospects. Becoming a public company means publicly discussing internal operations in much greater detail than a private company. Like the CEO, the CFO is unlikely to come from the ranks of the founding companies.

The senior management of the go-forward company are also expected to develop an acquisition program for further industry consolidation. Post-IPO, the new public company is expected to act much like a typical acquisitive assembler, sequentially folding other distributors into its operations through friendly takeovers. The initial group of founding companies is the "platform" onto which further acquisitions will be added. Consider Metals USA, which went public last July with $387 million in combined sales. Through a series of acquisitions, the company now has more than tripled in size to $1.2 billion in sales today.

It is interesting to note that many IPO roll-ups generate surprisingly little funds for an acquisition strategy. Most of the money is used to purchase the founding companies and leave them debt-free. In fact, four of the deals listed in Table 1 (Metals USA, ARS, PalEx, and Pentacon) generated no cash proceeds from the IPO that could be used for future acquisitions. For the other transactions, the funds dedicated to future acquisitions averaged 25 percent of the total offering size. The remaining funds for acquisition either come from revolving credit lines established by the public company or from future cash flow.

The Role and Compensation of the Sponsor

Almost every IPO roll-up to date has been facilitated by an outside investment firm. Some firms, such as Notre Capital Ventures in Houston, specialize in these transactions. The popularity of these transactions has brought many new players to the market, such as BGL Capital Partners in Chicago.

Outside investors act as catalysts for the transaction. They identify potential founding companies and act as objective outsiders to make sure that the deal moves forward. Most sponsors also help to negotiate the valuation of each founding company.

A sponsor with a reputation for putting together successful IPO roll-ups will be able to attract prestigious investment banks and get the attention of potential investors. The sponsor can help to line up a revolving credit line to fund the acquisition program. Most importantly, a sponsor advances the legal and accounting fees required to go public.

These fees can be substantial. For example, American Residential Services paid $3.6 million in accounting and legal fees for their IPO, which raised $63.0 million. Additional fees include investment banking underwriting fees and selling concession. (The "selling concession" allows the underwriting bank to act as a distribution intermediary, buying your stock at a discount and then reselling it to the public at a higher price.)

In exchange for these services, the sponsors are very highly rewarded. Since the sponsor usually incorporates the holding company prior to IPO, they initially hold all of the shares in the company. As I describe above, some of these shares are paid out as consideration for the founding companies. The sponsor retains the remaining shares, typically 10 to 15 percent of the total outstanding shares.

At the time of IPO, these shares are valued at the market price, giving the sponsor a paper gain that is referred to as "capital appreciation." Excluding IDG and Integrated Electrical Services, neither of which had an outside financial sponsor, the other deals listed in Table 1 generated an average of over $20 million in capital appreciation for the sponsors. While these fees may seem very steep, a deal's success may hinge on partnering with the right sponsor.

Instead of using (and paying) a sponsor, the founding companies can come together on their own and self-fund the IPO expenses. This eliminates the need for an external private equity source. Self-funding is possible because the majority of the accounting, legal, and banking fees are paid from the IPO proceeds. In other words, these fees are not paid unless the IPO actually occurs. Industrial Distribution Group followed this model. Barth Smith Company, a Chicago consulting firm with a focus in industrial distribution, assisted the founding companies of IDG with the combination in exchange for professional fees and less than 1 percent of the total outstanding shares.

Consolidation Fast-Track or House of Cards

If the strategic rationale is sound, then an IPO roll-up creates a dominant competitor almost instantly. Yet there must also be a compelling strategic rationale for the transaction. Here are a few hard questions to ask yourself about the prospects for an IPO roll-up in your line of trade:

- Will customers and supplier value the services and resources of a large, national company in my line of trade?
- Is this consolidation driven by business reasons, or is it an attempt to jam together different companies for a quick stock market profit? (In other words, is the IPO

roll-up trend a fad that will burn out during the next stock market correction?)

- Does my line of trade have the fundamental triggers for consolidation in wholesale distribution?[3]
- Will it be possible to integrate the different founding companies? Do I respect the owners of the other founding companies?
- Are there compelling acquisition targets for our new platform company?

An IPO roll-up can be a vehicle for tremendous wealth creation for the owners of the founding companies. The owners in the founding company can share in the success of the new venture through stock appreciation.

However, the transition from a private to a public company has been traumatic for many owners. Disclosure requirements and the need to deal with Wall Street create many issues. Rather than being an exit strategy, an IPO roll-up is really a mechanism to recommit to your business. There is also the chance that the new larger company will not be able to successfully integrate all of the different founding companies.

Keep in mind that stock prices fluctuate substantially. Industrial Distribution Group went public at $17.00 per share in September, reached a high of $23.25 in September, and traded at $19.50 on March 18, 1998. And as Table 1 shows, American Residential Services has seen its stock price decline by 43 percent in the past 18 months.

Here are a few questions to ask yourself to see if an IPO roll-up is right for you:

- Am I willing to recommit to building my business? Are the senior executives in my company ready for the challenge?
- Can I handle the risk that my stock may not go up?
- Can I accept oversight from holding company executives?
- Am I prepared for the disclosure requirements associated with a public company?

Increasingly, more distributor owners will consider the roll-up option. This article has only addressed a small fraction of the complex management and financial issues in these transactions.

TABLE 1   SELECTED CONTRACTOR AND DISTRIBUTION-RELATED IPO ROLL-UPS

Company (Symbol)	Business	IPO Date	No. of Founding Companies	Combined Sales at IPO ($M)	Amount Raised ($M)	Change in Stock Price*
American Residential Services (ARS)	Residential HVAC maintenance & repair	9/25/96	8	$114.6	$72.5	−43%
Metals USA (MUI)	Metal service centers	7/10/97	8	$387.0	$67.9	+70%
PalEx (PALX)	Pallet manufacture	3/20/97	5	$52.0	$25.9	+73%
Comfort Systems (FIX)	Commercial HVAC installation and maintenance	6/27/97	12	$167.5	$91.2	+52%
Industrial Distribution Group (IDG)	MRO distribution	9/23/97	9	$251.1	$64.5	+15%
USA Floral (ROSI)	Floral distribution	10/9/97	8	$175.5	$74.8	+77%
Integrated Electrical Services (IEE)	Electrical contractors	1/27/98	15	$312.7	$104.7	+25%
Quanta Services (PWR)	Data/communication contractors	2/11/98	4	$108.1	$45.0**	+38%
Pentacon	OEM fastener distribution	3/9/98	5	$151.8	$52.0***	+16%

*Change in stock price since IPO (as of March 18, 1998).
**Quanta could raise as much as $51.75 million if the underwriter exercises its full over-allotment option.
***Pentacon could raise as much as $59.8 million if the underwriter exercises its full over-allotment option.

With the current pressures for consolidation in the channel, it seems inevitable that there will be a parade of roll-ups—at least while Wall Street smiles on industrial distribution.

---

1. Despite this year's superior performance, there has been substantial volatility in consolidator stock market performance. For example, the SMM Twenty Index increased by 41 percent in 1996, more than double the S&P's 1996 gain of 20.3 percent. However, the Index's 1997 performance was substantially below the overall stock market.

2. To read more about the role of marketing and purchasing alliances as a consolidation survival strategy, see my article "How Good is Your Consolidation Survival Strategy?" *Modern Distribution Management,* November 25, 1997.

3. For a discussion of the forces triggering consolidation, see my report *Consolidation in Wholesale Distribution: Understanding Industry Change.* The report is available from NAW [National Association of Wholesaler-Distributors] by calling 202-871-0885.

Appendix 5

Canadian Venture Capital

T he Canadian venture capital industry operates in a very similar fashion to the United States venture capital industry. The only major difference is that one source of financing for venture capital funds is so-called labor-sponsored venture capital. Certain entities associated with Canadian labor unions are entitled to solicit venture capital funds from the public. An example of such a fund is Working Ventures Canadian Fund, Inc.

The Canadian Venture Capital Association (CVCA) reported that a total of $886 million went to first time financings in 1997, up by 28 percent from the prior year. However, much of the growth in 1997 was driven by a very sharp increase in follow-on financings. A total of 738 follow-on financings were completed in 1997, which together absorbed $955 million, accounting for 52 percent of the industry's disbursements.

Early-stage activity continued to grow in 1997 with 305 companies that are still in the early stages of their development capturing $659 million or 36 percent of total disbursements.

Canadian Venture Capital Association

The CVCA maintains an Internet Web site at http://www.cvca.ca. This Web site contains important information concerning the CVCA, which should be checked by Canadian entrepreneurs interested in raising venture capital.

Full members of the CVCA are comprised of venture-capital companies with funds under management and available for investment. The following are the full members of the CVCA:

CODE: #: Link to CVCA Web site

@: E-mail only

X: Not Online

\# ACF Equity Atlantic Inc.

\# Acorn Ventures Inc.

\# AgriVest Capital Corp.

X Bank of Montreal Capital Corp.

\# BCE Capital Inc.

@ Bayshore Capital Corp.

\# Business Development Bank of Canada (BDC) Venture Capital

X CAI Capital Croup

\# Capital Alliance Ventures

@ Cedarpoint Investments Inc.

X CIBC Wood Gundy Capital

X Clairvest Group Inc.

@ Crocus Investment Fund

X ELNOS

X First Ontario Labour Sponsored Investment Fund Ltd.

\# Fonds de solidarite des travailleurs du Quebec (FTQ)

\# Middlefield Ventures Limited

@ Miralta Capital Inc.

\# Norshield Capital Management Corp.

\# Ontario Municipal Employees Retirement Board (OMERS)

X Penfund Partners, Inc.

X Private Equity Management Corp. (PEMCO)

\# Priveq Financial Corp.

@ Quorum Growth Partners I, Limited Partnership

\# Retrocom Growth Fund Inc.

\# Royal Bank Capital Corp.

\# RoyNat Inc.

X Saskatchewan Government Growth Fund

\# Saskatchewan Opportunities Corp.

\# Schroders & Associates Canada Inc.

@ Scotia Merchant Capital Corp.

@ Hargan Ventures

X Helix Investments (Canada) Inc.

X Highgate Venture Capital Fund

X Horatio Enterprise Fund

X IPS Industrial Promotion Services Limited

@ Interquest Incorporated

@ Investissements Novacap Inc.

\# J. L. Albright Venture Partners Inc.

\# LIBORBANK Financial Group

\# McLean Watson Capital Inc.

\# MDS Capital Corp.

\# Mercator Investments Ltd.

X TD Capital

@ Tamarack Group Ltd.

\# Triax Growth Fund Inc.

X Trillium Growth Capital Inc.

X Trilwood Investments Ltd.

X Vencap, Inc.

@ VenGrowth Funds

\# Ventures West Management Inc.

@ Whitecastle Investments Ltd.

\# Working Opportunity Fund (EVCC) Ltd.

\# Working Ventures Canadian Fund Inc.

\# XDL Capital Corp.

Statistical Surveys

Tables 1–6 contain statistics provided by the CVCA concerning Canadian venture capital activities, based upon the responses of the surveyed members:

TABLE 1 INVESTMENT BY STAGE OF DEVELOPMENT*

	1997					1996				
INVESTMENTS		COMPANIES		AMOUNT		INVESTMENTS		COMPANIES		AMOUNT
#	%	#	%	$(Mil)	%	#	%	#	%	$(Mil)	%
Stage										
Early Stage										
596	44	305	38	659	36	375	43	204	39	344	31
Expansion										
585	43	371	47	949	52	393	45	245	47	573	32
Acquisition/Buyout										
57	4	36	5	98	5	40	5	31	6	98	9
Turnaround										
75	5	48	6	36	2	62	7	36	7	63	6
Other										
53	4	34	4	79	4	11	1	9	2	15	1
Total										
1,336		794		$1,821		881		525		$1,094	
	100%		100%		100%		100%		100%		100%

*Reprinted with permission of the Canadian Venture Capital Association.

TABLE 2   VENTURE CAPITAL INVESTMENT ACTIVITY
BY REVENUE OF INVESTEES*

| | | 1997 | | | | | | 1996 | | | |
INVESTMENTS		COMPANIES		AMOUNT		INVESTMENTS		COMPANIES		AMOUNT	
$(Mil) #	%	#	%	$(Mil)	%	#	%	#	%	$(Mil)	%
$0 – $1											
369	41	173	38	391	33	279	44	145	40	249	33
$1 – $4											
243	27	123	27	215	18	136	22	75	21	112	15
$4 – $9											
111	12	61	13	159	13	96	15	66	18	157	21
Over $9											
176	20	98	22	423	36	118	19	73	20	234	31
Total**											
899		455		$1,189		629		359		$751	
	100%		100%		100%		100%		100%		100%

*Reprinted with permission of the Canadian Venture Capital Association.
**Excludes investments for which investee revenues not reported.

TABLE 3   VENTURE CAPITAL INVESTMENT BY SECTOR*

| | 1997 | | | | 1996 | | | | | |
| | INVESTMENTS | | COMPANIES | | AMOUNT | | INVESTMENTS | | COMPANIES | | AMOUNT | |

INDUSTRY	#	%	#	%	$(Mil)	%	#	%	#	%	$(Mil)	%
Biotechnology	166	12	79	10	203	11	133	15	54	10	159	15
Medical/Health Related	127	9	56	7	180	10	85	10	37	7	111	10
Communications	114	8	59	7	140	8	65	7	42	8	95	9
Computer Related	358	26	191	24	466	26	195	22	117	22	222	20
Electronics	115	8	61	8	119	7	81	9	46	9	87	8
Energy/Environmental Technology	47	3	37	5	53	3	31	4	17	3	30	3
Industrial Automation & Equipment	29	2	17	2	35	2	22	2	15	3	45	4
Total (Technology)	956	70%	500	63%	1,197	66%	612	69%	328	62%	749	69%
Consumer-Related	68	5	56	7	97	5	58	7	43	8	67	6
Manufacturing	155	11	112	14	222	12	115	13	83	16	123	11
Miscellaneous	187	14	125	16	305	17	96	11	71	14	154	14
Total (Traditional)	410	30%	294	37%	625	34%	269	31%	197	38%	344	31%
TOTAL	1,336	100%	794	100%	$1,821	100%	881	100%	525	100%	$1,094	100%

*Reprinted with permission of the Canadian Venture Capital Association.

TABLE 4   VENTURE CAPITAL INVESTMENT ACTIVITY
BY INVESTEE LOCATION*†

LOCATION	1997 #	%	$(Mil)	%	1996 #	%	$(Mil)	%
British Columbia	161	12	207	11	109	12	103	9
Alberta	66	5	61	3	30	3	42	4
Saskatchewan	76	6	51	3	61	7	42	4
Manitoba	40	3	88	5	28	3	39	4
Ontario	415	30	704	39	255	29	467	43
Quebec	517	38	546	30	332	38	325	30
Atlantic Canada	23	2	22	1	22	2	27	3
Foreign Countries	68	5	142	8	44	5	49	4
Total	**1,366**	**100%**	**1,821**	**100%**	**881**	**100%**	**1,094**	**100%**

*Investee location defined as place of principal facility.
†Reprinted with permission of the Canadian Venture Capital Association.

**TABLE 5   VENTURE CAPITAL INVESTMENT ACTIVITY BY NUMBER
OF EMPLOYEES IN INVESTEE COMPANIES*

		1997					1996			
INVESTMENTS		COMPANIES		AMOUNT		INVESTMENTS		COMPANIES		AMOUNT
# Employees										
#	%	#	%	$(Mil)	%	#	%	#	%	$(Mil) %
0 – 24										
452	33	246	31	413	23	269	31	146	28	179	16
25 – 49										
204	15	91	11	263	14	158	18	83	16	198	18
50 – 99										
136	10	66	8	220	12	95	11	52	10	146	13
100 – 199										
69	5	38	5	107	6	48	5	28	3	104	10
200 – 499										
43	3	21	3	179	10	19	2	15	3	52	5
500 – 999										
7	1	6	1	15	1	7	1	5	1	22	2
≥1,000										
10	1	8	1	30	2	1	0	1	0	5	0
Did not report										
445	33	318	40	593	33	284	32	196	37	388	35
Total										
1,366	100%	794	100%	1,821	100%	881	100%	526	100%	1,094	100%

*Reprinted with permission of the Canadian Venture Capital Association.

TABLE 6   NUMBER OF INVESTMENTS AND AMOUNT INVESTED*
Private vs. Public Companies

| | 1997 | | | | 1996 | | |
	INVESTMENTS	AMOUNT			INVESTMENTS	AMOUNT	
	#	%	$(Mil)	%	#	%	$(Mil)	%
Private								
	1,163	85	1,479	81	765	87	893	82
Public								
	203	15	342	19	116	13	201	18
Total								
	1,366	100%	1,821	100%	881	100%	1,094	100%,

*Reprinted with permission of the Canadian Venture Capital Association.

List of Investors Responding to the Survey

ACF Equity Atlantic Inc.

Acorn Ventures Inc.

Ag-West Biotechnology/ICAST

Agri-Food Equity Fund

BC Mercantile Corporation

BCE Capital Inc.

BDC Venture Capital
Division

BioCapital Inc.

Caisse de depot et placement,
Private Investments Group

CI Covington Fund

Canadian Medical
Discoveries Fund

Canadian Science &
Technology Growth Fund

Canadian Venture Founders

Canadian Venture
Opportunity Fund

Capimont Inc.

Capital Alliance Ventures Inc.

Capital Monteregie Inc.

Cedarpoint Investments Inc.

Centerfire

Citibank Investment Capital
Division

Clairvest Group Inc.

Crocus Investment Fund

DGC Entertainment
Ventures Corp.

Investissements 3L

EnviroCapital Inc.

Environmental R & D
Capital Corp.

Exceptional Technologies Fund (VCC) Inc.

FESA Enterprise Venture Capital Fund

First Ontario Labour Sponsored Investment Fund

Fondacion, Le Fonds de developpement de la CSN pour la cooperation et emploi

Fonds Aerocapital

Fonds Agro-Forestier

Fonds de solidarite

Fonds Regional de Solidarite

Gestion Capital 07 Inc.

Gestion Capital Capidem

Gestion Capital de Developpement 04 Inc.

Gestion Estrie Capital Inc.

Helix Investments (Canada) Inc.

Highgate Venture Capital Fund

Horatio Enterprise Fund

HSBC Capital Canada Inc.

Innovacap Capital Corporation

Innovatech Quebec et Chaudiere-Appalaches

Innovatech du Grand Montreal

Investissement Desjardins

Saskatchewan Government Growth Fund

Investissements Logisoft Inc.

Investissements Novacap Inc.

J.L. Albright Venture Partners Inc.

Manvest Inc.

McLean Watson Softech Fund

MDS Health Ventures Pacific Inc.

MDS Health Ventures Inc.

Middlefield Group

Miralta Capital Inc.

Neuroscience Partners, LP

Le Societe d'investissement du Mouvement Acadien Ltee

Neuroscience Partners, Inc.

Penfund Partners, Inc.

Pinnacle Group

Placements Ger-Ben Inc.

Private Equity Management Corp.

Priveq Financial Corporation

Quorum Growth Inc.

Retrocom Growth Fund

Royal Bank Capital Corp. (RBCC)

RoyNat Inc.

Seed Management Inc.

SOCCRAT

SOCCRENT

SOQUIA

Sportfund

TD Capital Group

Technocap Inc.

Telsoft Ventures Inc.

The Health Care and
Biotechnology Venture Fund

The B.E.S.T. Discoveries Fund

Triax Growth Fund

Trillium Growth Capital Inc.

Tourism &
Entertainment Fund

The VenGrowth
Investment Fund

Ventures West
Management Inc.

Whitecastle Investments
Limited

Workers Investment Fund

Working Opportunity Fund
(EVCC) Ltd.

Working Ventures Canadian
Fund Inc.

INDEX